# Contemporary Feminist Fiction in Spain

# New Directions in European Writing

Editor: John Flower, Professor of French, University of Exeter.

As the twentieth century draws to a close we are witnessing profound and significant changes across the new Europe. The past is being reassessed; the millennium is awaited with interest. Some, pessimistically, have predicted the death of literature; others see important developments within national literature and in movements cutting across frontiers. This enterprising Series focuses on these developments through the study either of individual writers or of groups or movements. There are no definitive statements. By definition they are introductory and set out to assess and explore the full spectrum of modern European writing on the threshold of a new age.

ISBN 1350-9217

*Previously published title in the Series*

**Allyson Fiddler**
*Rewriting Reality: An Introduction to Elfriede Jelinek*

# Contemporary Feminist Fiction in Spain

## The Work of Montserrat Roig and Rosa Montero

C. Davies

**BERG**
*Oxford / Providence, USA*

First published in 1994 by
**Berg Publishers Ltd**
Editorial offices:
150 Cowley Road, Oxford, OX4 1JJ, UK
221 Waterman Street, Providence, RI 02906, USA

**Library of Congress Cataloging-in-Publication Data**

A catalogue record for this book is available from the Library of
Congress.

**British Library Cataloguing in Publication Data**

A catalogue record for this book is available from the British Library.

ISBN  1 85973 086 8

Cover picture based on a painting by Isabel Villar.

Printed in the United Kingdom by SRP, Exeter.

# Contents

# Acknowledgements

I am grateful to the following for permission to reproduce and translate excerpts from works by Montserrat Roig and Rosa Montero: *Aprendizaje sentimental*, C 1981 by Montserrat Roig. *Ramona, adiós*, C 1980 by Montserrat Roig. *Los hechiceros de la palabra*, C 1975 by Montserrat Roig. *Tiempo de cerezas*, C 1978 by Montserrat Roig. *La hora violeta*, C 1980 by Montserrat Roig. *¿Tiempo de mujer?*, C 1980 by Montserrat Roig. *Mujeres en busca de un nuevo humanismo*, C 1981 by Montserrat Roig. *La ópera cotidiana*, C 1983 by Montserrat Roig. *La aguja dorada*, C 1985 by Montserrat Roig. *La voz melodiosa*, C 1987, by Montserrat Roig. All reproduced with permission from Mercedes Casanovas. *Dime que me quieres aunque sea mentira*, C 1992 by Montserrat Roig. *El canto de la juventud*, C 1990 by Montserrat Roig. *Noche y niebla. Los catalanes en los campos nazis*, C 1978 by Montserrat Roig. All reproduced with permission from Edicions 62 S.A.

*Crónica del desamor*, C 1979 by Rosa Montero. *La función Delta*, C 1981 by Rosa Montero. *Te trataré como a una reina*, C 1983 by Rosa Montero. *Amado amo*, C 1988 by Rosa Montero. *Temblor*, C 1990 by Rosa Montero. *El nido de los sueños*, C 1991 by Rosa Montero. All reproduced with permission from Agencia Literaria Carmen Balcells S.A. *Bella y oscura*, C 1993 by Rosa Montero. Reproduced by permission of Editorial Seix Barral, S.A.

# Preface

Two important critical works in English have come to my notice since the completion of this book. The first is Stephen M. Hart's *White Ink. Essays on Twentieth-Century Feminine Fiction in Spain and Latin America* (Tamesis, London, 1993) which includes brief but lucid studies of Montserrat Roig's novel *L'hora violeta* and Rosa Montero's *Temblor*. The second is an extremely informative M.Phil thesis entitled 'Too Much History and Not Enough Story: Montserrat Roig's Literary Output of the Seventies and Its Critical Reception' (University of Birmingham, 1993) by Neus Real Mercadal. It offers a wealth of material regarding the critical reception of Roig's work in Spain quoting, among other such gems, the following remark by Manuel Vicent in the Sunday supplement of Spain's leading newspaper, *El País* (11/I/1981, 29): 'In this country where the male writers are ugly and the female poets are fat, Montserrat Roig brought to literature, more than anything else, a pair of nice legs . . .' (1). This corroborates what I had found elsewhere. Clearly, the book by Hart and the thesis by Real Mercadal make for essential further reading.

I would like to thank literary agents Carmen Balcells and Mercedes Casanovas for their help with the research for this book. I am particularly grateful to Vanessa Knights, always generous and enthusiastic, who kindly sent me a copy of Rosa Montero's paper 'La aventura de escribir' ['The adventure of writing'], read at the University of Cambridge in October 1993, her lengthy interview with Montero on that occasion (now in press), and the seminar discussion which followed the paper. Several interesting points emerged from these items but, unfortunately, too late to be included in this book. No doubt Vanessa Knights will give a full account of her findings in the PhD thesis she is currently preparing at Cambridge on Montero's work. I am also very grateful to my sister-in-law, Angeles García Reales, who first introduced me to Montserrrat Roig's novels in the heady days of post-Franco Madrid, to Carlos Sánchez, to Josep-Anton Fernández, to Dr. Anny Jones, to Professor Alex Longhurst whose perceptive comments on the manuscript much improved the final draft of this book and, last but not least, to Rosa Montero herself for her time and assistance, particularly for allowing me to see her unpublished paper 'Escribiendo en la luna' ['Writing on the Moon']. Needless to say, any errors in the book are entirely my own.

I would like to express my appreciation to Queen Mary and Westfield College, University of London, for a term's leave which allowed me to finish the book, and to my colleagues in the Department of Hispanic Studies who covered my teaching. Richard Fardon, Sarah, Anna, and Tom, as always, helped in a thousand different ways. The staff at the Biblioteca Nacional, Madrid, the University of London Library, and Queen Mary and Westfield College Library have always been helpful and courteous. Above all, however, on this occasion thanks are due primarily to my former and current students at the University of St. Andrews and Queen Mary and Westfield College for the many hours of discussion they shared with me over six years on various 'Women Writers' courses. This book was written with those students in mind and it is dedicated to them.

Part of Chapter 3 was presented at a postgraduate seminar in the Department of Spanish and Portuguese, University of Cambridge, 1993. All translations into English are my own.

London, March 1994

# Introduction

The aim of this book is to introduce the narrative fiction of Montserrat Roig and Rosa Montero, two of Spain's most popular and distinguished contemporary women novelists, to a broader public. The book should interest not only academics but also readers generally who are curious to know about women's writing outside the confines of their own culture and language. It does not presume a knowledge of Spanish or Catalan and all quotes are translated to English. The novelists' work will not be discussed primarily within the context of post-Franco literature, as is usually the case in Spain, but rather from a predominantly feminist and woman-centred perspective. Hopefully, this approach will redress some of the masculinist bias and condescension still very noticeable in most critical works, anthologies, and literary histories published in Spain. In this sense the book continues the informative work of the mainly female academics in the United States who have clearly distinguished a tradition of Spanish women's and feminist writing.

Examples of Spanish male critics' lack of understanding abound. Take José Luis Castillo Puche who writes (incoherently and with paternalistic aplomb) in an article on the contemporary novel:

> As yet, we have not said anything about a group of women who, although worthwhile, are still rather stuck in precisely their woman's condition and have not renounced their personal war, the war of their sex, writing novels of a feminist kind, something that's no longer of interest, although there are among them writers with varying degrees of depth of inquiry.[1]

He refers to Roig and Montero among others, misquoting the title of the latter's novel as *Operación Delta*. Ramón Acín refers to the

---

1. J. L. Castillo Puche, 'Situación de la novela española actual', in Samuel Amell (ed.), *La cultura española en el posfranquismo*, 49–56, p. 53.

extraordinary and irrefutable popularity of Spanish women novelists in the 1980s thus:

> On the other hand their strength and force has given rise to the term 'feminine literature' and its possible discussion or debate, following Anglo–American models. It is difficult to believe they should be corsetted under such a tag, due more to the usual need to label things, or to publishers' propaganda, or perhaps, to a lesser extent, to the ideological positionings of feminist ideas.[2]

Rather than keep to the traditional demarcations between and within national literatures, my approach prioritizes women's literature in Spain on its own terms and within an international, gender-defined literary framework.

However, situating Roig's and Montero's novels in the wider perspective of contemporary Spanish narrative helps situate them with regard to the novels of other women writers. Fiction published in Spain between 1976 and 1982 is usually referred to as fiction of 'the transition': the transition between Franco's dictatorial regime and a democratic Spain. Franco died in 1975, but the democratic constitution of 1978 was not consolidated until after the unsuccessful army coup of 1981 and, arguably, the Socialist victory of 1982. According to Santos Alonso, the great majority of the novels published in these six years dealt with the existential, routine, psychological or amorous vicissitudes of one individual character and did not tend to experiment with narratorial perspective: 36 per cent were written in the third person, 34 per cent in the first person, and 13 per cent in the third and first persons.[3] Broadly speaking, these characteristics apply to Roig's and Montero's novels, at least until the late 1980s. Santos Alonso includes Montero's first novel in his section on the narrative of daily life but insists, erroneously, on what he believes is its autobiographical content (39–40). The post-transition novel, that is, the novel of the 1980s, is divided by Juan Ignacio Ferreras into seven categories. Most of Roig's novels fit into the first category: novels which deal with the Spanish Civil War (1936–9) and the post-war period (1939–75) from a new position of free speech and detachment (although Ferreras does not include novels written in Catalan).[4] However, none of the other categories in his

2. R. Acín, *Narrativa o consumo literario (1975–1987)*, p. 45.
3. Santos Alonso, *La novela en la transición*, pp. 131–3.
4. J. I. Ferreras, *La novela en el siglo XX (desde 1939)*, pp. 88–116.

typology (historical, erotic, intrigue, experimental, reflexive) would seem to apply wholly to the work of either Roig or Montero, except one: new realism. According to Ferreras it is this tendency of 'enriched' (116) or 'renewed' (128) realism which in 1988 'not only remains open and in full evolution and renovation', but is also the main source for the development of new types of novel (91). One of the new types was the realist-reportage bestseller dealing with themes hitherto taboo, many of these concerning women. Obviously, such narrative is well-suited to authors who are also journalists, such as Roig and Montero. The work of these two authors, then, falls well within the predominant realist and socially oriented narrative practice of the late 1970s and 1980s in Spain. Here too Ferreras places the work of another popular woman writer, Soledad Puértolas (118).

Ramón Acín stresses the fact that the popularity enjoyed by women novelists in Spain in the 1980s was due to public demand for novels about women, 'Rosa Montero and Montserrat Roig climb to the highest seats of honour in the ranking of bestsellers' (45), and he includes Esther Tusquets and Carme Riera in his list. But the feminist novels of Esther Tusquets are quite different from those of Montero and Roig. They continue the experimentation with language and the psychological import of, for example, Luis Martín Santos and Luis Goytisolo. According to Ferreras's or Alonso's typologies Tusquets's work is experimental and reflexive discourse. Her narrative belongs to what Pablo Gil Casado calls the 'dehumanized' Spanish novel, that is, narrative which is solipsistic, intimist, private, egocentric, the reverse side of the social novel because it 'systematically avoids dealing with human problems as a collective preoccupation, of a here and a now'.[5] Within the 'dehumanized' novel, Tusquets's and Ana María Moix's narrative is of the psychological and erotic type. Contrast this classification with the remark made by Haro Tecglen in 1978 to the effect that Roig's *El temps de les cireres* [*Tiempo de cerezas*] (*A Time for Cherries*) had arrived just in time on the desolate scene of Spanish narrative fiction because it was a 'human' novel and 'we have reached the depths of dehumanization, coldness, and distance'.[6] Similarly, Alex Broch includes Roig's first novel,

---

5. P. Gil Casado, *La novela deshumanizada española (1958–1988)*, p. 9.
6. *El País- Suplemento*, no. 64, 31 December 1978, pp. 1, 11. Quoted in José María Martínez Cachero, *La novela española entre 1936 y 1980*, p. 388.

*Ramona, adéu* [*Ramona, adiós*] (*Ramona, Goodbye*), in his typology of Catalan narrative of the 1970s in the section 'novels of the family and social circles'. He points out that this kind of novel, characterized by its historicity, was one of the most predominant in Catalunya during the 1970s. Roig's novel draws 'a dialectical relationship between social history and the individual development of each character, and this shows and explains the developing political and clearly nationalist awareness of women'.[7]

The typologies favoured by male Spanish critics hardly take into account the wide range of questions raised and objectives pursued by feminist narrative. Elizabeth Ordóñez gives further examples of these critics' uneasiness or short-sightedness (*Voices of Their Own*, 15) and adds 'when women's narrative is included in studies of the novel, it often appears curiously unmanageable' (15). A more useful approach is offered by Biruté Ciplijauskaité in her book *La novela femenina contemporánea (1970–1985)* where she sketches a typology of contemporary female-authored European narrative written in the first person. The novels she discusses are divided into four main, overlapping categories: consciousness-raising; psychoanalytical; historical; experimental-erotic. Roig's work falls clearly into the first and third sections, while Montero is included in the last in order to underline her metafictive narrative strategies and her rejection of existing social and literary structures. According to Ciplijauskaité, Roig shares with Doris Lessing, Olivia Manning and Jeanne Bourin a propensity for the *roman-fleuve* (35), with Christa Wolf, Margaret Atwood and Margaret Drabble consciousness-raising objectives, and with Lessing, Beatrix Beck and Barbara Frischmuth self-reflexive techniques (69–71). Ciplijauskaité borrows Graziella Auburtin's categorization of (French) women writers and divides those in Spain into two large groups, one oriented towards theory and the other to social issues; she places Montero's narrative squarely in the second (195). Montero, like Christiane Rochefort and Emma Santos, privileges the message of her novels rather than the style (188–9); like the Italian author Dacia Maraini and the German Svende Merian, she writes polemical socio-political bestsellers (191). Although such classifications are inevitably schematic they are useful methodologically. As in France, the two broad

---

7. A. Broch, *Literatura catalana dels anys setanta*, p. 76. See also Gonzalo Sobejano, 'La novela poemática y sus alrededores', *Insula*, 464–5, 1985, p. 1, p. 26.

groupings (theoretical-psychological/socio-political) generally hold in Spain, at least as far as individual novels are concerned; the authors themselves often avoid pigeon-holing by writing different kinds of novels. Robert Spires singles out Lourdes Ortiz whose work spans what he identifies as the 'polarity between discourse (metafiction) and story (mystery fiction)', between 'process' and 'product', in all post-Franco fiction, by both male and female authors.[8] The novels of Roig and Montero are similarly wide-ranging but their common insistence on the significance of history, society, and politics from an overtly feminist perspective suggests Ciplijauskaité's groupings are not unfounded.

In the introduction to her book *Women Writers in Contemporary Spain*, Joan L. Brown writes 'literature by women in modern Spain, though united by important gender-based commonalities, is characterized even more by its diversity'. She asks if it is thus legitimate to separate out fiction by women: 'For Spain, the answer is yes. At present, this affirmative action is necessary to bring outstanding, underappreciated literature to the attention of a wider readership' (23). But this should not be the only reason for distinguishing female-authored narrative in Spain. Those 'gender-based commonalities', the *sine qua non* of a female literary tradition, are crucial in a reading of the polyphonic, eclectic works of women novelists. Fiction by women in Spain which articulates female experience is necessarily non-hegemonic. And if the writer supports the general objectives of the Women's Movement, that is, she critiques patriarchy and sexism and questions the ideological underpinnings of femininity, if she is engaged in the transformation of dominant gender relations in society and considers the practice of writing a means of doing this, then she is perforce a feminist writer.

There is no shortage of women writers in Spain today but the majority dislike intensely any suggestion that they are feminists or that they are writing feminist fiction. This applies as much to older and well-established figures such as Carmen Martín Gaite

8. R. Spires, 'Lourdes Ortiz: Mapping the Course of Postfrancoist Fiction', in Joan L. Brown, *Women Writers of Contemporary Spain*, 1991, 198–216, p. 200. Angeles Encinar studies the twelve female-authored short stories included in Ymelda Navajo's *Doce relatos de mujeres*, Madrid: Alianza, 1982 and discovers two unifying aspects: first, the themes of love and death which are inextricably related (love signifying sexual freedom and death extreme rebellion against the system); second, the metafictional mode.

as to the younger novelists of the post-transition period. In an interview in 1991 an American academic asked Mercedes Abad (aged 30), Cristina Fernández Cubas and Soledad Puértolas if they were feminists, and suggested it was strange for so many Spanish women writers to declare they were not. Mercedes Abad said she had never written with the intention of voicing women's rights issues and that in her view social class was as important as gender;[9] Cristina Fernández Cubas remarked, 'None of our books can be considered feminist' and 'literature and feminism have nothing to do with each other'. She denies there is any discrimination against women in Spanish literary circles and deplores the fact that foreign critics apply to Spanish women writers schemes which do not apply (158). Interestingly, she reveals that what she understands by 'feminist' is to be active in a feminist organization. Púertolas opts for the androgynous model declaring that she writes as a person not as a woman (159). Púertolas and Fernández Cubas both hate the idea of feminist theory, the latter declaring there is too much in Spain already (161). All three rejected classificatory tags or labels. Other writers speaking on other occasions are less incisive. Marina Mayoral (b. 1942), for example, also repudiates the label 'feminist', but believes her feminist sympathies are 'profound' (Brown, 194). Lourdes Ortiz (b. 1943) was once active in the Spanish Communist Party and the feminist movement but left both (Brown, 199). Tusquets (b. 1936) 'disavows a direct engagement with the feminist movement' (Brown, 160). On the other hand, the Catalan author Carme Riera shows great interest in French feminist theory and claims she would never have written her novel *Una primavera para Domenico Guarini* if it were not for these readings. But even she admits her new priority is to write good literature, no matter what her ideas, and to continue defending women's rights as a person, not as a writer (Nichols, 192).

Monica Threlfall believes Spanish women writers do not want to be labelled or classified as feminist because this might suggest they should write in a certain way and attract only a certain type of reader. In other words, women writers stress their literary freedom as individuals in the same way any male author would. It is also symptomatic of a general attitude to feminism in the arts. If a writer says she or he is socialist readers do not necessarily

9. In an interview in *Mester*, XX, 2, 1991, p. 157.

*Introduction*

expect social realist novels. But in Spain, writes Thelfall in 1985, feminism is still associated with over-commitment bordering on obsession, blinkered vision, small-minded cliques, difference politics, the defunct Feminist Party, or the restricted interests of Anglo–American women academics who, it is felt, try to impose their own critical paradigms on Spanish women in yet another form of cultural imperialism. If women writers did refer to themselves as feminists this would suit the male Spanish literary critics who could then legitimately separate women into a category of their own. Women writers want to be considered as good as male authors. According to Threlfall, if there were more women critics who considered male-authored books in the same way as male critics consider female-authored books then the story might be different.[10]

Montserrat Roig and Rosa Montero have been selected for study on several counts: they represent the new generation of women writers emerging in the post-Franco period and publishing their first novels in the 'transition'; they both write bestsellers about woman in society using a predominantly realist format; they are both middle-class professionals sympathetic to the Left; they are approximately the same age – Roig is five years older than Montero – and were born after the Civil War; they are both journalists; but, more importantly in my view, they are both declared feminists. Moreover, their work represents feminist fiction written in the two main languages of Spain: Catalan and Castilian Spanish. Their narrative thus points to two literary traditions and two nationalities. Yet both authors write within the framework of the Spanish state, draw on recent Spanish history, and are concerned with contemporary Spanish society from a woman-centred perspective. Montero writes in Spanish and locates her novels in Madrid; Roig writes in Catalan and closely identifies with the city of Barcelona. Before discussing the feminism espoused by both authors the prickly question of language needs to be broached.

Roig is bilingual: she writes her fiction in Catalan, the rest of her prose in either Catalan or Spanish. Her novels were translated almost immediately into Spanish, and it is in that language that they have reached the majority of the peninsular and international

10. M. Threlfall, 'The Women's Movement in Spain', *New Left Review*, 151, May–June, 1985, pp. 44–73.

public. This study (which makes use of the Spanish translations compared to the Catalan when necessary) is more concerned with Montserrat Roig as a woman writer than as a Catalan speaker. Roig's contribution to women's literature and feminist ideas in Spain and further afield is important and should be divulged to an international public. The import of her work straddles language barriers and involves the kind of cross-cultural analysis relevant to today's feminist criticism. As Maggie Humm writes, 'passing across the borders of languages is a way of making the arbitrariness of national cultures very visible'.[11] Roig recognized this when she brought the Russian writers she admired so much to the attention of the Spanish and Catalan public.

It should never be forgotten, however, that one of Roig's main purposes for writing at all was to write in Catalan. She aimed to prolong the Catalan literary tradition, brutally interrupted after the Civil War, and contribute to it with contemporary works about women. Her love for her mother tongue comes across clearly in her essays and novels, not only in the carefully-wrought language she writes, but in the strong, inevitable connections she makes in her fiction between language, national identity, and selfhood. When discussing the women's issues raised in her narrative the reader should be ever mindful that these gender-related questions are being focused through the medium of the Catalan language which, as a minority and recently persecuted language, sheds its own special vindicatory light on all other topics raised. For Roig, Spanish is the language of 'power and domination, while the language of love and affection' is Catalan (Nichols, 147). In her essays and articles Roig returns again and again to the problems she faced when she set out to write novels in Catalan.'I write in a half-born language and I live between chaos and isolation', she writes in the prologue to her first collection of stories, published in Spanish as *Aprendizaje sentimental* (*Sentimental Education*), on p. 8. Interesting in this respect is her essay 'Voices and Dialogue'.[12] Here Roig refers to the enormous chasm produced during the Franco regime between the Catalan spoken at home and the written Catalan enshrined in great works of literature. Catalan literature belonged to the pre-Civil War period. The language of

---

11. M. Humm, *Border Traffic. Strategies of Contemporary Women Writers*, Manchester, 1992, p. 22.
12. M. Mayoral (ed.), *El oficio de narrar*, Madrid, 1990, pp. 69–80.

the great Catalan authors, Roig's literary fathers and mothers, was impeccable, authentic, and perfect, and this inhibited her as she came to write after the long literary silence. Josep Pla and Mercè Rodoreda were 'my masters, my classics, and yet, they paralyzed me verbally'(72); the Catalan of neither Pla nor even Rodoreda was appropriate to the Catalunya of the 1970s. In Barcelona the situation was particularly difficult because the popular, spoken Catalan of the urban streets, the language Roig needed for her novels, had died. The working classes were mainly Andaluz and spoke Spanish. Even after the regularization of the status of the language in the late 1970s these immigrant workers learned Catalan at school, writes Roig, as she had once learned Latin. Television had replaced the tradition of storytelling; it had supplanted 'oral literature and has given us instead a packaged substitute' (80). Roig points out that most of the Catalan authors writing in Castilian are from Barcelona (Esther Tusquets, Juan and Luis Goytisolo, Ana María and Terenci Moix, Juan Marsé, and so on), while those writing in Catalan are from the rural areas. The textual trace of this problem, typical of a diglossic situation, is lost in translation. For instance, in the short story 'Mar', one of the characters parodies American film stars and switches from Catalan to Spanish. A different kind of problem is found in *Tiempo de cerezas*, where the maid who is Andalusian should speak in Spanish, but has to be read in Catalan. Roig was faced with a situation very similar to that confronted by the novelist Manuel Puig (of Catalan and Italian descent) writing in the same years in Argentina. He too was inhibited, by the literary language of the great Spanish masters.[13] Both authors came across an ingenious, age-old solution. Roig explains: 'I realized I did not only see the characters [in my novels] but that I also heard them. I heard their voices, sometimes in monologues, sometimes in duets, or through a chorus' (79). She, like Puig, realized the voices she heard were women's voices. The male characters seemed to express abstractions and concepts and they were able to write the written Catalan of the classics. But it was the female characters who saved the language by speaking it, that is, by telling stories. Roig writes: 'We all hear voices. They are in the air. It is just a matter of listening

---

13. Saul Sosnowski, 'Manuel Puig. Entrevista', *Hispamérica*, 1, May 1993, pp. 70–2.

to them' (80). To liberate a polyphony of voices in a democratic project is another of Roig's purposes for writing:

> It seems to me that literature has a role which nothing can substitute: to free the voices of the world, the old voices, in the face of the VOICE . . . the one that restricts our imagination and denies us the right to dream for ourselves. (80)

This gives some indication of the complex textual interweaving of national language, narrative voice, gender roles, and the constitution of a collective and personal identity in Roig's boundary defeating work.

Both Roig and Montero, then, are writers who are also declared feminists. The type of feminism they espouse is not radical feminism ('feminismo de la diferencia' in Spanish), nor overtly psychological, nor the feminisms associated with the better known French theorists, nor lesbian feminism. Generally speaking, they tend towards hetero, socialist, and political feminist positions. However, once again such categorizations taken out of the contemporary Spanish context over-simplify. The following section will analyze in greater detail what Roig and Montero seem to understand by feminism in the context of women's emancipation and the Women's Movement in Spain. Roig has written at length on this subject, Montero to a lesser extent, but both authors share a number of basic assumptions and preoccupations which can be gathered, following Roig, under the heading 'humanist feminism'.

### Humanist Feminism

> It's not the superficially hysterical scream of a handful of women dissatisfied with their own lives; it is not the public expression of feminine bitterness. It is the stuggle to achieve a new human identity starting from the biological fact of having been born a woman; it is to reach with men towards a new and better category: the category person (Montserrat Roig, El feminismo, Barcelona, 1984 (1981), p. 5).

In 1981 Montserrat Roig published an illustrated book in a popular series meant for a broad public. It was called *Mujeres en busca de un nuevo humanismo* (*Women in Search of a New Humanism*). The book had a second edition in 1984, but the title was changed to *El feminismo*. This illustrates the rapidly changing attitudes towards feminism in the Spain of the 1980s. The book is a succinct, informative account of the Women's Movement, not only in Western Europe (including Spain) and North America, but also in the socialist countries (Cuba and the USSR) and the Third World. Roig discusses briefly the ideas informing feminism, from John Stuart Mill, through Lenin, to the three great contemporary theorists: de Beauvoir, Friedan and Millett; she then goes on to analyse the general situation of women in the world with relation to the family, work, consumer society, rural and urban economies, education, female sexuality, psychoanalysis, motherhood, and mental illness. This book is interesting on two counts: first, it indicates Roig's perception of the need for a defensive legitimization of feminism in the face of a generally hostile public which she hopes to achieve by means of a largely objective, sociohistorical account; second, it shows her own broad knowledge of the subject. She quotes from the translated works not only of the above mentioned authors but also from the work of, for example, Sheila Rowbotham, Margaret Mead, Elizabeth Cady Stanton, Alexandra Kollontai, Rosa Luxemburg, Clara Zetkin, and Evelyne Sullerot.

In 1980, Roig points out, the word 'feminist' is still perceived as a threat in Spain and is associated with aggression towards men, frustration, and macho women, the 'amazons of a future matriarchy' (4). She explains what, in her view, feminism really means. It is 'a rigorous and exhaustive analysis of the reasons for the centuries old oppression of one part of Humanity'; it does not imply a break with men as human beings, 'but with the idea created through History that the male is the superior, intellectual being by definition and woman the other side of his mirror'; it is a liberating philosophy but 'the freedom of women does not imply the slavery of men, in the same way that men cannot dream of freedom if they continue to oppress women'; feminism means the 'recuperation of women's words and of their own collective and individual history, so that women can reconcile themselves with their own sex and with the other sex, without taboos, without restrictive laws, without paralyzing fears'. Ultimately, Roig believes the analysis of one's own female experience 'leads to the fullest comprehension of a feminine reality' (5). Not all women are the same, she claims, nor do they resist in the same way; what could unite them all is the knowledge that oppression is not their destiny but culturally constructed, that there are reasons and causes for their situation, and that the condition of women is both universal and specific.

In an earlier publication, *¿Tiempo de mujer?* (*Woman's Time?*), 1980, which brought together a number of previously published essays and articles, some published as early as 1976, Roig launched into a more impassioned, often personal attack on cultural conventions and traditional role models in Spain.[14] Again, she deals with the history of the liberation movement, particularly in Britain, and – in the section 'We Women' (which was published as the introduction to a medical book on contraception[15]) – the mystique of motherhood and the oppression of the Catholic Church. She suggests shared parenting as a means of resisting 'phallocracy' (95) and the family unit: 'in marriage love becomes anthropophagy. We don't want the freedom of the other. Before freedom we want destruction' (295). In the section 'What Sex is God', Roig discusses pornography, the effects of sexual repression in Spain, sexuality and the sex/gender system, and she includes several interviews with Spanish transvestites. She attacks sexist French philosophers in 'Why there have been no women geniuses' using several arguments put forward by Doris Lessing in *The Golden Notebook*. The impact of Lessing's book in Spain is incontestable, particularly on women writers. Roig admires Lessing because she examines both the collective and individual consciousness:

> In *The Golden Notebook* several women try to reach totality after having disintegrated in a multiple cosmos. In a difficult and conflictive process of introspection, Doris Lessing tries to reconcile the artistic, the psychological and the literary. Out of the failure of an ideology which purported to reach totality in abstract, Lessing's protagonists choose to be fragmented and broken up in a more concrete world . . . In Lessing's novel all the women are trying to forge an independent

---

14. *¿Tiempo de mujer?* (*Women's Time*), 1980, is stylistically much more interesting than *El feminismo*. It is a pot pourri of interviews, personal reflections, and short essays on women's issues. Again, Roig shows her wide knowledge of feminist theory. Works of the following authors are listed in the bibliography: Eva Figes, Adrienne Rich, Anais Nin, Erika Jong, Annie Leclerc, Marie Cardinal, Doris Lessing, Shulamith Firestone, Nora Ephron, Virginia Woolf, Juliet Mitchell, Susan Brogger, Foucault, and Masters and Johnson, all in translations published throughout the 1970s.
15. Eugeni Castells, *El derecho a la contracepción*, Barcelona, 1978.

*Introduction*

world in the midst of a civilization that is disintegrating. Lessing shows us the world of men, which is as broken as that of women, and asks herself, 'Is it possible to fly there?'. Perhaps only after assuming dichotomy, failure, inner fragmentation will the pieces slowly come together, or perhaps never. But we have to be aware of this and, above all, express it. (161–2)

After all, 'feminism attempts to reconcile being a woman and being a person' (164).

Roig's clarification of what feminism ought to be was important for Spanish women in the early 1980s. They were having to adapt to a radically new situation. 'Feminism' might well have been a threatening word still, but the progress made in the area of women's rights was undeniable. At the risk of over-simplifying, in ten years (1976–86) Spanish women went from having no individual rights to enjoying the same rights as women in the European Community. This speedy and concentrated political reform was impelled by an exuberant Women's Movement in the late 1970s. The new Constitution of 1978 provided the framework for equality before the law and specifically ruled against sexual discrimination. Legislation to secure equality in the workplace (1980) and in the family (1981) followed shortly, including a polemical divorce law (1981) whose stormy four-year passage through parliament contributed to the defeat of the Centre government. The Socialist victory of 1982 made way for the actual implementation of legislation. The abortion law (1983) was delayed until 1985 when it was passed, although in a more restricted form than originally envisaged. In 1983 the Women's Institute was set up under the directorship of a socialist feminist and two years later had at its disposition a budget of £3.5 million. By the mid-1980s the divorce rate was 0.5 °/00 (a figure still lower than the European average), women constituted about 30 per cent of the workforce, and female representation in parliament was around 6 per cent. Attitudes to women's role in society had changed markedly. In a 1975 survey of just over 2,000 respondents, 82 per cent had believed household jobs should be done by women and 79 per cent that women should be at home when their husbands returned from work. But in 1987, 47 per cent of the respondents of a larger survey believed in shared household duties, shared parenting and equally fulfilling jobs for both partners compared to the EEC average of 41 per cent (Moxon-

Brown, *Political Change*, 68–78).[16]

Paradoxically, following these reforms, the embryonic feminist movement fell into disarray. As Moxon-Browne states, 'the Spanish state has, in a very direct sense, co-opted a large part of the feminist movement' (79). Second-wave feminism in Spain was never politically strong; it reached a peak of activity between 1975 and 1979, and then dissolved as an independently organized movement. It exists today as a collection of numerous groups and collectives linked informally, in the women's sections of the parliamentary political parties and trade unions, in local neighbourhood and housewives' associations, and in state institutions. The two main problems which were never resolved in the Spanish movement and which led to irreparable, internal dissension were, first, the question of double-membership, and, second, the conflicting ideas of difference politics and politics of equality. In a way, the mainstream double-militancy position, in which women were both members of left of centre political parties and feminist groups, was a victim of its own success. As we have seen, the 1978 Constitution and the Socialist victory of 1982 provided the working framework for the implementation of most of the legislation that women had campaigned for, except women's control of their own reproduction (Monica Threlfall could still write in 1985 that 'no woman has yet had a legal abortion in Spain' (64)). But social democratic reform did not go far enough. The founding of the Women's Institute, for example, smacked of tokenism. Why, then, was there not a strong, independently organized feminist movement in Spain? Why did the feminist movement peter out in the early 1980s? And why was feminism seen to be synonymous with radical, man-hating positions?

First, there was no Spanish first-wave feminism as such mainly due to the strength of right-wing, Catholic ideology in the

16. Other figures, however, were not so encouraging. In 1987 Spain boasted the highest percentages of unemployed women in the EEC: 50 per cent of economically active women in the 15–24 age group and 22 per cent in the 25–49 age group were unemployed (cf. 15 per cent and 10 per cent in the UK respectively). Spain also had the highest percentage of non-active women (59 per cent) in the EEC (cf. the EEC average of 42 per cent). In 1988 only 8.2 per cent of Spanish women without children lived alone, compared with the EEC average of 19.6 per cent, and in 1989 70 per cent of Spanish women with a spouse were non-active by the age of 45. The pattern is still that women work throughout their twenties and leave their jobs (for good) when they marry or have children. *Women in the European Community*, 1992, p. 108, p. 127, p. 68, p. 32.

dominant classes and among women themselves. 'Feminism arrived late and badly in Spain' wrote Roig (*El feminismo*, 13). The absence of a powerful, free-thinking middle class in a primarily rural economy is crucial in this respect. The rights women did secure briefly in the 1930s during the Republic and before the Civil War, including the right to vote (1931) and the complete equality of women in Catalunya (1935), were not due to pressure from a Women's Movement but to political manoeuvrings and the support of the centre-left Radical and Socialist Parties. Allegiance, then, to left-wing parliamentary parties which again in the 1970s and 1980s pushed to provide a democratic framework for women's liberation is perfectly understandable. The oppressive, patriarchal, Catholic, military dictatorship under Franco, in which even the most basic of human rights were denied to the whole population, delayed women's liberation by decades. 'Ironically, Spanish women voted for the first time in 1933, twelve years before women in France, and again in 1936, before losing all their political rights until 1977' (Moxon-Browne, 68). In Franco's Spain women who protested about the role they were allotted in a fascist society were considered left-wing. The women who remained in the country (that is were not forced into exile) retreated from the public scene into the home and the church; they depended entirely on their father or husband, and their confessor. Special emphasis was placed on women's role as mothers not only to comply with Catholic doctrine but also because the country needed a work-force. Women were expected to produce as many offspring as possible; prizes for large families encouraged this. Condoms and all forms of contraception were illegal. In the 1950s, increasing numbers of women entered educational institutions, but their instruction was in the hands of the Church and the Feminine Section, set up after the war by the sister of the founder of the Spanish Fascist party (Falange), Pilar Primo de Rivera. All women were obliged to have a certificate of Social Service (the domestic equivalent of military conscription for men) without which they could have neither a passport nor a driving licence, nor study at university. Any counter-hegemonic women's groups were to be found in the illegal trade unions and underground political (predominantly Communist) parties (Durán, 396–7). In Spain, it was inevitable that the issue of women's rights should be identified with the political left and civil rights. This shaped the nature of Spanish second-wave feminism; the women's movement entered the arena of democratic debate only after Franco's death, more than ten years after its counterpart in the rest of Western Europe.

Second, most Spanish women had a deep aversion to all-women organizations which reminded them of Fascist ideology and organization and Catholic doctrine. Women endured the Feminine Section for forty years. It stressed the importance of mothering and 'natural' feminine attributes (care, nurturing, sensitivity, passivity, suffering) and, like the Catholic Church, insisted on sexually segregated schools. It is hardly surprising that the difference politics of radical feminism did not go down well in Spain. Add to these two factors the relatively low percentage of women in the work-force and the undeniable influence of the Catholic church, then it is not surprising that the cultural parameters of Spain gave rise to a different set of problems and solutions in the Spanish Women's Movement than in that of the United States and Britain, for example.

The two tendencies in the women's movement in the Spain of the late 1970s and 1980s were, and still are, irreconcilable. On the one hand were the grass-roots organizations of the radical or 'difference' feminists who were opposed to patriarchal structures and men as a class and were not aligned with parliamentary political parties. Organized on the basis of discussion groups and collectives, they aimed for consciousness-raising on specifically women's issues, such as abortion, contraception, and rape. This tendency has always been weak in Spain: it is identified by some as extremely revolutionary and, as we have seen, by others as right-wing. But it does constitute a resilient social movement (if not a political organization) which by its very flexibility can adapt to circumstances. The other, stronger tendency, often referred to as liberal, socialist or social feminism, was associated (to a greater or lesser degree) with the trade unions and parliamentary parties. It aimed to reform the system through legislation and believed in collaboration with fair-minded men. Obviously, it was hampered or even annulled by the very political and social male-centred forces with which it collaborated. A third tendency, the Feminist Party set up by Lidia Falcón based in Barcelona, is now defunct. After the debacle of the 1979 feminist congress which was attended by over 3,000 delegates but where no agreement was reached on aims and strategies, the Spanish women's movement was further weakened and fragmented.

*Introduction*

The failure of the feminist movement, then, was mainly due to internal dissension and to state reform during the 1980s: 'The political system, by accommodating many of its earlier demands, had effectively spiked the guns of the mainstream feminist movement' (Moxon-Browne, 78). Lidia Falcón points out that women who were militant feminists during the 1970s tended to follow different directions in the next decade: some were satisfied with their gains, others were incorporated into well-meaning but under-funded state institutions, others – who were dissatisfied with the chaos in the Women's Movement – joined political parties, peace organizations or the green party (Falcón, 1992, 499). However, she places the blame not only on internal dissension (independence v. double-membership; socialism v. difference; hetero v. lesbians; housewives v. professionals; atheists v. Catholics) but also on the traditional 'enemies' of feminism in Spain: the Church, the political parties, the judiciary, the media, the medical profession (429–31). The result was that, despite some fifteen years of consciousness-raising, in the 1991 general elections only 13 per cent of the MPs voted to Congress and Senate were women, and only 33 per cent of the female work-force was in employment, compared with the EEC average of 44 per cent (238).

In *El feminismo*, Montserrat Roig could not be aware of the difficulties the Women's Movement would face in the 1980s. What then were her conclusions regarding feminism in her 1981 publication? She calls for a profound reappraisal of the role of the family unit: 'feminists question the family . . . because it is at the core of their annulment as social beings' (37). She underlines the need for female self-reliance and independence. Women should resist their own insecurities and their propensity towards victimization as well as men's reluctance to forego privilege: 'only those women who respect themselves can opt for their own freedom and independence.' She rejects essentialist positions. Women should remember they are no better than men. They too can be cruel, competitive, dogmatic and intolerant when given the opportunity: 'To be a woman today is not easy. But neither is it easy to be a man . . . what is really difficult is to behave like and to be considered human beings, men as well as women'; 'to be a woman and at the same time a person is not an easy task' (62). She proposes on-going debate; it is the kind of feminism which 'doubts and reflects' that makes more meaningful advances. Feminism will achieve women's liberation as long as 'it stems from

Introduction

a new, humanist vision of the world'. Roig's credo in 1981 is humanist feminism:

> the day that men and women are no longer mutilated, the day when sex does not condition people's full development, the day when male domination and supremacy pass to the Annals of History..., the day when communication between the sexes is born out of mutual respect between free human beings, that day there will be no need for feminism. (63)

In interviews given in 1984 and 1985 Roig's views can be seen to have changed little; she states a preference for the work of Juliet Mitchell, for example, because Mitchell tried to unite feminism and socialism. But Roig's tone is no longer optimistic:

> I can't hear the feminine [sic] world right now, it is silent. There are only a couple of loonies like me saying anything. ... I want the feminine world to speak, to demand its rights ... How can they [women] accept these things and think everything is alright? ... With each day I get the sensation of belonging to a minority, I wouldn't say mad, but almost ... My generation has waged a war without ever going to war, and that's worse because everything we had hoped to do is dissolving ... We've been losing bit by bit. At the same time I think we women have given up; there shouldn't be just a few illuminated nuts like me who live – as far as possible – in accordance with our ideas. Well, it's no good being so pessimistic. Feminism has left something; it's frozen or hibernating for the moment but we did reach a ceiling in our demands for women's rights, and perhaps that was totally mad. What we were hoping for was a complete, radical change in people's way of living – not just in their public but also in their private lives – and that was much more difficult to achieve. But I'm sure something has remained ... (Nichols, 169)

In the elections of 1986 Roig (a member of the Catalan Communist Party until 1980) was so disgusted by the major political parties' indifference to a programme for women that she debated, in an article published in *El Periódico*, whether she should vote at all or simply go to the beach (Falcón, 236). This sentiment was echoed by Rosa Montero in the elections of June 1993. 'I won't be supporting anyone', she stated, 'I think they are all pathetic.'[17] Optimism had given way to disenchantment.

Like Roig, Rosa Montero is a declared feminist. For the reasons

17. In *Cambio 16*, 10 May 1993, p. 26.

outlined above she too is unsympathetic to radical feminism and essentialist positions. She explained in an interview in 1985:

> I have considered myself a feminist for a long time; but feminism for me is not an ideology. Which does not mean I agree with that right-wing movement [postmodernism?] which avoids ideologies altogether and ends up nowhere. What I mean to say is that for me feminism is something more basic, more animal-like, it's a way of being in life, something definitive, defining. (7)[18]

She claims her feminist consciousness developed not out of theoretical enquiry but from empirical observation, and her novels are feminist in as much as they represent her feminist vision of the world. In a 1986 interview Montero added that the world is sexist, and therefore should be reflected as such in literature; women writers should face up to this: 'women express the world very differently from men, and they need to tell it in a way which is often completely different too' (Alborg, 73). From her early days of journalism Montero made her feminist position quite clear. Her book of interviews, *Cinco años de País* (*Five Years of País*) (Madrid, 1982), which collects pieces published in the press between the first general elections in democratic Spain (1977) and 1982, is extremely interesting in this respect. Montero is an aggressive defender of women's rights and she provokes her interviewees into revealing their deepest prejudices. She engages in a heated debate with the anti-abortionist opera singer Montserrat Caballé; Caballé believes feminist organizations are for people with 'complexes' (249). She sympathetically interviews the founder of the Feminine Section, Pilar Primo de Rivera, who deplores divorce, extra-marital relations, contraception, and abortion but who, Montero suggests, was nevertheless marginalized by the Franco regime. She prods the infamous industrialist José María Ruiz Mateos into declaring that a woman's mission is the home and the family, and the then leader of the Spanish Communist Party, Santiago Carrillo, into admitting he is something of a womanizer. Throughout her work, Montero is obviously concerned about a whole range of issues relating to sexual politics and patriarchal relations. Like Roig, she stresses the importance of female self-reliance. She believes interpersonal (heterosexual) relationships can be mutually destructive: 'if we [women] don't know how to live with

18. In *La mujer feminista*, 21, November–December 1985.

ourselves . . we will only have anthropophagous relationships, just because we are frightened of being alone' (*La mujer feminista* (*The Feminist Woman*), 8). She is also strongly critical of cultural conventions and modes of behaviour in which Spanish women have been traditionally educated, such as romantic myths and mystique, and masculine-defined sexual relationships. In a talk delivered in 1992 entitled 'Escribiendo a la luna'('Writing on the Moon') Montero reminds her audience that machismo is still rife in Spain (as in all Europe) and attributes sexism in Spain to the Catholic Church, eight centuries of Islamic 'occupation', and forty years of Francoism. Yet she recognizes the enormous progress women had made in the previous twenty years; in the early 1970s married women could not open a bank account, buy a car, take out a passport, or have a job without their husband's permission. In 1970 women in the work place were still rare creatures. Speaking from personal experience as a journalist Montero writes:

> I remember . . . when you arrived at the office most men tried to find out if you were a virgin or not, and, depending on what they thought, they adopted two attitudes: if they thought you were a virgin they became insufferably paternalistic and would tell you exactly where to put your commas; if they imagined you weren't a virgin they hassled you interminably, because if you had been to bed with someone, then why not with them, seeing they were so marvellous? (3)

However, as previously mentioned, Montero, like Roig, believes the Socialist Party's reforms have not gone far enough. The two ministerial posts 'invented for' women in 1988, for example, were 'ridiculous and outrageous [una chorrada indignante]' (*La Tribuna*, 58).

Monica Threlfall wrote in 1985, 'Spanish feminists have often asked themselves "Where are we going?" and the answer has chiefly been, "We don't know"' (72). Her conclusion was that the gender struggle 'in private life rages on. The democratization of inter-personal relations, domestic arrangements and emotional life is a vital complement to the reforms in Spanish society and politics, and the impetus for initiating this can only come from the women's movement' (73). On the basis of her analysis Threlfall suggested two specific contributions Spanish feminists could make to femininst thought and writing without copying Anglo–American paradigms: an analysis of the relationship between

*Introduction*

women and Catholicism, and between women and totalitarian ideologies and the gender relations therein subsumed (60). Both Roig and Montero engage with these questions in their fiction, but as we shall see, their range of vision goes much further. In many ways, their narrative responds to the changing attitudes of and towards women in Spanish society over a twenty-year period. Their work is always woman-centred but never separatist. Generally speaking, Roig explores how the past inheres in the present, Montero how the present inheres in the future. For these writers the sexual revolution could be nothing less than a revolution at all levels of society.

# Part 1

# Montserrat Roig: History, Nationalism and Female Identity

# 1

## *Maternal Circles and Family Lines: the Narrative of the 1970s*

*F*or over twenty years, between 1970 and 1991, the Catalan author Montserrat Roig repeatedly explored the implications of the social and historical construction of feminine identity in both fiction and non-fiction. Her untimely death from cancer at the age of forty-five brought her ground-breaking project to a premature end. Her fiction is written in Catalan and it is with the Catalan literary tradition that it engages. But although her novels and short stories are to do with Catalan history and national identity, they are primarily about woman's position within the culture and society of Catalunya, and by extension of Western Europe. Roig's work was almost immediately translated and published in Spanish and reached a popularity outside Catalunya equalled only by her earlier female compatriot, the novelist Mercè Rodoreda, whose woman-centred narrative also surmounted the barriers of language in its portrayal of women's lives in post-Civil War Spain. Roig is conscious of her literary role-model but although she quotes extensively from Catalan authors in her fiction (the intertextual affirmation and revision of the Catalan literary tradition being one of its main characteristics), she does not quote Rodoreda or, indeed, any other important Catalan woman writer publishing earlier this century (for example, Maria Aurèlia Capmany). This may well point to a clichéd anxiety of maternal influence, or to the language problems posed by 'classical' female-authored texts in Catalan, pointed out in the Introduction. It does suggest that Roig looked outside Catalunya for literary models and found them in Virginia Woolf or, in the case of *L'hora violeta* (1980) [*La hora violeta*, 1980] (*The Violet Hour*), in Doris Lessing's *The Golden Notebook*, 1962, (although Roig read Lessing's novel after writing *La hora violeta*, Nichols, 161).[1] Her fiction, then, while rooted in Catalunya and crucially involved with the fortunes of Barcelona this century, to the extent that the city becomes a collective character in the dramatis personae, nevertheless appeals to women living in a similar social milieu (a large, European city in decline) responding to similar problems concerning personal identity and political commitment.

Roig's fiction draws on the European realist tradition, bringing to mind not only the social dramas of the nineteenth-century Catalan and Spanish realist authors (particularly the tortured self-questioning of Leopoldo Alas's Ana Ozores in *La Regenta*) but also the British Victorian and Edwardian family sagas.[2] This is not surprising. The world of Roig's fiction is the urban, bourgeois family; her female characters are firmly located in a social formation they paradoxically perpetuate yet simultaneously resist as it threatens to swallow them up. Generation after generation, the self-identity of these women is formed vis-à-vis the social and cultural norms and expectations they encounter within traditional, middle-class family roles. There is no way out. Despite participation in left-wing politics and the women's liberation movement, despite consciousness-raising, economic independence, sexual freedom, travel, and the extension of women's horizons in all directions, the protagonists of Roig's novels are impossibly caught up in a web of assimilated assumptions involving heterosexual relationships, mothering, and home-making which they consistently resent. They resent and reject these roles almost begrudgingly, in spite of themselves. The women of the 1970s are enmeshed in an impossible situation that invalidates traditional feminine models yet can offer no new arrangements for women's self-fulfilment and happiness. Again, the similarities with Lessing are striking: here too is a search for

---

1. Enric Bou in *Historia de la literatura catalana*, II, ed. Martí de Riquer et al, Barcelona, 1988, refers to Roig's use of monologue as 'deliberate imitation of one of the techniques characteristic of Mercè Rodoreda', p. 405.
2. As C. B. Cadenas suggests, rather than a saga, Roig writes a 'counter-saga' in which women are the protagonists. See C. B. Cadenas, 'Historia de tres mujeres', *Nueva Estafeta*, 1980, p. 76 and C. Bellver, *Women Writers of Contemporary Spain*, ed. Joan L. Brown, 1991, p. 222.

'something new' which never quite materializes. And the problem is not just men, 'machismo' or even patriarchal social structures. The problem has to do with women themselves. There are no simple answers to the questions raised in Roig's work. The female characters work round and round their conundrum in an open-ended process, and although the deferral of narrative closure does suggest possibility for change, the overall mood – again like Lessing – is bleak.

Usually included in the Catalan literary generation of the 1970s, Roig made her reputation as a novelist with the trilogy published between 1972 and 1980: *Ramona, adéu* (1972) [*Ramona, adiós,* 1980] (*Goodbye, Ramona*); *El temps de les cireres* (1977) [*Tiempo de cerezas,* 1978] (*A Time for Cherries*); and *L'hora violeta* (1980) [*La hora violeta,* 1980] (*The Violet Hour*). This traces the fortunes of the women of two Barcelona families, the Miralpeix and the Claret, during this century. Two later novels, *L'òpera quotidiana* (1982) [*La ópera cotidiana,* 1982] (*The Everyday Opera*) and *La veu melodiosa* (1987) [*La voz melodiosa,* 1987] (*The Melodious Voice*) pick up the stories of one or two members of these families, but more tangentially, and explore new directions. Roig has also published two collections of short fiction: the early *Molta roba i poc sabó . . . i tan neta que la volen* (*Lots of Washing and Not Much Soap . . . and They Want it So Clean*), 1971, translated into Castilian as *Aprendizaje sentimental,* 1981 (*Sentimental Education*), and her last work of fiction, published while she was ill, *El cant de la joventut* (1990) [*El canto de la juventud,* 1990] (*The Song of Youth*). These, too, interrelate with the novels. Finally, two works of drama were published posthumously in one volume: *Reivindicació de la senyora Clito Mestres. Seguit de El Mateix Paisatge,* 1992 (*The Vindication of Mrs. Clito Mestres. Followed by The Same Landscape*).

Montserrat Roig was not only a writer of fiction and drama; she was a committed investigative journalist. She first came to public attention through television with a series of interviews in the programmes 'Personatges' and 'Líders'. Apart from numerous collaborations in leading Spanish and Catalan newspapers and reviews (including *Serra d'Or, Avui, Mundo Diario, Triunfo, Cuadernos para el Diálogo, El País* and the leading Spanish feminist publication *Vindicación Feminista*) she has published other books of non-fiction which are worthy of attention in the context of this study: *¿Tiempo de mujer?,* 1980 (*Woman's Time?*); *Mujeres hacia un nuevo humanismo,* 1982 (*Women Towards a New Humanism*); *Els* *catalans als camps nazis*, 1977 [*Noche y niebla: los catalanes en los campos nazis*, 1980] (*The Catalans in Nazi Concentration Camps*); *Mi viaje al bloqueo*, 1982 (*My Journey to the Blockade*); *L'agulla daurada*, 1985 [*La aguja dorada*, 1985] (*The Golden Spire*); and, finally, the more intimate *Digues que m'estimes encara que sigui mentida*, 1991 [*Dime que me quieres aunque sea mentira*, 1992] (*Tell Me You Love Me Even Though It's Lies*). This corpus of non-fiction, privileging feminist and social concerns, interweaves with her more self-conscious fictional work often through an autobiographical interface enabling the reader to interpret the novels and short stories, at least partially, as testimonial fiction. In this way Roig's prose dissolves demarcations of genre. Short and long fiction, documentary, journalism, autobiography, and lyrical introspection merge in a constant rewriting of the self-in-history. Hers is one consistent and coherent attempt to explore and make sense of woman's place in contemporary society and of society itself through the written word. 'This writer's life and work were mixed together in one unmistakable drama' wrote Enric Bou shortly after Roig's death (*El País*, 12 November 1991, 41), while Maruja Torres, in the same issue, attributed Roig's belief in 'el valor testimonial de la palabra' [the first-hand experience value of words] to the silence enforced on her father, the writer Tomás Roig, during the Franco régime (29). Roig herself in a 'Confession' preceding her first collection of short stories describes how she made the decision to be a professional writer: 'I shut myself indoors with the desire to make that leap: to pass from the informal, intimate pages [of a diary] I had kept since childhood to write free-standing pages, detached from my navel' (*Aprendizaje sentimental*, 11), but the connection between self and society was never lost. Her death, although expected after a year-long illness, was no less shocking and caused consternation in Catalan and Spanish literary circles not only because of the value of her work but also – as a number of correspondents pointed out – because she represented a position, a socialist and humanist politics and ethics, that was becoming as increasingly unfashionable in a market-oriented, postmodern Spain as in Western Europe as a whole. She has died, wrote Maruja Torres, at a time when 'we can't afford even one casualty in the ranks of those who purposely *look* with a moral eye', who 'relive history [for us] so we don't have a falsified version'. In Roig's fiction, this 'history' was largely the cyclical repetition of a matrilineal and matronymical her-story.

## Aprendizaje sentimental (Sentimental Education)

There is no better introduction to Roig's novels and to the notion of cyclical patterns in her work as a whole than the first collection of short stories *Molta roba i poc sabó . . . (Lots of Washing and Not Much Soap*, 1971), published in Spanish in 1981 with the title *Aprendizaje sentimental (Sentimental Education)*. The collection won her the coveted Víctor Català prize. Published in Catalan four years before Franco's death, this is clearly an important text for the feminist reader. Many of the issues broached in the novels are first sketched in what is a rather off-beat collection of short prose pieces: stories, snatches of conversation, vignettes, and letters. Roig refers to them in the dedication as 'this mixture of sentimental miscellanea, scenes of Barcelona, and magazine stories'. In fact, several pieces were incorporated into the novels almost verbatim, others suggest material which was excluded from the novels possibly because it was not developed sufficiently. Quite remarkably, the order of the stories anticipates the chronological development Roig's literary output would take over the subsequent twenty years. Of the fifteen stories, four have to do with Ramona Jover and Ramona Ventura and at least three with Ramona Claret, all main characters in Roig's first novel, *Ramona, adiós*. The short preludes thus complement the novel by allowing the reader further insight into the main characters. It is as if, while establishing the groundwork for her later fiction, Roig had at her disposition a complete family history which she dips into and only partially reveals to the reader, who has to actively reconstruct the private and public worlds of these fictional women through snippets of information. The first story, 'Brief sentimental story of a Madame Bovary from Barcelona, born in Gràcia and educated according to our soundest principles and traditions', indicating important Flaubertian connections, cleverly incorporates two perspectives and modes of dicourse: a series of enthusiastic letters from the young Ramona Jover to a friend told in the first person, and the third-person narration of, presumably, her granddaughter, attending Ramona's funeral. The 'cut and paste' technique effectively juxtaposes the excitement of the once youthful Ramona – telling of school-days, her first night at the opera, her honeymoon in Paris – with the more serious reflections of the granddaughter. Her grandmother's life was wasted, the latter muses darkly; society and the Church slowly sucked away her vitality and grandeur, reducing her to the comfortable mediocrity she was expected to be. The narrator addresses her dead grandmother; her aim will be from then on to 'try to reconstruct for you the perfume of history' (47), to recuperate and preserve through memory that untold, insignificant life. This was Roig's lifelong project. She returns to it explicitly in her last published book of essays, *Dime que me quieres aunque sea mentira*, 1992, in the chapter 'About windows, balconies and galleries'. Here she refers to the many 'Madame Bovarys of Barcelona' who 'dreamt of other worlds which were often scented with the aroma of the "folletín" ' (155), the middle-class ladies who looked at the world passing them by from the windows and balconies of the magnificent nineteenth-century houses in Barcelona's 'Eixample' district, who lived their lives in the dark interiors and hall-ways.[3]

The story, 'Ramona Ventura is invited to a fraternity banquet and she marvels at how the erudite annoy each other in the Year of Hunger, 1953', shows up post-war Catalan intellectuals as self-important, mean-minded hypocrites who only manage to impress the likes of the naive Ramona. 'Yellow, or Señora Adela Torrents's biographical tale' is a letter sent by Adela from the world of the dead to her friend Ramona Jover. Adela sketches her empty, useless life, marked by complete submission to husband and Church, her poverty, and her last years in an old people's home during the Civil War. The titles of these stories and other extracts, such as 'One of the numerous strolls that Mundeta Claret took through Barcelona when she was young', suggest Spanish picaresque literature and the work of Cervantes, but they also point to a conscious, ironic use of the nineteenth-century 'folletinesque' tradition of cheap, short, sensationalist novels. 'The Mysteries of the Fifth District. About how the thief and murderer Perot Andreu recounts his life and miracles' is a clear, parodic reference to the French 'Mystères' of Sue and de Kock. More significantly, it is a witty parody of Camilo José Cela's renowned post-war novel, *La familia de Pascual Duarte* (1944) [*Pascual Duarte's*

---

3. The Eixample is a fine example of nineteenth-century middle-class town planning. The district was originally designed by Ildefons Cerdà on a grid pattern with wide streets crossing narrower ones running from the mountains to the sea, and two diagonal avenues traversing the district to relieve the monotony. Much of the architecture is 'modernista' (art nouveau). 'The Eixample architecture reflected the bourgeoisie's drive and optimism, and coincided with the renaissance of Catalan nationalism.' See, M. Vázquez Montalbán, *Barcelonas*, London, 1992, 73–9, p. 78.

*Family,* 1967], presented to the reader with the simplistic annotations of a pedantic editor. 'Doña Patricia Miralpeix, an unhappy Pygmaliona' could belong to *Tiempo de cerezas.* It consists of a letter written in 1933 by Patricias's aesthete husband, Esteve, to a friend. Esteve writes how surprised he is that Patricia should resent a certain 'ritual' he indulges in which consists of him telephoning his wife and commanding her to 'prepare herself' for his homecoming; she should lie on the bed naked, hold a lily in one hand, and make sure Schubert's 'Ave Maria' is playing on the gramaphone. That is all he asks. So why should she be so annoyed when he gazes at her for half an hour and, at the height of his ecstasy, writes a poem? Pygmalion-like masculine constructions of feminity that do not take into consideration women as subjects of desire and the ensuing tragedy this provokes is a theme Roig returns to explicitly in *La ópera cotidiana.* 'About how a maid in the Ensanche tries to feel at ease in our beloved Barcelona' could be about Mari Cruz, from *La ópera cotidiana;* 'Monologues of a Barcelona couple who spend their evenings as is expected of them' from *La hora violeta;* and 'Jordi Soteres demands help from Maciste' from *La voz melodiosa.* In *Dime que me quieres,* Roig explains how she wrote this story, one of her first, in the bar of the Faculty of Arts in Barcelona University surrounded by 'lots of young students who wanted to construct a world that was different than their parents' and, at the same time, who made the weakest of them drunk just for a laugh'. The 'Maciste' in question, Jordi Soteres's hero, is the Maciste of Vasco Pratolini's *Cronada dei poveri amanti.* Roig adds, 'the protagonist dreams of the past because it was better' but that in his monologue 'Jordi Soteres insinuates there is no better world anywhere, unless in the imagination'. The theme of the innocent character, rejected by the 'hordes', educated 'in the faith and nostalgia of his grandfather', and unable to live in the present is the subject of *La voz melodiosa,* but when Roig wrote the novel, she says, she had forgotten about the story (164–5).

Even Roig's reference in her 'Confession' of 1978 to the 'poor, grey bureaucrats' of censorship (13) is elaborated in a later story entitled 'Before I deserve to be forgotten', signed 1988. These interlinking prose pieces indicate, once more, the intricate web woven by Roig in a fiction which defies beginnings, endings, and other generic or formal constraints, and which returns again and again to the same issues. The Valencian author Joan Fuster makes this point in the prologue to *Aprendizaje* when he claims that Roig 'interferes' with the idea of 'literature' as 'encoded genres'; that she did not recognize boundaries between fiction and documentary (18), and Roig does so herself when she quotes from the Argentinian novelist Ernesto Sábato, 'You write better when you repeat one single theme throughout your life' (13).

As if to underline this subversion of traditional literary form, *Aprendizaje sentimental* has several false starts. The fifteen stories are shielded from the reader by an armature of quotations and other prefatory matter: the 'Justification' of 'an apprentice writer' dated in 1971; another 'Justification' dated 1978; a 'Prologue' written by Joan Fuster, who Roig much admired; a dedication to her parents, to Papitu [Josep] Benet and Joaquim Molas; and a quote from Faulkner. The first story is prefaced by another lengthy quote from Josep de Sagarra. On the one hand, this ploy is symptomatic of an inexperienced author leaning on figures of authority to introduce her to the reading public. It also deliberately inserts Roig's motley collection into the Catalan literary tradition, with overtones of contemporary, foreign influence, and it is a form of asking the reader for indulgence. In the 1971 'Confession' a forthright Roig explains how writing is her form of feminist resistance to social and cultural conditioning. She recalls her ten years of Convent school education among girls who (unlike herself) were pretty, delicate, slightly fearful of the world, and always disposed towards martyrdom. These 'Little Lambs of the Lord' became the 'future moral battleaxes of our dazzling middle class' (8). A middle-class student at University, she found she was not accepted on equal terms by male political activists, 'possibly because of physiological or class defects, who knows'. So she turns to writing, in Catalan, 'a language half born'. In the 1978 prologue (three years after Franco's death) Roig is much more explicit. By this time she has decided to make writing her profession but she is more aware of the difficulties, 'A "young lady" who writes? Come on! You, with those legs. How dare you get involved in such an enterprise, it has nothing to do with you?' (10). Her decision was due partly to a rejection of the role of 'little woman' which Catholicism and Francoism had imposed on her, partly due to revenge against her own sex 'that I still didn't love', and to revenge against the 'sex with a capital "S", the male one' (12). What seems inconceivable today is that this short book of innocent stories should be censored: thirty pages were cut in the first edition (1971).

Doña Censorship eliminated . . . what must have most wounded her impotency: sex, politics, and religion. I can imagine the sexual misery of the poor, grey bureaucrats obliged to cut words and situations, making quite apparent with their attitude the mediocrity and the fear they were immersed in. They were sons of the Francoist 'coitus interruptus'. (13)

As mentioned above, Roig returned to this subject years later in her short story, 'Antes que merezca el olvido' ('Before I deserve to be forgotten'), published in *El canto de la juventud* (1990), where she shows a more sympathetic attitude towards the state censor. What brings the stories together is the focus on women's lives, on Barcelona, and the ironic, penetrating gaze of the narrator. The Jordi Soteres/Mundeta Claret relationship in particular functions in several stories as a paradigm through which to touch on questions relating to feminism, class politics, and the role of the writer. Thus, 'Jordi Soteres, apprentice author and former student leader, writes an Allegory to explain to his friend, Mundeta Claret, who's in charge round here', seeps of left-wing male chauvinism. The novels were needed to explore these issues in greater depth, but once the novels are read two of the stories in the collection stand out in retrospect. One, 'How Mundeta Claret's sentimental education began', provides the key to Roig's lifetime, narrative project. Mundeta, the modern Madame Bovary, is about to have sex with a student she hardly knows while Jordi, her boyfriend, is doing military service. How should she play this scene? Should she play the seductive vamp or the coy maiden? Whatever role she does choose, she is well aware that her attitude that night depends on 'the years, months, days of education she had received since birth'. She also knows that whatever she does, she will be sorry afterwards:

> Because that was her destiny. Hers, and the destiny of so many others who had been born under the same star: to go through life advancing and retreating. And using only one defensive weapon: guilt. (162)

The other key story, 'Before the Civil War' (title in English in the original), reminiscent of Margaret Drabble's fiction, is of particular interest to British readers. Signed 'Bristol, November 1973', it is a first-person account of a typical 1970s party (in Collingwood Street, near Whiteladies Road). Roig skilfully points out the limited possibilities of communication between young people, so-called rebels against the establishment, who remain profoundly

ignorant of each other's cultures. The female narrator, a politi-
cized, young Catalan (whose perspective is that of an outsider to
British culture) tries in vain to explain the awful significance of the
Spanish Civil War and the importance of her Catalan roots to a
North American drop-out (who has no views on Nixon) and to her
either indifferent or alienated British peers. The story centres on
the drunken Bishan 'an Indian born in Uganda, with an English
education' for whom the narrator feels sympathy, 'Poor Bishan . . .
You don't feel Indian, you don't live in Uganda, you don't like the
English' (192). But all she receives from Bishan – who classifies her
'European' – is abuse:

> you European, you make me sick, you don't have to explain anything
> to me, I don't want my children . . . to live on your continent, to learn
> anything from you. You think you're very intelligent, right? But you
> don't understand a thing, because your world has nothing to say [. . .]
> I am lost for words. Me, European? Have I got to say it all again? My
> sermon about 'before the civil war'? The Indian without a homeland
> looks at me furiously, he feels aggressive towards a country which is
> just as foreign to me. (195)

What the narrator has that Bishan lacks is a city, a community, a
culture, a homeland, a history, a language, and a cause; in other
words, an identity. But it is not hegemonic or European; it is
oppositional, belligerent, and Catalan.

*Aprendizaje sentimental*, then, ushers in the central themes and
narrative techniques Roig would explore in future years. The
wasted lives of middle-class women; the constraints of bourgeois
family life and marriage; the detrimental effects of the Catholic
Church and authoritarian state ideology; male dominance in the
worlds of art and oppositional politics; the hardships faced by
working women; women's popular culture and leisure pursuits
throughout the century; patriarchy's double standards; women's
secular ignorance of all matters political and sexual; and women's
passive acceptance of their fate; these are the main topics covered
in this exercise in consciousness-raising. No less problematical are
the new choices facing the liberated woman of the 1970s.

Montserrat Roig left no doubts about her preference for realist
fiction. In her early book of collected interviews, published in
Spanish as *Los hechiceros de la palabra* (*Wizards of the Word*)
(Barcelona, 1975), which engages with sixteen celebrated Spanish
and Spanish American authors, she makes a strong case for

realism in the face of a swing in Spain towards fantasy and experimental narrative. One of the questions she puts to her interviewees is whether they prefer the work of the acclaimed realist novelist Camilo José Cela or the experimentation of Valencian author, Juan Benet; and she interviews both Cela and Benet. This book, like *Aprendizaje sentimental*, is introduced by a justificatory 'confession' where Roig explains how she hoped to learn from the established writers she interviewed. But she excuses herself on three counts: her obsession with a historical reality (post-Civil War Spain), with Catalan literature, and with realism. She adds, 'realism in literature is the formula which interests me most because it seems to me that reality and everything it covers, which is immense, is more exciting than anything else' (16). When Juan Benet suggests that after a period of dogmatic realism (in the Spain of the 1950s and 1960s) it was not surprising that writers should turn to fantasy, Roig bravely begs to differ. She believes not all realism is dogmatic, that there are many modes of realism, and that anti-realist dogmatism is equally harmful. 'Your attacks', she adds, 'are directed against what was written in the years when young gentlemen cleansed their guilty consciences by writing social novels. But to go on and dismiss all realism . . .' (26). Juan Benet, she concludes, is afraid of certain words which new generations of writers also hesitate to use. He avoids terms such as 'commitment' and 'realism' because he feels quite at home in his escapist labyrinth (27). In other words, Roig associates a revaluated realism with a courageous feminist 'littérature engagée'. In her interview with Joan Fuster, she refers to writing as 'a profession which in Spain today is almost heroic', especially if the writer focuses on experienced, familiar reality:

> these days it is easier to be 'cosmopolitan' and to denigrate 'localists' [such as [Josep] Pla and Fuster]. It is easier, and more profitable, for us to be ignorant about what is ours and knowledgeable about the culture of others. It is easier not to be curious about what you can touch, yet pretend to know what you can't even see because that way we don't have to know about anything at all. (204)

Through these interviews in the early 1970s it is possible to glimpse the programme of what would be Roig's Catalan narrative project during some twenty years: to write realist narrative fiction, which nevertheless incorporates new techniques, to put across in straightforward language a clear set of ideas and a point of view, and to focus on experienced reality (middle-class family and university life) in Barcelona. She did this in the face of possibly more fashionable modes of writing for a deeply felt, ethical commitment. Such commitment was to the Catalan language and culture which, for Roig, was inseparable from a duty to procure social justice by means of progressive politics.

It is interesting to note that women's issues are hardly mentioned in these interviews, even in the conversation with arguably the greatest female Catalan author of the twentieth century, Mercè Rodoreda (who, it is true, hardly has a reputation for feminist views). To Roig's question, 'What do you think of the current Women's Liberation Movements?', Rodoreda answers cryptically, 'I think woman is sufficiently important so as not to have to think about that at all' (62), and then, more forthrightly:

> All this about 'women's rights' is literature. From the social point of view I'm not interested, and from the personal point of view I've won the battle. A woman always ends up winning, if not through work, then through motherhood or love. (63)

Yet the following snippet of conversation is important as Roig will return to the subject repeatedly. She discerns in Rodoreda's work an 'internal battle between man and woman', a kind of 'latent aggression on the part of the woman against the man' which Rodoreda only partially admits to. Roig then adds:

> It seems to me that you put forward the idea that relationships between men and women are impossible.
> And do you think they are possible?
> Well, I don't know.
> Perhaps not impossible but difficult.

Unlike Rodoreda, it seems, Roig was extremely conscious of the fact that she was a woman from the start of her career, and was thus well aware that she was writing against the grain in Franco's Spain. This early feminist consciousness perhaps accounts for the fact that Roig did not often refer to or quote Rodoreda, her seemingly obvious literary 'mother', although she does admit to being impressed by Rodoreda's female character Aloma, over and above all others with the exception of Madame Bovary (*Hechiceros*, 52). She names one of her own characters Aloma in a story 'La división' ('The Division') published in a collection of short stories

(*El canto de la juventud*) in 1990. Yet although Roig would show more predilection for male, Catalan authors a feminist perspective is evidenced in her very first publications.

## Ramona, adéu [*Ramona, adiós*] (*Goodbye, Ramona*)

Roig's first novel was published in Catalan in 1972, three years before the death of Franco, and in Spanish in 1980. Described by Ignasi Riera as 'a compendium of parallel and symmetrical situations', it sketches key moments in the lives of three generations of women: Ramona Jover (1874–1970), her daughter, Ramona Ventura (1909–), and her granddaughter, Ramona Claret (1949–).[4] All three share the same rather old-fashioned, provincial proper name, while amongst friends and family they answer to the (equally mundane), Mundeta. Their different patronyms are less important and point to diversity within a continuum. As one critic put it, the main themes are developed 'in triplicate', affirming Roig's 'concept of time and her idea that everything is repetition, no matter what historical period'.[5] Women, not men, are 'the determinants of genealogy' (Bellver, 1991, 221).

The novel opens with a disturbing scene, a first-person narration (written in italics and so separated from the main text) symbolical of a descent into Hell. A pregnant woman searches the ruined streets of a devastated Barcelona, systematically bombarded during the Civil War by the Fascist–Nationalists, looking for her husband. The date is 17 March 1938. The anonymous woman picks her way through the darkness, through the freezing, starving remnants of humanity, to the morgue where she is faced with the carnage of war, the unrecognizable faces of dismembered men, women and children, and she is violently sick. While she waits in the morgue expecting her husband to be brought in dead (there has been an explosion at the place where he was to meet an associate) an old man shows concern for her and they begin to talk. In the midst of the suffering and devastation compassion, friendship and, above all, communication is established. This is a

---

4. Ignasi Riera, 'The many memories of Montserrat Roig', *A Montserrat Roig en homenatge/Homage to Montserrat Roig*, Barcelona, 1992, p. 44.
5. Enric Sullà, 'Sobre *Ramona, adéu*. Fuga en gris', *Serra d'or*, 1973, p. 468.

working man, an Anarchist, the kind of person the middle-class, politically naive woman would never have wanted or been allowed to talk to before the War. He is looking for his nephew, and as he sits with the woman through the night he tells her his story: one of workers' demonstrations, clashes with the police, and the love for his young son killed at the front. For her it is at once the revelation of new knowledge, and the reminder of a past romance, the significance of which is deferred. The scene ends, 'I explained to him that I had no idea what politics were until the day the Republic was proclaimed' (32).

The above scene functions as a prologue to the novel. It is completed in what amounts to an epilogue placed at the end of the novel where the first-person account (again in italics) continues and represents the newly enlightened woman's emergence from Hell, darkness, and despair. The reader can now identify her as the most insipid of the three women of the novel, Ramona/ Mundeta Ventura, the second-generation woman who throughout the book seems to hold out least possibilities for social regeneration and feminist consciousness. In this closing scene she comes away from her conversation with the old Anarchist, after facing up to her own irrational class prejudices, a different woman. She comes out into a new dawn and into a defiantly hopeful city. She has not found her husband Joan, dead or alive, and continues to be deeply worried by this until – in the final lines of the novel – she sees an old woman fighting with a dog for a crust of bread. As she runs to help her in the 'battle' for survival Mundeta Ventura finds herself thinking, 'I could live my whole life without knowing what has happened to Joan' (190). She does not find her husband and, as a consequence, she finds herself and meaning in her previously purposeless life.

Wrapped around the novel like a book jacket, placed at its beginning and end like a pair of bookstands, this divided scene encloses the fragmented sections of the main body of the text which plunges the reader back and forwards in time, to and fro across the city of Barcelona, mapping crucial moments in the lives of the three women. It is both a supplementary and the central episode of a novel turned inside-out. The narrative's kernel becomes a sheath lending coherence and giving form to the various narrations in the novel and providing a clue to interpretation, an answer to the many questions posed. Only by reading the novel as a whole can the full irony of this wrap-around scene be appreciated. Mundeta Ventura's bullying, unscrupulous husband did not die; he had intended passing over from Republican Barcelona to the 'other side', hence his mysterious meeting, but he had no need to because, in the end, the Fascists won. Franco's victory spells out a living death for Mundeta. Like all other women in Spain, she is expected to shape herself, her activities, and aspirations to fit the restrictive model of a pious, passive angel-of-the-home enforced on women by a right-wing, militaristic, Roman Catholic patriarchy. The night in the morgue is crucial for her because it is her one and only glimpse of what otherwise might have been. Her taste of emancipation, human solidarity, political awareness and hope for the future, made possible by the temporary removal of a stifling order represented by Joan, is brief indeed. In later unpropitious circumstances the experience is relegated to memory, never to be revealed, not even to her own daughter. Without a purposeful role in society to lend it coherence Mundeta's life remains, like the narrative, dipersed and fragmentary. Her unfulfilled self is inchoate: 'In fact, I'm made up of snippets, of tiny insignificant occurrences', she admits as she converses with the old Anarchist, and that is how she stays.

The rest of Mundeta Ventura's story, told by a third-person narrator in eleven short sections, is analogous to the history of twentieth-century Spain. It hinges on the Civil War (1936–9) and two important dates: 1931 (the year the Republic was proclaimed), and 1934 (the year of the Revolution in Asturias). In 1931, Mundeta, a silly, awkward middle-class girl aged twenty-two, is on her way to a chocolate parlour with her mother when the Republic is declared. The panic and celebration she witnesses in the streets are her first inkling of social and political reality for which she is totally unprepared. In 1934 she meets her first and only true love, the radical Ignasi Costa. He speaks to her of literature and politics; they make love, but soon after Ignasi commits suicide for mismanaging an arms delivery to the revolutionaries in Asturias. Although Mundeta loses her virginity, in libertarian pre-war Barcelona this is of no great significance. Only with her marriage to Joan and the subsequent victory of the Right does her secret become a stigma. Joan finds out on their wedding night and holds her 'sin' against her, like the sword of Damocles, for the rest of her life. The destructive power Joan Claret and the Francoist state apparatus he represents exert over Mundeta, to which she succumbs (incomprehensibly for the rest of the family), reduces her to a pathetic shadow, derided by all, including (paradoxically) her own mother and daughter.

One of the most important themes of the novel is this lack of communication between successive generations of women, between mothers and daughters. If Mundeta Ventura seems an unlikely candidate for a 'romantic adventure', her respectable mother hides a similar secret, revealed to no one. The sharing of their experiences could have helped mother and daughter understand and objectify their personal feelings, and made them aware that their desires and disillusions were not aberrant but part of a general pattern faced by all women, particularly of the middle classes, at that time. As it is, their most intimate memories are never shared; they erect walls around their private selves in true bourgeois fashion. As Elizabeth Rogers suggests, this 'immense lack of knowledge', the gaps and silences in the novel, and the misinformation imparted by the women to each other, are structuring devices resulting in the suppression of 'a hidden female history which can be re-covered, re-membered, and revealed only through language' (Rogers, 1981, 105–6).

The grandmother Ramona Jover's story is interspersed throughout the novel and hidden in short extracts from her diaries which cluster around important moments between December 1894 (just before her marriage) and January 1919 (the date of her husband's death). There is little to tell during those twenty-five years of uneventful married life to a good but boring man. The high point is a platonic 'affair' with a student when she is twenty-seven. Eight consecutive snatches from the diary point to the intensity of the period between April and June 1901. But the 'idyll' ends before it has begun when the couple meet for the first time in a park, the young man attempts to put his hand down Ramona's dress, and she runs away. Subsequent entries are the reflections of a middle-aged, forty-four year old woman musing on the monotony of life and the disappointments of marriage. 'I don't know why I'm getting married', Ramona writes on the eve of her wedding. Then she answers her own question: 'A woman needs a man at her side, so as not to be alone, so as not to be laughed at by everyone' (42). Marriage, she deceives herself, is freedom, enabling her to escape from her mother's social ambitions and her control over what she reads. It is the freedom to experience the presence of a 'divine lover' (43) who, like Jesus Christ, will cover her body with kisses and tears. But twenty-five years later she writes,

> When I think about our marriage, I think Francisco has loved me too much. His love has been faithful but bungling, boring, and he hasn't awakened in me any feelings other than understanding and acceptance of us living together of necessity . . . He has never made me shake with the fear of losing him, I've never been afraid of being left alone, he hasn't sparked my imagination . . .. I've lived my life pursuing vain chimeras, illusions that only existed in my mind. My intuition told me that his love, so sure, so ordered and thorough, would only fill me with disgust and monotony. I've always felt myself pulled to other worlds, unknown and distant, impossible to attain. (179)

These are worlds impossible to express in words. Ramona Jover, craving for excitement, resents domesticity, her husband, and her daughter but never shows her feelings. Compromise is her mask; but her diaries are historical and personal documentation and they voice her albeit submerged resistance.

It is hardly surprising that the third and youngest Ramona, a contemporary of the novel's implied reader, should rebel against these past models of (what she interprets as) submissive female passivity in an abusive patriarchal order. If the grandmother's self-identity is constructed on the basis of autobiographical fragments extending a quarter of a century and the mother's through a first and third-person account of experiences during a short period in the 1930s, Ramona/Mundeta Claret's sense of self hinges on the events of one significant year, 1969. Her story (again, dispersed in short sections throughout the text) is told by an omniscient narrator in the third person. Again, it is one of unreciprocated love. At the age of seventeen Mundeta Claret meets Jordi Soteres (a character who reappears in various guises in Roig's novels) in the midst of the historical 1966 student protests of Barcelona University. He is her first lover and her story concerns (again) the fraught relationship between a naive, middle-class girl and a politically active radical. Through a series of flashbacks, this relationship is reconstructed with hindsight up to its present moment of crisis. Jordi, a proponent of 'free-love' and non-commitment, sleeps with Mundeta's friend and Mundeta, in revenge, takes on the role of prostitute. After a night of sex with a stranger, during which she has hurt no one but herself, and faced with no viable alternative, Mundeta takes the decision to leave

Jordi, leave home, and leave Spain. Hence the title of the novel, *Ramona, adiós*. Of course she rejects the norms and values of the conservative, Catholic culture which shaped her mother and grandmother (she knows nothing of their secret cores of resistance) but she is at a loss when she realizes that young male radicals of her own generation, theoretically working for a 'liberated' future in which the kinds of restrictions placed on previous generations of women would no longer apply, do no more than manipulate these newly acquired social and sexual freedoms for their own sexist interests. Women are no better off. Paradoxically, Mundeta aches for the kind of stable relationship her grandmother deplored, she wants to be needed, but she cannot establish any meaningful communication with Jordi because there is no common ground. She is as disgusted with her own feminine passiveness as with Jordi's sexist behaviour, and she is as thoroughly disillusioned with left-wing, Marxist or equality politics as with the so-called sexual revolution:

> The relativity of life that Jordi went on about so much – How absurd and sad! They had imagined a rational and scientific concept of the world, a concept that resolved any error, any problem, and at the first signs of change they had crashed against that concept like a stag bumps his hard and stubborn antlers against an unexpected tree. They had reacted like millions and millions of people inhabiting the universe, with vulgarity, without a bit of ingenuity or a glimmer of originality . . . Not her, or anyone like her, or anyone like Jordi would change the world. By simply leaving home, by bragging about not believing in God, by making free-love, by taking part in University politics . . . No, it wouldn't be them who'd change it [. . .] To feel . . . perhaps that was it. She was tired of defending theories she had never ever felt. To feel, even if just a little. (182)

Her grandmother glimpsed escape in an unconsummated romance, her mother defied tradition with a brief affair, but to escape the cyclical repetition of a meaningless life Mundeta Claret must actively break up her relationship altogether and leave the country.

Thus, the three key dates which mark these women's moments of self-awareness, 1901, 1934, 1969, each separated by a generation of some thirty years, are important dates in the history of Spain (the post-1898 Disaster period, when Spain lost Cuba, the last of its colonies; the pre-Civil War years; the post-1968 student rebellions). But a linear concept of time, either personal or national, is denied by the cyclical fragmentation of the text. The women experience time as stasis or repetition; they work through the same situations, problems and preoccupations throughout the century and are trapped by the same Romantic myths. Although the material conditions of the youngest Ramona allow for an independent decision regarding her life, she can find no alternative means to extricate herself from the treadmill endured by her mother and grandmother in Spain, so she opts out altogether. The novel suggests that fissures in the dominant culture produced by social or political upheaval do create situations in which women can glimpse other ways of being. But as the forces of reaction close ranks women have little option other than to bury themselves and their desires in family domesticity and traditional roles. The role of history can be interpreted from another angle. References to dates of national importance 'serve only to emphasize that . . . women live apart from official History . . . History is consciously identified as a male enterprise'; for women it is intrusive.[6] The fragmentation of the novel also points to a split female self of heterogeneous identity. One reading might consider the three Ramonas to be facets of one paradigmatic character whose immediate historical context changes, but whose means of self-definition in bourgeois culture remains consistently lacking; and when change is mooted it is class and not sexual politics which are on the agenda.[7] Female identity is in process, but always defined by others save during brief moments of revelation or epiphany. These women are oppressed by the bourgeois class and Catholic religion and above all by male dominance. However, if women are portrayed as having failed in their existential project of self-fulfilment, if they are marginalized by national history and linear time, and are confined to domestic space except when they escape (to the park, the streets, to another country), if they are shown to have assimilated the ethos of privacy to the point of resisting communication even between mothers and daughters, they are nevertheless representative of the latent impulse for social change.

Their potential to deconstruct and reconstruct society is manifest in the very structure of the novel which dismantles and

6. Elizabeth Rogers, 'Montserrat Roig's *Ramona, adiós*: A Novel of Suppression and Disclosure', *REH*, 20, 1986, p. 109.
7. C. B. Cadenas, 'Historia de tres mujeres', p. 77, refers to the novel as the single story of a 'Mundeta-paradigm'.

reassembles the traditional conventions of mimesis (showing) and diegesis (telling) associated with this typically middle-class genre. Fragmentation defies closure; there is no last word, no ending. The novel thus challenges the generic conventions from which it developed and the tight-knit (masculinist) ideologies, of the Right and the Left, these subsume because they lack the potential to respond to women's needs. Conversely, the collective socio-political experience is voiced from a feminine perspective and is incorporated into feminine experience. The novel asks to what extent and in what ways were women affected by these momentous historical and national events and what were women's responses? The answer is fairly negative. Women are clearly on the margins of power, they take no initiative, and they are made aware of politics only through the men in their lives. The male characters, for their part, closed up in the hegemonic discourses of their particular socio-historical contexts and the patriarchal structures of their gender's own creation, are inevitably blinkered. Francisco and Joan represent the softer and harder faces of Catholic capitalism respectively, and Jordi the Marxist alternative. But these seemingly diametrically opposed ideologies give rise to similar sexist and classist hierarchies. They are the two sides of the same bourgeois coin. Women have no place in this system. Yet, for the moment, there is no way out. Hence their constant hankering for something different, something strange or untoward, in a chaotic, amorphous text enclosed between a wrap-around morgue scene symbolical of their search for life in death.

### El temps de les cireres [Tiempo de cerezas] (A Time for Cherries)

None of Roig's subsequent novels are as historical as her first. *Tiempo de cerezas* (*A Time for Cherries*), 1978, the second novel in the trilogy, was written in the months following Franco's death (November 1975) and is set in one year, 1974. It was Roig's first novel of the 'transition'. The protagonist Natàlia Miralpeix, a double of Mundeta Claret, has now returned to Barcelona after spending twelve years in Britain, the home of all free women. Natàlia, aged 36, gradually picks up the threads of her previous life and finds a job as a photographer, a skill she learned in

England. However, the novel is not just about Natàlia. Her return affords a perspective on her family and through her eyes and memories (representations of the past and present) four stories are told.

One story is her own, her past relationship with Emilio Sandoval, a militant Communist student, her pregnancy and backstreet abortion (a common event in the Spain of the 1960s and 1970s), her growing political and feminist consciousness, and – above all – her fraught relationship with her father, Joan Miralpeix. Joan's story is the most moving and significant of the novel. It concerns his relationship with his wife, Judit, and her enigmatic friendship with the extravagant socialite-cum-radical feminist Kati, who committed suicide at the end of the Civil War. As with the relationship Jordi/Mundeta, Roig will return again and again to the Judit/ Kati motif of close female friendship and love between women. Joan's story both answers and raises questions in relation to *Ramona, adiós* and provides the main thread of continuation between the two novels. The third story is that of Natàlia's aunt, Patrícia Miralpeix, her life with her husband Esteve and her brief flirtation with the young poet Gonçal who – it turns out – is also her husband's lover. Patrícia's experiences were not included in *Ramona, adiós*, where she appears for the first time, but they follow a similar pattern of brief fulfilment of desire followed by loss and lifelong disappointment. Finally, the story of Silvia Claret (Natàlia's sister-in-law, eldest daughter of Joan Claret and Mundeta Ventura) is structurally important. Silvia is married to Natàlia's brother, Lluís, and this is the link which joins the families Miralpeix-Claret. In this way the 'great allegory of contemporary Barcelona' is taken one step further.[8]

Less formally experimental than the previous novel, *Tiempo de cerezas* is realist, third-person narrative divided into six parts each dealing with a character. However, Roig does make skilful use of focalization, free indirect discourse, and frequent shifts of point of view which approximate the characters to the reader. The four central sections tell the above four stories and privilege the past, but the first and last sections, focusing on Natàlia and Joan, are set in the present and the few days in which Natàlia returns home to find her father interned in a mental home. Thus, again, the first

8. Jordi Castellanos, 'Montserrat Roig i "El temps de les cireres"', *Serra d'or*, 1977, p. 397.

and last sections produce a wrap-around effect enclosing an open-ended narrative.

What is important in this novel is that all the characters, both male and female, are the isolated victims of corrupt, repressive authoritarianism, be it political or sexual. The pathetic Patrícia bullied by her husband, who married her for her money and spent it all before his death, has no other company than her paid employee, her maid Encarna. Communication between these women, despite their divergent cultural backgrounds, outweighs their class differences. Silvia, one generation younger, is similarly bullied by Lluís and relives her own mother's experience of passive submission in the role of aimless, monied, middle-class mother and wife. The occasional frenzied hen party, frequent masturbation, visits to the hairdresser and beauty salon, relieve her tedium and frustration. In *Ramona, adiós*, it was her mother, Mundeta Ventura, who roamed the morgues of bombed Barcelona; Silvia was the unborn child and, according to Ramona Jover (the grandmother) it was Mundeta's fright that led to Silvia's introversion (45). Evidently, the novel is making a strong case against the sexual repression of women in middle-class society and, particularly, in the nuclear family. This repression is accepted and transmitted by the women themselves from generation to generation.

However, the greatest victim in the novel is a man, Joan Miralpeix, who cannot come to terms with the death of the wife who saved him from a bullying father. He is as much a victim of male repression in the family as are the women, not only because of his brutal father (his mother dies when he was young) but also because of his uncaring son, Lluís, who puts him in a mental home. Joan is also a victim of the Civil War and the dirty business dealings of Joan Claret, his son's father-in-law. But even Lluís could be considered a victim of sorts; his authoritarianism is partially justified. He was ignored as a child by his mother who was totally absorbed in caring for her younger mongol son. Only the third-generation Màrius, son of Silvia and Lluís, seems to hold some hope for the future. He takes his cue from his rebellious, independent aunt Natàlia and he too looks to foreign cultures for 'something new'. Thus his penchant for the posters of Millais' 'Ophelia', Che Guevara, and the pop group 'Blood, Sweat and Tears'. Three couples, then, Joan and Judit, Patrícia and Esteve, Silvia and Lluís, represent the constraints of married life, while the two unattached younger figures, Natàlia and Màrius, point to change. In this novel it is clear that the middle-class family structure works for no one. All kinship relationships, between siblings, parents and children, husbands and wives, are fraught with tension and announce the inappropriateness of the Catalan bourgeoisie itself as a modern social system.

The various biographical strands converge and help explain the final outcome of a drama which gathers momentum as the novel progresses. Joan, the key family father-figure, is strikingly absent at the start of the novel. Although absent, his presence is maintained by his daughter Natàlia who repeatedly speaks of him, asking where he is. The novel, then is the daughter's search for the father. Joan appears only half way through the novel, and by the last section is shown slipping into a world of fantasy and memory to escape the unbearable present. Through free-indirect discourse and stream-of-consciousness Joan discloses he is not mad, merely lonely. He is broken by a life of disappointment during the Franco years and is devasted by Judit's death. Joan's love for Judit is the only example of the true, uncompromising, totally selfless love (hetero or homosexual) that the women in Roig's novels, particularly Natàlia, constantly pursue. Yet Judit, strangely remote after the suicide of her close friend Kati and the death of her retarded son at the age of four, never seems to have responded to Joan with the same intensity of feeling and degree of dependency. The final section of the novel, entitled 'Only Dreams', begins with a poignant scene in which an unknown figure admires a pair of silk stockings hanging from the back of a chair in a bedroom. The stockings have been selected by this person with care from a range of lyrical colours – orange blossom, rainy-sky grey, apple blush, ash grey. The sexual identity of the subject is deferred by means of impersonal verb constructions and the use of non-gender specific pronouns (almost impossible to recreate in English). It is only in the second paragraph that the reader realizes the figure is a man:

> the stocking was gathered up, fold by fold . . . First one stocking then the other. Foot stretched-out in the air, pointing like Odile in 'Swan Lake' or a Degas adolescent. Toes pressed together tightly, pointing down to the floor, and instep arched . . . Slowly the stockings were put on, first one then the other, slowly, stroking the skin along your leg. Until half way up your thigh. But there were no garters – you never dared to buy them. To see yourself in the mirror, the stockings

had to be held up with both hands. Your body was hunched, but the stockings so pretty . . . Each night they were stroked before going to bed. Stroked in the dark . . . While caressing the stockings, against your cheek, it seemed the light from the lamp was moonlight. And it is also then when it seems, that he is not so alone and that Judit, his Judit is nearby . . . (229)

This is, of course, an elderly Joan with his fetish, silk stockings, replacing a dead woman. Women's underwear gives him aesthetic and sexual pleasure; they are the object of his desire. What is more, as he dresses in drag, Joan becomes Judit; his masculine self is constructed, paradoxically, through the assimilation of her female sexuality. Judit is the mother-lover figure who rescued him from his father and who initiated him sexually when he thought he was impotent. His fetishistic transvestism (and other performances such as masturbating with a doll and collecting women's under-wear) suggests a psychological reading of the novel. In Freudian terms, Joan's masculine 'perversion', consisting of pleasure from a female sexual object which is associated with an inanimate object, points to failed homosexuality. His fetishism allows him to identify both with the pre-oedipal mother and the father and thus avoid psychosis. In short, it develops his sense of masculinity once Judit is dead. Clearly, Joan does not represent the kind of aggressive masculinity normally associated with an authoritarian regime; unlike the unscrupulous Joan Claret he is artistic and sensitive, and has a moral conscience. He has survived the 'dirty war'(162) and three years in a concentration camp, while most of his Republican friends were killed. But, like the women in the novel, he colludes passively with the system and relinquishes his former ideals and life-style in order to comply. The castrated male vegetates, he gets rich 'because to make money is a way of going to sleep' (162). This is what infuriates Natàlia, and this is why she calls him a coward. Ultimately, Joan is a victim of the same kind of socio-sexual repression as his daughter. But communication between father and daughter, despite their similarities, is sadly lacking as it is between all members of the family. After the war 'Judit and Joan closed themselves up, the spirit of one in the other' (164); the closed doors of their inner, bourgeois worlds are never opened up. It is a sad affair when an old man has to resort to stockings for comfort, companionship, human contact, and communication. His is the most extreme case of alienation in a society of commodity fetishism, where all

individuals are isolated one from the other. Only Joan believes he
'will never die' because he has 'his Judit' with him, in him: he is
Judit (244). Only true love makes life meaningful; but only the
mentally unbalanced believe in it.
   Female fetishism is no less important in the novel and suggests
a lesbian subtext. Judit starts to collect memorabilia, mainly dolls,
after her friend Kati commits suicide in 1939. When Judit suffers
an apoplexy in later life she turns increasingly to her dolls rather
than to Joan:

> Judit missed Kati and decided she wanted fetishes, all kinds of objects
> that she adored like small gods . . . Let's fill the house with fetishes!
> she said to Joan . . . The most important fetishes were dolls. Judit spent
> a long time buying dolls, dolls of all sizes, dressed or undressed, made
> of rubber, plastic or porcelain. She ended up hiding the dolls in her
> room . . . Judit pricked their eyes and broke their hands. And the more
> she made them suffer, the more she loved them. There was a big one
> with empty eyes that Judit caressed when she became an invalid . . .
> Look, the dolls that are boys have no sex, and she laughed with her
> bird-like giggle. Those years were sad and unsettled, frozen. (164–5)

Female fetishism is associated in psychoanalysis with female
homosexuality; that is, a woman disavows her own castration and
becomes the phallus. Judit takes the sexual initiative in her
relationship with Joan, and her ambiguous relationship with Kati
is the pivot point of both this novel and, more overtly, the next.
Thus there seems to be a suggestion of role reversal with a
demasculated Joan absorbed in a phallic Judit. These complex
sexuality and gender issues escape Natàlia's grasp; only the reader
has the privilege of witnessing certain scenes. Yet Natàlia grew up
in the midst of the family and was also a witness. The central
sections of the novel function as a remembering, as if through
double focalization Natàlia brings to consciousness those
memories which would give her the key to understanding her
father, her country, and herself.
   Closely associated with the theme of fetishism is photography:
like the novel itself, both sustain the illusion that something absent
is present. Natàlia learns her profession in England. She is
instructed by her boyfriend Jimmy's uncle, Mr Hill, who teaches
her to 'tell a photograph's story, give value to an image' (20). She
is given 'the tools to earn her living' (19) abroad, not in Spain, and
the first section of the novel hinges on the brusque contrast she
experiences between her liberated life in Bath and her re-encounter

with an inert and stagnant Barcelona. She had left Barcelona in 1962, shortly after the Grimau affair, in the aftermath of the violent anti-Franco student riots which she took part in but observed as if a film (111); she returns two days after the execution of the young Anarchist, Puig Antich. Before she left for England, Natàlia's eyes had been opened to the political situation in Spain by her boyfriend, Emilio – the sexist Communist. Through him she had her first glimpse of personal and social liberation: 'I don't see why the desire for pleasure and the desire to change the world should belong to some other time', he tells her (107) in true Marcussian fashion. He refers to this future 'spring of happiness' as 'a time for cherries', borrowing the phrase from a poem by the French Commune poet J. B. Clément (125). But Natàlia realizes there has been no profound change in Spain, despite consumer advances (hence the different opinions of Silvia who thinks things have changed for the better and the publisher Arcadi who thinks not (100)). The revolutionary 1960s had passed by with little trace. Natàlia, then, returns to the same, stagnant, corrupt society she had left, and she realizes the vision Emilio had given her was incomplete. There were still too many questions unanswered, particularly regarding their own personal relationship. The change that has occurred is in Natàlia herself, 'she was someone else, she was no longer afraid' (100), because she had learned a great deal in twelve years. Through Sergio in France and Jimmy in Bath she had discovered her body, her femininity. Sexual and political liberation, the New Left, and the Women's Movement had enabled her to develop a feminist consciousness. Photography symbolizes this new awareness, this new way of looking at things.

Natàlia focuses her gaze on Barcelona, the family, and gender relationships; 'she had learned to see a world that previously had escaped her' (35). Before she had left England Natàlia had wandered around Reading (where Oscar Wilde was imprisoned) taking photographs as if to capture, possess, and retain the memory of her newly acquired consciousness. Through photography Natàlia is placed in a position of domination. She can be the subject rather than the object of the gaze (as she had been under the gynaecologist's speculum). She can produce her own meaning, unlike her female relatives. She has the means to subvert traditional ways of seeing and, therefore, social and sexual relations of inequality. These memories, experiences, and attributes are what differentiate her from the women at home.

In a metafictional sense, photography also calls attention to the conscious narrator and to the very production of representation. Neither the camera's eye nor the narrator's point of view are objective but are part of an all-encompassing ideological construct. An unenlightened Natàlia could not see properly before she left Spain and her understanding was similarly impaired. Even on her return, Natàlia's and, by analogy, the narrator's vision is necessarily limited, framed selectively, and divorced from context. Thus there is an attempt to focalize through the eyes of others, through Patrícia, Silvia, and Joan, who reveal to the reader what they have hidden for so long from each other. Through free indirect discourse the narrator's and the characters' points of view merge. Yet the reality portrayed in the novel is still partial and incomplete. It constitutes another attempt to reconstruct a family history, yet another inconclusive glimpse into the family album. And in as much as a fetish and a photograph are illusions or fictions through which an absence is made present, we can see how closely related were Natàlia's and her father's (and the narrator's) quests to reconstruct and make sense of their lives. Natàlia searches for her father and the pre-war Catalunya he experienced and renounced. But she is too late. In a final, moving scene Natàlia visits her father in the mental home and swears to take him home. Their reunion is symbolical of her new understanding. However, Joan is lost without his wife and lives in a dream world, clinging to the past: 'life is a circle', he says, 'we always return to the starting point' (243). For him the starting point is Judit and her photograph which he keeps at his bedside. He lives through her presence, 'to see Judit there, in that yellowing portrait. . . to smell her hollyhock perfume meant that he was still alive . . . The photograph said: you're still alive' (244).

Joan's comment on the circularity of life points to the frequent references to whirlpools in the novel: the whirlpools of non-being which threaten to suck him under in his nightmares, and the whirlpools of history in the first section (entitled 'Remolinos' or 'Swirls, eddies, whirlwinds') which threaten to undermine Natàlia's enterprise. The epigraph to the first section, taken from Joan Vinyoli's Gorgs, points in that same direction: 'Lost time. Lost time. Lost time. To repeat the same words at greater depth is, perhaps, to go naked in order to find a pathway on the other side.' In fact, all the sections of the novel are glosses of their corresponding epigraphs, taken from the work of several Catalan authors, Apollinaire, and Shakespeare. Again, this suggests the source of renewal is to be found in the nation's past (Catalan literature) and in foreign (French and British) culture. The critic Jordi Castellanos points out that while the title of the novel refers to the future, the literary quotes inscribe the past in the present; they make 'the past an essential element in the future' (Castellanos, 399). Despite circular journeys and fallacious escapes a better future can be constructed, but only if the collective past is taken on board. In *Tiempo de cerezas*, it is a woman who is the catalyst in this reconstruction. She explores through her own and her family's experiences the hidden relationship between sex, death, power and identity. What she learns is that society is not informed by class relations alone, but more fundamentally, by sexuality. The private informs the public, and even in times of political upheaval, this is much more difficult to uncover and change.

# 2

## Colour and Music: the Narrative of the Early 1980s

he third novel of the Miralpeix-Claret trilogy, *L'hora violeta* (1980) [*La hora violeta*, 1980) (*The Violet Hour*) is arguably the most successful, the most ambitious, and certainly the one in which Roig writes most clearly as a feminist. It is structurally complex and, again, challenges linear chronology and the conventions of the realist novel by means of repetition, circularity, fragmentation, and self-conscious metafictional and metadiegetic discourse. At the time the book was published, not all critics understood the full import of this blurring of genres, the fusion of the personal and the social, and Roig's refusal to distinguish fact from fiction. Enric Bou, for example, writing in *Serra d'Or*, accused Roig of having produced 'a transposition of personal problems and obsessions in ways that aren't entirely fictional . . . she wrote about people, not characters, and that is when she writes carelessly and when she resorts to facile platitudes'. The fact that Roig's fiction is 'anchored in her personal reality' leads to a 'relative disquiet on the part of the reader', he adds. But the greatest disappointment for Bou is that she should have abandoned her chronicle of Barcelona for a work of 'militant' feminism.[1] More 'au courant' is David Ross Gerling, who points out the effectiveness of a 'collective female protagonist', exemplifying Roig's insistence on the 'oneness of all women', and of a narrative technique which 'portrays the flux and indeterminacy in the life of the contemporary Spanish woman'.[2] For Catherine Bellver, the women of *La hora violeta* are, more

1. Enric Bou, 'Un llibre cada mes. *L'hora violeta* per Montserrat Roig', *Serra d'Or*, 1981, p. 166.
2. David Ross Gerling, 'Review of *La hora violeta*, 1980', *ALEC*, 8, 1983, pp. 243–5.

precisely, a 'collective community of differing females' (1988, 156) who share similar experiences, and Roig's narrative technique a 'flickering montage of events and faces' (164) used to penetrate the superficiality of historical fact. Bellver adds:

> [Roig's] novels are not autobiographies, for they are not her life story. They are not existential vehicles of self-revelation . . . nor are they instruments of psychological exorcism . . . Fiction for Roig the Journalist is a means of documenting the features of the world around her, particularly as they relate to the psychological struggles of women.[3]

Bellver's comments are perceptive, although the insistence on documentary prose belies the lyricism of *La hora violeta*. In a later essay, the critic draws attention to Roig's vindication of women 'through the inscription in her novel of female-generated texts . . . Their fragmentary and incomplete nature only reconfirms the disregard, disdain, and darkness that have surrounded women's history' (1991, 232), a point which, apparently, eluded certain Spanish critics.

The novel is divided into five parts: an introductory chapter, 'Spring, 1979', followed by four parts or 'hours' ('The lost hour'; 'The novel of the violet hour'; 'The dispersed hour'; 'The open hour'), reminiscent of Doris Lessing's *The Golden Notebook* which is also divided into four (coloured) notebooks. The main action of the novel is set in 1979, during the 'transition' period between the death of Franco and the full restoration of a Spanish democratic constitution (October 1978). The first general elections held in Spain since 1936 took place that year. On one level, it traces the disillusion and disarray of the Left, paradoxically, after the legalization of the Communist Party (the main organization of opposition to Franco) two years previously. As the old order crumbles, so the oppositional strategies of the traditional Marxist camps are likewise invalidated. A new order is sought as the whole debate concerning the individual and society, and the interaction of personal and collective freedoms and responsibilities, is opened up. In Ross Gerling's words, there is a 'gradual accommodation to freedom of expression' (244). On another level, the novel is strictly woman-centred. The individuals

---

3. Catherine Bellver, 'Montserrat Roig: A Feminine Perspective and a Journalistic Slant', in *Feminine Concerns*, ed. R. C. Manteiga, 1988, pp. 154–5.

Colour and Music

who ask the leading questions and who set the agenda for change towards something different are women. Situated on the boundaries of power, these women can envision a shift away from patriarchy itself, whether it be authoritarian or progressive, but they are held back by their cultural conditioning and social identity. They try to bridge the illusory division between self and other, between the individual and society, but they founder when it comes to personal relationships with men. This was the point Emilio made to Natàlia in *Tiempo de cerezas* when he quoted from J. B. Clément's poem, 'Quand vous en serez au temps des cerises / Vous aurez aussi des chagrins d'amour' (125). The novel gives no simple answers to the problems it raises but does suggest that, as far as women are concerned, the base line for change is self-knowledge which necessitates an awareness of the construction of femininity in a phallocratic culture. Progressive strategies must take into account female subjectivity, desire, and personhood, as well as sexual relationships and class politics. No such truly humanist equality politics existed (then or now). The endless self-questioning of the female protagonists of *La hora violeta* ranges across seemingly insoluble issues such as how women see themselves, what they want from life, what their relationships with men are, and how they can collaborate on an equal footing with men to construct a better society for all.[4]

*La hora violeta* returns to the Miralpeix family (the Castilian edition includes a very useful family-tree) and fits further pieces of the family jigsaw in place. The three protagonsists, forty-one year old Natàlia the photographer (five years older than when she returned to Barcelona in *Tiempo de cerezas*), her younger friend Norma, a writer and journalist, both members of the Communist Party, and the young mother Agnès, are all clearly fictional constructs of a divided authorial self. As Norma the novelist points out, 'A person ['persona'] has more than a thousand faces and it's enough if a novel manages to bring out three or four' (12). The question which this novel, and the trilogy itself, returns to repeatedly is posed by Norma towards the end: how to make 'collective love individual love' (267), that is, how to integrate social concern and political commitment with one's own love life,

4. See, Catherine Davies, 'The sexual representation of politics in Hispanic feminist narrative', in *Feminist Readings on Spanish and Latin American Literature*, L. Condé and S. Hart (eds), Mellen Press, 1991, pp. 107–19, p. 111.

{ 55 }

how to break out of narcissistic compartmentalization, how to extend the love of one man or woman to a love of humanity.

Natàlia is breaking up with her lover, Jordi, who is returning to his wife, Agnès, and two children – although Natàlia believes he has found a younger lover. Norma has recently split up with her husband and also has two children. The plot is simple: after her father's death, Natàlia is given a diary belonging to her mother, Judit, and some letters sent to Judit from her close friend Kati. She wants Norma to write a novel about the relationship between the two (dead) women which, she hopes, will help her and Norma sort out their own problems. Norma would like to rise to the challenge, but is committed to writing other projects, seemingly more socially worthy and politically correct, such as a report on Catalan prisoners in Nazi concentration camps which involves interviewing one of the few survivors. Norma also faces writing alone, without her husband, and has meanwhile met a new man, Alfred, who is, of course, married. Like the layers of an onion, this story wraps itself around a core narrative, buried in the centre of the novel, which provides the key to the meaning of the whole trilogy. It is Judit's story.

The mother's story is told in the third section 'The novel of the violet hour', intended by Norma to be a novel in its own right entitled 'The violet hour', but finally published as only one part of *La hora violeta*. *La hora violeta* is not only about Judit's relationship with Kati, or even about Norma and Natàlia; it goes much further. Even the section 'The novel of the violet hour' does not only concern the attachment between Judit and Kati, which developed during the Civil War, but Judit's total absorption with her mentally retarded son, Pere, born in 1942. This section complements Joan's version of events as narrated in *Tiempo de cerezas*. In other words, Norma never gets down to telling the full story of Kati and Judit, but the other stories interrelate and weave a metafictional narrative web around the structural void. *La hora violeta*, with a technique similar to that used in *Ramona, adiós*, focuses synchronically on several periods or significant years in recent Spanish history. The novel is set in 1979, but the complex section 'The novel of the violet hour', based on Judit's diaries, refers analeptically to two historical periods: the immediate post-war years, 1942–8, during which Pere is born and dies, and the year 1958 (by which time Judit's life is a meaningless routine) functioning as a point of reflection for past events. Various scenes from the same day in 1958 are interspersed between the diary entries for the 1940s. Furthermore, several fragments throughout this section refer to Kati between the years 1936–8, to Judit in 1950, and to Patrícia in 1964, the date of Judit's death. Once again, the story told in 'The novel of the violet hour' is one of disappointment with life, particularly family life, which is portrayed as claustrophobic, restrictive, bleak and frustrating for men and women alike. The family romance, then, is totally subverted because the only times women manage to fulfil themselves throughout history, albeit momentarily, is outside the confines of the home or the boundaries of social convention.

The two most tragic figures of this novel, and indeed of the trilogy, are Natàlia's parents: the father Joan, who could not face the world without the wife he so much loved, and the wife and mother Judit, who dies broken-hearted because of her love and loss of Kati and of her mentally retarded son. Judit's diary notes centre on the summer of 1943, between 5 July, the day Joan is let out of prison, and 6 July, the day Pere is born. By the end of that month it is clear the child is retarded, and in early August Judit is told he will die in infancy. From then on she cuts herself off from her other two children, Natàlia and Lluís. She particularly dislikes Lluís, possibly because he desperately tries to impress her and thus represents thrusting post-war triumphalism (123). This unfair treatment creates jealousy and life-long incomprehension (indeed, the young Lluís tries to kill his small brother), the consequences of which are explored in *Tiempo de cerezas*. Neither Lluís nor Natàlia understand their mother's indifference towards them until Natàlia finds Judit's diary. In an important entry in May 1948 Judit explains how music is dead for her (she was a first-class pianist and taught music in her youth), as are Pere and Kati. All she loved in life is gone, and what is left is lifeless or (in the case of Joan) defeated. Judit dies in spirit in 1950; her last diary entry is for 1 November, All Saints' Day, of that year. The subsequent blank pages tell of the blank years the follow. Physically, she vegetates until her death.

'The novel of the violet hour' ends with three fragments: a monologue by Judit's sister-in-law, Patrícia Miralpeix, recounting Judit's recent death and scenes of her own childhood; and two short pieces on Kati, the independent free-thinker who during the Civil War fought at the front and helped set up children's homes, but who fell in love with an Irish soldier and when told of his death and the defeat of the Republic committed suicide. Paradoxically, the 'romantic friendship' between Judit and Kati (what 'The violet hour' was supposed to be about) is open-ended and ambiguous, but it is crucial for an understanding of the family's past and present. The untold story of the two women is absent and suppressed; it is a void in the centre of the trilogy which the reader must reconstruct and imagine. Judit is married with children; Kati detests men, but finally falls in love with Patrick and when he dies kills herself. The two women are seen together holding hands and, before she commits suicide, Kati asks Judit to go away with her; Judit refuses. Ten years later Judit imagines she hears Kati's spirit saying:

> I'll come back , Judit, I'll come back, and nothing will separate us, no law, no war . . . Fill your house with my ghost, Judit, fill it with my memory . . . don't let me out of you, Judit, love of my life, love of my death. I hear all this and I'm not sure if I am inventing Kati . . . But I know nobody can kill this memory in me, that I shall always take it with me. Like I took Pere's little hand. (163)

The fact that neither Norma while writing 'The novel of the violet hour', nor Natàlia while reading her mother's diary, nor even the author of *La hora violeta* can clearly voice and name this love between women suggests it cannot be articulated in words, in language as we know it. Poetry, music, and colour are possibly the only means of communication between women – including between the female author and reader – as the significance attached to music, skyscapes, and literature in the novel suggests. Ross Gerling links this 'fleeting, purple light of dusk' to impressionist painting and to Roig's impressionism in prose which produces an hypnotic 'dreamlike effect' (245). But it is significant that 'the violet hour' should also refer to T. S. Eliot's *The Waste Land*, as the novel's epigraph shows.

Love and solidarity between women is a subject that haunts the female characters of the novel. It is not a question of the lesbian love propounded in feminist collectives. Norma 'envied lesbians' (232). She remembers a discussion she had with a French lesbian writer who pointed out the great advantages of lesbian relationships: 'We don't have to establish any kind of alliance with the enemy, men. Our world belongs exclusively to women, and it really suits us.' But Norma 'could not put herself on the edge of the world of the concentration camp victim without feeling guilty'.

The same applied to all those men 'who had lost out through history. Nevertheless, she did find it much easier to love men in the abstract than actual men' (233). The problem is more complex than discovering a lesbian identity. It has more to do with the kind of solidarity a married man's lover should feel for his wife, and vice-versa. This is precisely the problem facing Natàlia, Agnès, and Norma. When Norma's lover Alfred speaks of his wife, Norma wonders 'How could she reconcile the passion of love with solidarity between women?'. She remembers the advice she gave Agnès when Jordi left her for Natàlia:

> You have to be yourself, she said, we can live perfectly well without men. We don't need them for anything ... And Norma didn't want to renounce Alfred, while his wife hated militant feminists because she knew one of them had taken her husband. (240)

The broader social implications of close, human relationships are foregrounded repeatedly. Kati, for example, represents a life force which died with free Spain: she meets Judit in 1931, the year the Republic was declared, and she dies at the end of the war in 1939. Pere, too, represents that life force which was mutilated and deformed by the war and its aftermath; Judit often refers to him as a child of the war. Patrícia Miralpeix admits to herself that the war broke them all. What models, then, can Natàlia, Norma, and Agnès find in the past to help them cope with the present and the future? How can they relate to a situation which, after forty years, is finally coming to an end? In what way does the end of Franco's Spain – after having destroyed the lives of the women of the previous generation – affect the lives of women in the 1970s? It is true, as Bellver points out, that 'unlike their earlier counterparts, these contemporary women are not destroyed physically by losses in love' (1991, 231), but can they hope for something different, something new, in a theoretically brighter future? Should they return to the pre-war 1930s for inspiration and re-engage with the buried traditions of progressive politics, libertarianism, and free love; should they take up the story where others were forced to leave off, or create anew?

The quest for answers to these issues is presented as a challenge by Natàlia to Norma in her opening letter in the first section of the novel, 'Spring, 1979'. Here, the fictional author Roig-Natàlia-Norma outlines the project she has set herself. Natàlia, intent on overcoming Norma's reticence to write about 'two middle-class women lacking in feminist consciousness' (11), starts by describing how, when she returned to Barcelona from abroad, she tried to recreate through memory the lemon tree of her childhood in what had been Patrícia's garden. This scene is recounted in *Tiempo de cerezas*.[5] Memory is imbricated in narrative, 'I don't think we are able to value reality until this has become memory', writes Natàlia, and 'Literature invents the past based on a few details that were real, though only in our minds' (13). The recreation of the past, which is memory, from a woman's point of view is not possible through realist representation. Natàlia discovers this with her photography: 'I am rather tired of . . .depicting a reality that is accurate and external. As if my eyes were a camera always looking out. I want to explore my own rhythm' (13). Her rhythm has to do with memories reconstructed from smells, sensations and colours. Norma, the writer, can do this with language. And although Norma, too, has been 'seduced' by realist narrative from a so-called objective point of view (Natàlia is referring to *Tiempo de cerezas*), at least she was able to create a fictional world. Natàlia is afraid to create at all: 'I know I will never achieve harmony between mental and sensorial experience and the reality which helps keep this alive' (21). Clearly, the fictional author is dissatisfied with her previous work and wants to try something more ambitious, more introspective, without losing sense of the social. Natàlia continues: 'It seemed to me that it was necessary to save with words everything that history, great History, that's to say, the history of men, had blurred, had condemned or idealized' (17). She declares her solidarity with Patrícia and Encarna above all, 'because great History has forgotten them more than anyone' (20). But women have also to narrate themselves and construct their own identity. Natàlia feels split 'into hundreds of fragments', dispersed amongst her lovers, unable to find herself. 'Lost in thousands of particles, made through men, shared out among the geniuses, what's left of us?', she asks, again foregrounding the void; 'For a man isolation can be the first step towards power or towards art. For a woman it is emptiness, madness, or suicide' (18). To narrate themselves women need to be agents in the construction of their own femininity. Norma

5. See Roig's comments on her use of a lemon tree to evoke the pre-war gardens of the Eixample district in Barcelona and of the character Natàlia's lost childhood in *Dime que me quieres aunque sea mentira*, Barcelona, 1992, pp. 48–9. The theme of the lost Garden of Paradise is recurrent in the work of Catalan women writers.

returns to this problem towards the end of the novel when she looks into a mirror and tries to see 'how she was outside the gaze of others' (251). She, too, is afraid, of 'entering into herself, afraid of finding herself empty' (251). How, then, is woman to be represented outside patriarchal constructions of femininty?[6]

One possibility ties in with the Judit-Kati relationship. Natàlia wants to understand herself by understanding her mother. As a girl, Natàlia hated her mother, 'I found her past, her failure as a mother annoying' (16). If *Tiempo de cerezas* was a quest for the father, *La hora violeta* is a search for the mother, for the lost maternal bond. Natàlia cannot explain her mother's love for Kati and leaves Norma to come up with an imaginary solution. She admits there are things she cannot share because 'We women have to keep deep inside us a good part of ourselves. If we give everything, we end up like a bee without a hive' (19). Of course, Norma is unable to come up with a definition of the Judit-Kati relationship either. Was it sexual desire, sisterhood, companionship? The question is left unanswered, the love unvoiced, because it cannot be categorized or labelled within accepted paradigms. What is clear is that the love between the women was intense and 'our times are too mediocre to live with intense feelings' (19).

'The Lost Hour' (Chapter 2) thrashes out the three-sided conflict between Natàlia, Jordi (her lover), and Agnès (Jordi's wife), to suggest (once again) that women have to look outside mainstream left-wing political organizations if they want change. What is on the cards in Spain is a complete restructuring of social relations, in the bedroom and in the chambers of government. Following the prefatory letter, the novel opens with Natàlia reading *The Odyssey* on a Mediterranean island. At the same time, she engages in a first-person lament addressed to an absent Jordi (ten years younger than her) who she is about to lose. She represents her personal drama in terms of the mythical figures of *The Odyssey*, identifying with the forlorn Circe and Calipso, who each loved and lost the hero Ulysses (Jordi) and suffered as a consequence. This long, poetic lament is interspersed with third-person accounts of events from the point of view of Agnès, the young Penelope. She has to

6. These questions are teased out at length in the essays and articles of ¿*Tiempo de mujer?* (*Woman's Time?*), Esplugues de Llobregat, 1980, particularly in the chapter '¿Por qué no ha habido mujeres genio?' ('Why haven't there been women geniuses?'), pp. 147–64, and 'Hija y nieta del silencio' (Daughter and granddaughter of silence), pp. 299–300.

endure the ignominity of staying at home pregnant and then bringing up her two children alone while her husband spends more and more nights with Natàlia. He finally leaves his wife altogether; the affair lasts a year. During that time Agnès, who has been on the verge of suicide, finds the strength to go it alone and turns abandonment into independence. Meanwhile, Natàlia, the self-declared independent, politically active, professional woman who attempts to deal with her emotions rationally, has had a hysterectomy to comply with the wishes of Jordi, a Communist who believes in sexual freedom and women's liberation (as did the Jordi of *Ramona, adiós*). When Jordi leaves Natàlia, she is alone and unable to have children. But should that matter? 'I don't know where loneliness ends and where independence begins' (68), she says during her rambling monologue. Any self-pity and false sentimentalism is avoided by memories of snatches of dialogue with Norma whose sharp quips reassert a feminist consciousness and challenge emotional reliance on men. Needless to say, the simultaneous perspectives of both Natàlia and Agnès reveal the would-be male hero to be no more than a shallow, self-conceited and irresponsible mediocrity.

The fourth chapter, 'The dispersed hour', develops the introduction, 'Spring, 1979'. It focuses on Norma and her husband, Ferran, who each give a first-person account of their marriage from quite different perspectives. Ferran, another active Party member (friend of Jordi) seems concerned only with Party organization at this crucial moment in Spanish history and in his personal life. But Ferran's and Norma's thoughts return insistently to their friend, Germinal, who disgusted by the turn of political events (in a gesture reminiscent of Kati's some forty years earlier) commits suicide rather than face the new order of things based on compromise. Throughout this section, Norma is writing (and finishes) the novel 'The violet hour'; she even comments on what she (and the reader) has already read from Judit's diaries and papers. The relationship Norma-Ferran is obviously a mirror-image of the relationship Natàlia-Jordi, but in this alternative, less emotional, more rational, working out of the same problem, personal feelings are of secondary importance. More important are questions relating to narrative practice and representations of reality. Norma is another fictional representation of the author Roig, so that 'The dispersed hour' deals on multiple metafictional levels with such conundrums as the social responsibility of writers, writing as escapism, literature as a means to social change, and the boundaries between fiction and reality. The author Norma-Roig is engaged in writing three works: 'The violet hour'; a book-length report on Catalans held in Nazi concentration camps; and a short story about the life cycle of the salmon. The second is a reference to Roig's book *Els catalans als camps nazis*, 1977,[7] and the latter a story, 'Mother, I don't understand salmon', included in the collection *El canto de la juventud* (1992). Norma also remembers how, three years previously,

> she was completely absorbed in a novel where Joan, Natàlia's father, fell in love with Judit, and Patrícia with the poet Gonçal Rodés . . . Norma could dream, dream she was being kissed as Joan had kissed Judit. On a windy, stormy afternoon. While the waves on the Sitges beach were being covered in foam. (201)

This, of course, is *Tiempo de cerezas*. She remembers how she wrote these love scenes despite her nagging social conscience. She should have been denouncing the fact that an old lady was shut up in a nearby home, wailing with terror, or that her neighbour's child had spent two months in hospital terrorized by nuns who refused him permission to go to the toilet. This tension between writing as a novelist and as a journalist underlines a major preoccupation voiced in the novel: the appropriateness of writing committed feminist or socialist fiction. Is not writing about the self as important to social change as documentary, especially if the pen is a woman's, asks Norma? Indeed, she is busily jotting down her own present experiences in this aptly named section 'The dispersed hour'. Similarly, Norma and Natàlia together represent the split identity of the fictional author: the former communicating in words, the latter in images. Writing and living, Art and Life, are inextricably intermeshed to the extent that Alfred, Norma's lover, accuses Norma of living her life as if it were a novel, of merely repeating a clichéd discourse.

In a structure which by now is familiar to the reader, the novel doubles back on itself in a wrap-around effect. In the last section,

7. Montserrat Roig, *Els catalans als camps nazis*, Barcelona, 1977. The book (over 500 pages long) was written between 1974 and 1976 in Barcelona, Bristol, and Paris. It is dedicated to the memory of Joaquim Amat-Piniella, author of *K.L. Reich* (written in 1946 but not published in Spain because of censorship), who died shortly after Roig interviewed him.

'The open hour', Natàlia brings her long lament, begun in chapter two, to a close. She returns to aunt Patrícia's house to wait, 'she didn't know what for'. To wait, the passive fate of women '(she would have liked to have told Norma that all the books and the meetings on feminism had been of no use at all. Now, the only difference was that she knew, she knew they were of no use)' (260). Natàlia is devastated but she hopes in time to get over her sorrow 'and look ahead towards History, to her time, to the collective hour . . .' (260). Meanwhile, Norma, after so much agonizing about social responsibility, ends up putting her personal life first. She treats the old concentration camp survivor, who gave her so much information, callously – despite her high moral ground. It would seem that the two politically conscious feminists have lost out all round in this novel, the title of which points to either a new light dawning or the sun setting on the past. They, like their men, are caught in the transition between the old and the new. Unlike the men, they are trapped in a void because patriarchy still goes unchallenged. There is, nevertheless, a final moment of exultation which is deferred until the last pages of the novel. An unrepentant Jordi asks Agnès to take him back:

> And Agnès hesitated before answering. After a while, she just said no. 'No what?', asked Jordi. But she just said no, no. She said, no, and her heart ached . . . It was as if she had finally crossed the front door . . .. She had crossed the front door and she said no. And Jordi tried to hold her tight, like before, and he asked her, 'Is there another man in your life? Do you love him, do you want to live with him?' And Agnès just smiled. (268)

The archetypal down-trodden, politically naive housewife and mother has learned to say 'no'. She needs no man.

The overriding conviction, then, to which Roig returns repeatedly in this and previous novels, one which is best illustrated in the scene where Agnès asserts her independence, is that self-knowledge, self-representation, and breaking out of masculine paradigms constitute a first crucial step for women (and men) as they restructure their bodies, desires and society as a whole. Despite the awful sensation of 'finding oneself empty' (251), as Natàlia tells Norma, 'Only when you know how to look at youself will you learn to look at what surrounds you. Perhaps then you will know how to love humanity and individual people at the same time' (252).

Colour and Music

## *L'òpera quotidiana* [*La ópera cotidiana*]
## (*The Everyday Opera*)

In an early interview with the novelist Juan Marsé (of humble 'charnego' origins, that is, born in Barcelona but of a family that was neither Catalan nor spoke the language), Roig admitted the following: she had read his bestselling novel, *Si te dicen que caí* (*If They Tell You I Fell*) and

> I realized there was a split, a difference, an abyss – something like that – between the world of the marginalized and Catalan culture. The two have nothing in common. And I hope one day the reasons for this mutual ignorance are analysed in depth, without emotional confrontation or absurd rivalries. (*Los hechiceros de la palabra*, 1975, 90)

Roig returned to this problem in her fourth novel, *La ópera cotidiana* (1982), published two years after *La hora violeta*. Once again, she returns to the Mirapleix family although this time tangentially. She was particularly interested in foregrounding a male character, 'a Catalan worker, who is very patriotic and yet cowardly; who has kept the language over the years, but with a kind of racism' (Nichols, 174–5). The structure of the novel – based on that of an opera – is complex, fragmentary, and carefully organized. This is an opera in which the protagonists are not primarily middle-class property owners but ordinary working people from Barcelona. Roig shifts her attention from the women of the claustrophobic Catalan bourgeoisie to women of other social sectors in Catalunya, theoretically worse off in as much as they are immigrants, usually Andalusian, and working class. In this way ordinary people are elevated to heroes in a drama which, as the title of the novel suggests, occurs every day. But it would be erroneous to say this is light opera or Spanish 'zarzuela'. The drama is tragic and the protagonists noble in their aspirations; they too feel 'excessive passions' (189), 'opera makes [their] dreams posible' (196); they too are doomed from the start by their cultural and historical circumstances and human weaknesses.

It could be said *La ópera cotidiana* is an addendum to the trilogy. Familiar figures reappear (Patrícia, Natàlia, Lluís, Silvia, and Màrius) and references to past events narrated in previous novels are plentiful. Indeed, the novel opens with Patrícia's musings on her brother, Joan Miralpeix, who died the previous year, 1979. However, this novel introduces a completely new set of characters, clustered into the stories of four lives: those of Patrícia, Horaci Duc, Mari Cruz, and Señora Altafulla. The narrative centres on Patrícia who lets the reader eavesdrop on her conversations with her ill-fated lodger, Horaci Duc. In passing, Patrícia refers to the disappointments of her own life (her husband's affair with her bisexual lover, Gonçal Rodés) and the tragedies she has witnessed which are now viewed from her perspective: Kati's suicide, Judit's illness, Pere's death. She presents Horaci's story to explain her fatalistic pessimism and her conviction that a malign, perverse evil exists in the world – an evil which cannot be defeated and is invisible until it strikes. Patrícia lives alone (her former maid Encarna is now married) and has taken on a home-help, a young Andalusian girl named Mari Cruz, whose story is told by an omniscient narrator. This way the lives of Patrícia, the lodger, and the home-help, cross. Horaci tells his own story in snatches to a patient and sympathetic Patrícia who, as narrator and interlocutor, provides the means by which the drama involving Horaci Duc and Mari Cruz unfolds.

It is interesting to note the explicit connections made between the written text and musical drama or opera. One of the prefatory epigraphs of the novel is taken from Manuel Valls y Gorina, *Para entender la música* (*To Understand Music*):

> we always find [in these operas] a perfect balance between an exact number of diverse yet related factors which may seem conventional, even trivial, individually, but in their scenic context and coherently articulated with the other components of the work, they acquire substance and meaning.

Roig dedicates the novel to those who 'initiated me into opera (and its fatal consequences)'. The structure of the book is based on that of classical opera. The 'Overture', or instrumental prelude, is voiced by Patrícia who is the instrument through which Horaci's story is told. The lengthy Part One consists of 'duets' (compositions for two singers or instrumentalists), the dialogues between Patrícia and Duc; 'cavatinas' (short solo songs), Mari Cruz's first-person monologues; and 'recicativos' (sung narrative, the basis of dramatic musical dialogue), the third-person accounts relating to Mari Cruz and Señora Altafulla. The short interlude or 'Intermezzo' gives one more example of each of these modes of narration: a third-person account of Señora Altafulla; a dialogue between Patrícia and Duc, and a monologue by Mari Cruz. Part

Two continues with Patrícia-Duc 'duets' and the sung narration of episodes of the lives of Mari Cruz and Señora Altafulla. But these two hitherto secondary characters now voice their own stories, not only through short solo songs or 'cavatinas', but also in full length 'arias'. The two-paged 'Chorus' is a third-person summing up of the outcome of the dramas for the four main characters.

The effect of such structuring is two-fold. First, as in *Ramona, adiós* and *La hora violeta*, fragmentation and constant shifts of focalization and modes of narration make for a kaleidoscopic effect which avoids the linear, unifocused narrative of classical realism. No one version of events is conclusive, more credible, nor less ambiguous than others; history is yet another discursive fiction. The reader is never sure what to believe; for example, was the death of Horaci's wife murder or an accident? Did Duc betray Paguès? Was Colonel Saura a hero or a traitor? Furthermore, each character's story is not self-contained but is immersed in a web of interpersonal relationships. The stories constantly mutate according to the subjects telling them and to the position of those subjects in the 'scenic context'. The dramatic climax (Maria's death) is constantly deferred, then reinvented (she did not die). The second effect has to do with the relation of verbal expression to music. Roig achieves polyphony and multivocality in narrative without sacrificing conversational, realist discourse readily understood by her readers. Arguably, the musical structure facilitates the outpouring of jouissance in lyrical prose, as we shall see. This way Roig creates a new form of literary expression which incorporates music, drama, and words, and attempts to bridge arbitrary divisions not only between the literary genres but also between the arts.

'We go on making people according to our relationships with them' (17), wrote Natàlia to Norma in *La hora violeta*, and the dire consequences of men shaping women according to their own preconceived images of femininity is precisely the theme of this novel. The young Horaci Duc, a humble but honest butcher, married an Andalusian woman, Maria, whom he loved intensely. He taught her the Catalan language and culture with such enthusiasm that she identified with Catalunya completely and in the post-war period became politically militant, much more than Duc himself who was cowed by Franco's regime. The couple had a daughter but their family life was shattered when Maria began to distribute radical propaganda, a dangerous task which Horaci was too frightened to take on himself. Believing Maria to be having an affair with Paguès, one of the underground organization's leaders who is subsequently caught and imprisoned, ravaged by jealousy and humiliation, Duc seemingly pushes his wife under a train. She and the small daughter are killed. Horaci can never put the tragedy and guilt behind him. When he meets Patrícia's home-help, Mari Cruz, herself a young Andalusian immigrant (who first worked in Paris as a maid and later looked afer old ladies such as the Señora Altafulla), he confuses her with the dead Maria and falls in love. Their sexual relationship, described in lyrical, erotic scenes suggestive of the 1975 film *Last Tango in Paris* (explicitly mentioned in *Tiempo de cerezas*), is doomed from the start. Horaci is living in the past; he cannot accept Mari Cruz as she is (free, modern, disrespectful of social and sexual taboos) and constantly tries to fit her into his generation's concepts of womanhood. When he suddenly disappears Mari Cruz leaves Patrícia's home for a life of prostitution on the streets. What could have been a workable relationship is, once again, destroyed by ghosts of the immediate post-war past, by sexual and social roles foisted on men and women, and by mutual incomprehension between the sexes.

However, the ghosts of the past and romantic idealization can also provide a reason for living. This is the case of the old Señora Altafulla and her dead lover, the Republican Colonel Saura, executed after the Civil War. Their love story (and her progressive degeneracy) is re-enacted in scenes, 'who knows if invented or recreated' (71), in the theatre which is her bedroom. She explains to Mari Cruz, 'In the Colonel I found the ideal man I had imagined when I was a girl . . . Who knows if he found the same in me' (164). The point is, that unlike Horaci Duc and Maria, this couple decided to part 'so that our relationship wouldn't become routine'; 'if things had been otherwise, perhaps our dream would have shattered' (163). Romance, remembered and imagined, is what keeps Altafulla alive. She plays at being La Traviata in Verdi's opera, romance is her escape; reality (marriage) shatters fantasy and love. Mari Cruz is thus led to believe in romance; 'you want to be free and independent and at the same time have old-fashioned dreams' (188), Duc tells her. He suggests, 'You dream what you desire, it's a way of tolerating the suffering of being awake' (189). But, as Akiko Tsuchiya shows, romance is a pernicious verbal fiction. All the characters of the novel – even Mari Cruz – end up trapped in Romantic plots, 'their individual tragedies are intimately linked to the failure of their fictions'; they 'find themselves drowning in the madness' of their linguistic constructions (1990, 155). Roig makes the point of linking these Romantic fictions to the Catalan cultural myths, linguistic purity and Republicanism. As these myths of the older generation disintegrate in the contemporary world the younger 'charnegos', such as Mari Cruz, are abandoned to their fate. In Roig's words, 'Mari Cruz is a girl who begins to live through the [Romantic] memories of others, they're not her own. And so between them [Horaci, Señora Altafulla, and Patrícia] they destroy her. It's always the old people who tell her stories; she can never tell her own' (Nichols, 175).

The construction of gender and national identity through verbal fictions relates to the theme of Pygmalion. Horaci's problem is he cannot control the ideal woman of his creation when she comes alive. Once married, he keeps Maria at home like a pet cat. She is the perfect housewife, as is expected of her, but she is bored and increasingly resentful. Her bid for independence is construed by Horaci as sexual infidelity, although there is no proof and the episode is unresolved. When Maria becomes politically active she escapes Duc's control completely. What galls Horaci is that the behaviour of this creature shaped to his own desire is perfectly logical; she shares her love of Catalan culture and language with others and actively defends her newly acquired nationalism. Horaci cannot conceive of Maria as an autonomous person rather than a dependent woman. He describes her to Patrícia thus: 'she was the enigma of the feminine personified . . . she had that mystery that made a man lose his head.' Patrícia retorts, 'When I look at a woman, even if she has got pretty eyes . . . I don't see any mystery'. He answers, 'That's because you're a woman' (35). For Duc, woman is an object of fantasy and desire to be possessed. He traps the unsuspecting Mari Cruz in these same patriarchal representations of femininity. But, ironically, their sexual encounter leads her to self-discovery. Certainly Duc's love-making with Mari Cruz is a mind-shattering experience for them both. Unlike the symbolical phallus figures Mari Cruz had dusted in the French poet's Parisian apartment, which meant nothing to her, the discovery of her own body and sexual pleasure proves to be a profound revelation. The love scene – the most erotic Roig wrote

– is recounted in moving, lyrical prose centering on the word 'entretelas' (Castilian), 'voraviu' (Catalan), meaning interlining, inmost being, heartstrings. Mari Cruz does not speak Catalan but she uses this Catalan word, learnt from Señora Altafulla, to express inexpressible jouissance (*Dime que me quieres*, 171):

> Kneeling down I started to lick his sex with the tip of my tongue, first little by little, as if it were a flower on the point of opening, slowly, and I closed my eyes to concentrate better on what for me was a new miracle . . . I shut out the image of the phallus poet, all the marble phalluses, the great phallus of the desert, . . . because this sex belonged to me, I would suck it, destroy it.. and I don't know who was speaking, me or him, Maria, Maria, said his sex, I am Maria and I'll swallow you, like the bee sucks the pollen from the flower and with my sting I kill you, Maria, Maria . . . and his sex was so inside me it seemed as if all of me were part of him. The magician lay me down on the floor and made me open my legs and he licked my interlinings and that's when I tasted heaven, I wanted to be him, all him, he must come deep inside . . . and the magician said, ride, and I galloped on him while he, he thrust me with his sex and he was brute-macho and I was brute-female, and we stayed like that for a long time, only panting, moans, skin, sweat, no words . . . and he touched my interlinings from behind, and that's when I screamed endlessly, a long moan, as if an electric current ran through my spine, a current I couldn't stop, couldn't stop, until I wanted to cry with happiness. (120–1)

The fusion of the two bodies, the release of a feminine libido, makes for a new feminine language. Mari Cruz embarks on a journey of self-discovery through desire; she liberates herself through her body. As Bellver writes, in this novel 'female sexuality emerges as a source of inner energy, as a means of self-fulfilment, spiritual nourishment and regeneration' (Brown, 236). Akiko Tsuchiya, however, in her perceptive study, suggests that Mari Cruz deludes herself into thinking she 'has found a new and somehow more authentic language that corresponds to her desires', because ultimately (unlike Maria) she is 'mastered by Horaci's paternal discourse' and his concept of the essential feminine self. Tsuchiya adds, 'if female sexuality can liberate women's language . . . Mari Cruz, as the victim of phallic domination, is reduced to silence' (Tsuchiya, 150–1). Horaci abandons Mari Cruz and she returns to poverty.

Roig's novels, then, while clearly anchored in history and

rotating around key dates are nevertheless fluid, boundary free, inconclusive, unforeclosed accounts. The boundaries between fact and fiction, dream, myth, and reality are blurred. This is not diachronic, master narrative, but an attempt to create her-story by piecing together what at first sight may seem trivial snippets, but which in the great scheme of things are of crucial importance. Women's lives are foregrounded in this novel, but once again there is a male tragic figure.[8] Duc cannot conceive of woman outside the parameters of masculinist discourse; she is nature which he must cultivate: '[Maria] was a jewel to be polished, and I felt like the sculptor who can model a work of art with primitive clay'(36). The independently thinking Galatea, of Pygmalion's creation, learns to despise her master, just as Patrícia – the 'Pygmaliona' of *Tiempo de cerezas* – had despised Esteve. These women refuse to be statues of man's making. Yet it should be remembered that Horaci, too, is a product of the patriarchal, authoritarian regime of Franco's Spain. He hates what he has become, what they made him be:

It's their fault. They are the ones who obliged me to play a role since I was born, obliged me to have courage, to believe in someone else's ideas . . . They are the ones who entered the ruined city on a dark January day, the ones who condemned me to live, . . . who prohibited the language I spoke, who were proud to enslave it, who compelled us to be martyrs and heroes though we weren't, . . . they are the ones who forced me to have a faith I didn't have, who made me convert Maria into another woman, not to know how to love her as she was, made me transform her, to make her be born anew, just to prove this land would never die, this land of sorrow . . . they are the ones who shattered the dreams of my youth, who turned my belief in myself, my faith in life, to shit, who didn't let me breathe . . . They and the History that constrained me . . . They, who haven't let me be a man, but a waste, refuse. (211)

'Language is power', wrote Roig, referring to the imposition of Castilian on Catalan speakers.[9] In this novel it is the Catalan imposition of their language and cultural myths on non-Catalan speakers which is brought into question. Horaci's patriarchal

8. For a harsher opinion of Horaci Duc's character, see Catherine Bellver, 'Montserrat Roig and the Creation of a Gynocentric Reality', Brown ed., pp. 234–5.
9. *Dime que me quieres*, p. 42.

wielding of linguistic authority over the young girl Maria, replicating the authoritarianism he experienced as a Catalan worker under the Franco regime, leads to disaster. On the other hand, Mari Cruz learns Catalan, 'the lost language of magic' (*Dime que me quieres*, 43), not from Duc primarily but from a woman – Señora Altafulla. The language, as in the word 'voraviu', enables her to free herself from sexual repression. By finding a language of her own she gains self-knowledge.[10] In the early 1980s Catalan was no longer a persecuted language and the Catalans could aspire to autonomous government. The tricky question of the interrelation of language, gender, nationhood, and power had to be reassessed. As Roig herself pointed out, to lose our mother tongue is equivalent to losing a grandmother; 'the nation is not only childhood [memories], but neither is it just language. The nation is the two at the same time. If we cannot remember one and use the other, we lose our breath' (*Dime que me quieres*, 38). She would continue exploring the psychosocial problematic of nationality, language and sexuality in her next novel.

10. Biruté Ciplijauskaité writes: 'Her self-fulfilment as a woman is identified with the creation of an authentic language and the destruction of old myths. Through the sexual act she reaches a word which is hers only', *La novela femenina contemporánea*, 1988, p. 56.

# 3

## The Same Old Song: the Narrative and Drama of the Late 1980s

'*Je* suis moi-même la matière de mon livre', writes Roig, quoting Montaigne (*Hechiceros*, 214) in an attempt to capture succinctly the essential Joan Fuster. But no sentence could be more appropriately applied to Montserrat Roig herself. Her work does not distinguish between fiction and non-fiction or, more precisely, between autobiographical fiction and fictional autobiography, documentary or make-believe. Montserrat Roig, Mundeta Claret, Natàlia Miralpeix, Norma, Agnès, are all refractions of the same decentred self in fiction, and are all further reduplicated and dispersed as writer, narrator, addressee, interlocutor, witness, journalist, mother, lover, and wife in the works of non-fiction. The self-reflecting refractions of Roig's prose break down traditional genres and blur the edges of the books themselves, so they spill over into each other. Nowhere is this more evident than in her moving (auto)biographical documentaries: *Rafael Vidiella o l'aventura de la revolució* 1976 (*Rafael Vidiella [founder of the Catalan Communist Party] or the Adventure of the Revolution*), *Els catalans als camps nazis* 1977 [*Noche o niebla: los catalanes en los campos nazis*, 1977] (*Night and Mist. Catalans in Nazi Concentration Camps*), and *L'agulla daurada* 1985 [*La aguja dorada*, 1985] (*The Golden Spire*).

The latter was published by the popular publishing house Plaza y Janés in their series 'Biographies and Memoirs'. Roig explains in a short prologue that she spent two months in Leningrad/St Petersburg in 1980, invited by the Moscow publishers 'Progress' to write a book on the Nazis' siege of the city between 1941 and 1945. 'In 1980', she writes, 'I fell in love with the city of Leningrad . . . This book is the story of my passion' (14). It is a skilfully written, moving account of her experiences during the process of historical research, an account which also incorporates the final commissioned report. The book is dedicated to Roig's two sons, Roger and Jordi, in the hope that 'they can live in a world without frontiers'. In what is both a historical reconstruction and a personal encounter with another culture and another literature, Roig manages to reconstruct events from the points of view of those who were involved in the siege, men and women who are prepared to share their memories. She also incorporates her own readings on the subject as if she were engaged in an academic project, relying heavily on two books, *El libro del bloqueo* (*The Book of the Blockade*) by Zenaida Vladimirovna and *Los 900 días* (*The 900 Days*) by Harrison E. Salisbury, her main sources of background information from which she quotes extensively. This draft is then supplemented with her readings of Russian literature (in translation), particularly the poetry and biography of Pushkin, the poet of St Petersburg. The effect is one of a multi-layered prose narrative involving three main threads: the nineteenth century, focusing on anecdotes about Peter the Great, Rasputin, and Pushkin's unhappy marriage; the siege of the 1940s involving reportage, further anecdotes from a series of personal experiences during the siege, and a large corpus of gruesome statistics (in December 1941 53,000 people died of hunger and in January 1942 4,000 people died a day); and, finally, the present day movements and thoughts of the author/narrator in 1980. However, as in all Roig's books, there is no facile experimentation; on the contrary, the final version of these overlapping historical and personal discourses is deceptively simple. The book is framed by Roig's journey to and from Russia, and her arrival and departure from Leningrad. She recounts her first moments of homesickness, nostalgia for creature comforts, tension and unease. A fraught relationship with her young interpreter, Nikolai, does not help. Gradually she penetrates the city, its parks, monuments, buildings, rivers, and colours. Presiding over them all is the golden spire of the Admiralty, the first thing she sees from her hotel window and which gives its suggestive name to the the book. More importantly, the narrator's female persona gradually becomes immersed in the people she meets, taking on at times a different identity. She identifies so strongly with the city and the people that she relives their memories as her own and her self merges into the personae of those who lived through the siege. The book ends with Roig back in Catalunya:

I longed for the self I had left behind, for myself, which no longer belonged to Barcelona . . . I longed for myself lost in the streets of Dostoievski . . . Everything disappeared. I am left with only the sensations. No it's not true: they are here with me. They exist. I have seen them. On the other side is another half of ourselves. For two months I dreamt it was possible to live without frontiers. (250)

The strange experience of existing in a kind of time tunnel, of being lost in the past, allows the narrator to see through the eyes of others and yet to be ever conscious of the images and representations she is presenting to the reader. Readers must construct their own mental image of the city under siege, the people in it, and the strength of human resistance and dignity in the face of appalling adversity from these representations. There is no room for sentimentalism. This is also the case of Roig's last novel, *La veu melodiosa* (*The Melodious Voice*), which also tells of strength and moral fibre through the collective voice of a specific urban setting, this time the inimitable Barcelona. For the first time, however, in this novel Roig strains the conventions of realism to the limits of credibility.

### *La veu melodiosa* [*La voz melodiosa*] (*The Melodious Voice*)

*La voz melodiosa* (*The Melodious Voice*), 1987, published in Catalan and Castilian in the same year, is somewhat different from Roig's earlier novels. Drawing on symbolism and allegory, it is open to multiple interpretations. Roig described it as a novel which 'is not fantasy but where everything is imagined . . . It is based a little on the book of Job; I wanted to find a parallel between that book and the present' (Nichols, 184). The novel's epigraph, taken from the great Catalan poet Ausiàs Marc, relates the 'melodious voice' to death: '. . . for when man is tied to pain / melodious is the voice of death'. The melodious voice also refers to love and harmony (17) and to the 'music' of the Catalan language (29).

The novel is divided into four unequal parts, each introduced with an epigraph from the Book of Job connoting steadfastness in the face of hardship. This strange tale, set in the mid-sixties, is told in the present by the middle-aged, disillusioned Virginia (sometimes speaking in the first person and at others focalized through a third-person narrator), who represents a group of characters, including the inevitable Mundeta Ventura and Jordi Soteres. Virginia – the metafictional teller of tales (98), the 'famous theoretician of love' (101) – is both an individual and a collective voice; she speaks from hindsight of her student days and of a group of friends to whom she belonged yet became detached. One of the group was the young man known as l'Espardenya [Alpargata] (canvas sandal) whose real name is never revealed.

In January, 1938, this boy is born in war-ravaged Barcelona to the daughter of a wealthy, cultured Catalanist, Señor Malagelada. The mother dies and the boy is brought up by his misanthropic grandfather and the maid Delors until he is six. He is never allowed out of the house, or to meet anyone other than the people at home, or to look into a mirror, because he is deformed and ugly. He is schooled by a series of exceptional governesses and teachers (Republicans without work in Franco's Spain) who are instructed not to mention his appearance or anything suggesting conflict and pain. At twenty-three he demands to go to university and, being extremely well-read and intelligent, stands out among his mediocre contemporaries. He becomes attached to a group of students (Mundeta, in love with Jordi, Virginia, and Joan Luís) who use him as a buffoon. But he puts up with their mockery and is allowed to join the clandestine students' political 'Platform' because of his complete command of Catalan. He writes their pamphlets but is not invited to participate in any organizational procedures, debates, or decisions. However, unlike the others, he takes it on himself to teach the homeless poor – put up in barracks outside Barcelona – to read and write, and on one visit falls in love with a young girl who is repeatedly abused by her father and who subsequently disappears. On a May 1st demonstration, which turns out to be a police ambush, he is the one picked on by the police, beaten up savagely, and tortured in prison because of his involvement with the poor. He gives away the names of the others on the 'Platform', who are also imprisoned, and is further ostracized because of this 'treachery'. When he is released he goes to see his grandfather, who never visited the prison, only to find his grandfather has died. But the grandfather leaves a note on the back of a photograph telling the boy the truth of his birth: he was born of a loving but incestuous relationship between father and daughter, between the boy's grandfather and his mother. In a short epilogue, we are told how Mundeta and Joan Luís have done well out of life. The young man, who calls himself Alpargata as a sign

of humility, has become a poet. Virginia has shut herself away for
twenty years and still awaits his call.

The story, bordering on the inverosimile and magical real (note
the pointers to Melquíades, the magical figure of Gabriel García
Márquez's *One Hundred Years of Solitude*, 39, 55), invites an
allegorical interpretation. Clearly, it is an indictment of the
progressive politics of the 1960s, divorced from the real problems
and the real poor of the everyday world. Such politically correct
élitism is represented by the group of silly students who read the
'correct' books but who shy away from positive and practical help
for the very people they are supposed to be defending and who
they really despise, people like the dirty, overweight, illiterate
women Alpargata teaches to read. The police pick on Alpargata
precisely because of these potentially dangerous activities, and not
on account of his involvement with the students. For the latter,
politics is a game which comes to a dirty end with the sacrifice of
the 'scapegoat' (73), Alpargata. Included in this indictment of the
politically correct is the so-called sexual liberation of the Left.
More importantly, the novel questions eugenics and a humanist
education which avoids facing and compromising with the ugly
side of human nature and social reality. The harmonious
environment created for Alpargata by his grandfather is artificial.
Señor Malagelada is a eugenist, a God-figure; the 'creator of things
and people ... invented a new reality' (67), he even changes
people's names (the housekeeper Delors [suffering] is renamed
Leticia [happiness]; all the female teachers are renamed Mónica
[solitary woman] and the male teachers Alfred [man of peace]).
This may work in the inner sanctum of the bourgeois family home
in the Paseo de Gracia (*Dime que me quieres*, 168), but the experiment backfires. Life is not poetry; amongst the lilies on the
University lake float scraps of newspaper and fag ends. By
shutting out human imperfection the grandfather provides an
erroneously conceived education for his grandson. Again, the
protagonists are deluded by verbal fictions, be they nationalist
discourse, Catalan poetry or left-wing propaganda.

As far as morality and aesthetics are concerned, *La voz melodiosa*
sets up and deconstructs a series of hierarchical binaries: ugliness-
beauty, altruism-selfishness, ignorance-knowledge, progressive-
regressive, lies-truth, appearance-reality. The Romantic adage
'Beauty is Truth' certainly does not hold here. Alpargata, the
martyr, the Christ figure – noble, sincere, thoughtful, and active

– is all that humanism could expect from a person, yet he is ugly and deformed; he is likened to a fish, a fly, and a cockroach. What the novel seems to be considering is a new order of things, a new humanism. For Freud, though not for eugenics, the prohibition of incest supposedly gave rise to civilization. In this novel from incest is born the most civilized (and the least beautiful) of men. Mores and values are supposedly passed on through the literary canon of the classics. But the high moral ground established by Señor Malagelada, founded on texual borrowings from the Catalan literary tradition, fails. An idealist who 'did not want to accept the idea that the ideal Catalunya no longer existed' (*Dime que me quieres*, 168), he committed the error 'of thinking that we can make the world according to our own standards' (*La voz melodiosa*, 157). To use the powerful quote taken by Roig from Goya, 'the sleep [or dream] of reason engenders monsters', if out of the sleep of reason, that is, irrationality, come monsters, so too do monsters come out of the dream of reason, or idealism. Nevertheless, a new Catalan culture and politics has yet to be created through language in accordance with the modern world, and the poet's role in this enterprise is more important than the politician's.

Through Alpargata the two worlds of Catalan culture meet. One is the anachronistic, pre-Civil War Barcelona of the grandfather who, rather than concede to the barbarism of Franco, creates a 'small paradise' (17) where only Catalan is spoken and read in order to save the boy 'from the evils of the outside world through poetic language' (29). Here the aesthetics, ethics and wisdom of the great humanist tradition are taught and prolonged. Through that bourgeois, liberal, nationalist culture (30) Alpargata learns knowledge, compassion, and hope; he learns that 'the world is beautiful and humanity good' (67). He is protected from the hypocrisy and defeatism of Franco's Spain (50). The other, contemporary world is the arena of student politics at Barcelona University where Alpargata learns about violence, deceit, pain, and cynicism. His knowledge of reality leads to self-awareness. He also learns, not through the students but through the wretched of the earth, about passion and its loss. Alpargata is the incarnation of the long tradition of Catalan humanism hidden from view between 1938 and 1962 which resurfaces to merge with contemporary progressive culture. The students read Marx, Sartre, Simone de Beauvoir but, at the end of the day, know less than Alpargata about human feelings and values; for the students 'it was considered bad taste then, and now, to be sorry for the poor' (106). The fact that Alpargata is deformed suggests, as Horaci Duc pointed out in *La ópera cotidiana*, that Catalan culture – hidden, restricted, threatened – was similarly distorted, not intrinsically perhaps but certainly when reflected by the deformed world in which it existed. Alpargata is only ugly to those who see him that way. The clashing of the past and the present is symbolized by the episode of the 'well' or cave, when the innocent Alpargata is beaten up by the police, crucified by his friends, and tortured in prison. That short time 'represented a change of epoch' (96); the four students die and are reborn as different people when faced with the clash of ideals and reality. They lose their idealism and become opportunists or defeatists. Alpargata is the only one of the group who was 'prepared to search for what none of us would look for, that is, the beauty that was still in the world' (97). In *Dime que me quieres*, 1992, Roig recalls how this type of male character, 'the innnocent individual rejected by the tribe' had appeared in her early story 'Jordi Soteres reclama la ayuda de Maciste' ('Jordi Soteres demands help from Maciste') in *Aprendizaje sentimental*.[1] The closed space of the Faculty café where 'a crowd of students tried to build a different world . . . and at the same time got the weakest one drunk just to laugh at him '(*Dime que me quieres*, 164) in the story, became the Faculty patio in *La voz melodiosa*, now 'the emblem of a cruel and disordered world' (166). The story was written 'in situ' and identified with the nostalgia of the older generation, while the novel – written over fifteen years later – depicts that once idealistic world from the perspective of hindsight, through the 'disfiguration and distortion' of memory, as something both fearful and naive.

What, then, is the importance of women in this novel? First, the metafictional narrator Virginia-Roig returns to a familiar theme: left-wing politics is a game by and for men; women have no part but they superficially participate through their personal relationships with men. As Natàlia told Norma in *La hora violeta*, 'they say I joined the Party through the vagina' (64), or as Virginia admits in this novel:

---

1. Roig writes in *Dime que me quieres*, p. 166, that the character Alpargata was based on two people she knew at University, the poet Josep Elias, who was later to die of cancer, and a tall, dark student who later committed suicide.

> None of us liked the world the way it was, but we didn't know how
> to put it right either. We girls were all from convent schools and we
> only had one thing on our minds: to lose our virginity. We read French
> books on sexuality and we didn't know anything about sex. (76)

Second, the novel insists on the deception of the sexual revolution
leading, in theory, to women's sexual liberation. Sexual freedom
was appropriated by men for their own ends and caused women
great unhappiness. Mundeta goes to the May 1st demonstration
only to show Jordi Soteres that 'she too believed in liberty'; for
the same reason she went to bed with Joan Luís. Both acts were
to show others that she was a free woman, but 'she didn't want
freedom' (122). Virginia is mortified when her boyfriend Joan Luís
sleeps with Mundeta. She tries to convince herself, 'One night with
a man is only one night. Love made her sick, sex was annoying.
She would finish reading Simone de Beauvoir . . . They were the
new women, they had buried their grandmothers and mothers'
(91). She remembers Joan Luís's words, 'You're not the only one,
darling . . . Sex is like drinking a glass of water' (92). But Alpargata
rejects this way of thinking furiously, and tells Virginia 'You have
a jewel in your hand and you don't know how to polish it' (94).
He uses the same image as Horaci Duc in *La ópera cotidiana*
referring not to woman as pliable matter but to heterosexual love.
Virginia admits that if she told Joan Luís she needed him she would
lose him; popular romance is out, 'You only say "I need you" in
films' (94). And, of course, such things as personal feelings are
never discussed by the 'Platform'.

Finally, the fact that the female narrator is the only member of
the group to understand Alpargata suggests an alliance between
all those men and women who are marginalized by power games
and share human values and ideals. Both Virginia and Alpargata
experience patriarchy. Franco's was authoritarian, apparently that
of the Marxist Left was no less. Similarly, Malagelada represents
a liberal, bourgeois patriarchy, inflected by paternalistic paro-
chialism. Within this space Alpargata does not know his
mother (who died) but is nevertheless brought up by a woman
(Leticia/ Delors) who teaches him domestic tasks, fairy tales, old
ballads, dreams, fantasies, and 'the goodness of the world' (27).
Señor Malagelada never knew his mother either, which indicates
the lack of women's input to the Catalan cultural tradition. But,
ironically, it is this outmoded pedagogue who represents the most

radical views on gender differences in the novel. When he is told his daughter has had a son he says, 'What difference does the sex make?' Sex is always a burden' (19) and he admires the poet Ausiàs Marc because he demythifies the feminine:

> he was a poet who understood women. He distanced himself from the troubadors . . . he brought woman down from the heavens and converted her into a human being, with vices and virtues . . . He never hid what was dishonest or shameful in woman because he knew she belonged to earth. (31)

Towards the end of the novel, after his grandfather's death, Alpargata comes to realize the full import of certain lines of poetry written by Rainer Maria Rilke which he read at the age of twelve in *Letters to a Young Poet*, a book given to him by his grandfather:

> men and women, freed from misleading and repugnant feelings, will search for each other as brothers and sisters and not as enemies. Then . . . we would all unite as human beings to endure sex together, simply and patiently, as a burden foisted upon us. (157)

'Sex is a burden' and only when 'we men and women regard each other as brothers and sisters will we be able to bear it' (158). This is the grandfather's lesson to Alpargata and, apparently, the conclusion Roig had reached by the end of her last novel.

### *Reivindicació de la senyora Clito Mestres. Seguit de El Mateix Paisatge (Vindication of Mrs Clito Mestres. Followed by The Same Landscape)*

In 1987 TV3 in Catalunya commissioned Roig to coordinate the production of thirteen stories written by local writers to be filmed as one hour television dramas. Only ten were filmed eventually including her own script 'El mateix paisatge' ('The same landscape'). This was shown on television for the first time in 1987 and was published as a text posthumously in 1992. The same volume, *Reivindicació de la senyora Clito Mestres. Seguit de El Mateix Paisatge* (Barcelona, 1992), included a dramatic monologue written by Roig which had been commissioned in 1990 by the Centre Dramatic of the Catalan Generalitat that wanted to stage five monologues written by contemporary Catalan novelists. The title of Roig's piece was 'Reivindicació de la senyora Clito' ('Vindication of Mrs Clito Mestres') and it was staged for the first time at the Romea Theatre in June 1991. Both television script and play were to be the only works of drama published by Roig. This is surprising as she had been closely associated with the theatre since her youth. Her sister Glòria Roig is a well-known actress, in fact, 'Vindication' was expressly written for her. As Josep M. Benet points out in his informative introduction to the volume, both pieces had to keep within strict guidelines: 'The Same Landscape' was to be based on film techniques, that is, on visual images rather than on verbal discourse; 'Vindication' had to be a monologue sustained without a break. It is interesting to see former themes cropping up again now streamlined and distilled for greater dramatic impact. Roig shows a quite remarkable dramatic skill unusual in novelists.

'The same landscape' consists of thirty-two sequences set in the late 1950s including three flashbacks to 1936 and one flashforward to 1977. It dramatizes the encounter of two unlikely characters in two distinct Barcelona settings: Rafael, a homosexual, living in misery, and moving in the underworld of nightclubs, drugs, and petty crime; and Joanna, an elderly spinster who, though poor, hails from a relatively wealthy family, and lives alone in the Eixample. She is seen watching Rafael's act in the music hall, El Molino, and then helping him after the show when he has been beaten up in the street. She takes him home, they chat, and they discover a common love of music and art. They also realize they both come from the same small town, Sant Esteve, and together they remember the sea, the landscape, the cherry trees, and tomato plants. This budding friendship is cut short when Rafael is denounced to the police and imprisoned; he revisits Joanna six months later, a broken man, protesting his innocence. It is at this point that Joanna reveals all; she was the one who denounced him to revenge herself and her family. It was no coincidence that they should meet; she had been following him for years. Her revenge concerns an incident during the Civil War when Joanna's father was shot in cold blood before her and her mother's eyes, because of supposed right-wing sympathies. The perpetrator was Rafael's brutish father accompanied unwillingly by his young, effeminate son. Joanna was a girl and neither she nor her mother (a seamstress who the father had married despite family objections) ever recovered from the experience. The mother goes mad and dies seven years later; Joanna plans her lifelong revenge. But the shooting also had a marked effect on the young, sensitive Rafael who swore never again to take part in violence. Joanna tells her version of events to an astounded Rafael who will return to prison for a further two years. She says she is happy and can now begin to mourn her dead; she even paid off Rafael's young lover to leave him. But the script then jumps to 1977 and to an alcoholic Joanna sitting at a bar. She has lost out too.

Joanna and Rafael, then, represent the innocent victims of both sides of the Civil War living in Spain in the late 1970s. They are also examples of how a patriarchal society marginalizes unmarried women and gay men. Neither the homosexual from a poor, peasant family, nor the poor, elderly spinster from a middle-class background fit into the model of the nuclear family propagated during the repressive Francoist years. Of course, the script is predominantly a commentary on the 'Transition' itself. The late 1970s may well have been the period of national reconciliation, but personal tragedies are not so easily forgotten. Hence the importance of the dates in the script, inscribed on the tombstones of Joanna's parents. However, to forget past grievances seems to be the only solution envisaged in the text; in refusing to reconcile herself to events taking place forty years previously Joanna ruins her own life as much as Rafael's. The long-standing effects of the war, the figure of the lonely spinster, and the dialogue she engages in with the younger, long-suffering man reminds the reader of *La ópera cotidiana*. There, too, the spinster was a victim of society and the war though indirectly. Here Joanna is given a character far stronger, more lethal, and more tragic than that of Patrícia Miralpeix. The message is clear. The drama is an indictment of the irrationality and the absurdity of war, the atrocities of which are prolonged through a lifetime in memory. There was no justice in Joanna's father's death, but neither was there justice in her victimization of Rafael. The script is a warning for those who think slates can be wiped clean easily.

The monologue, 'Reivindicació de la senyora Clito Mestres' also belongs to a middle-aged woman. Clito is a one-time actress, living in the Eixample, whose life has been wasted meaninglessly. The play is set in the actress's dressing room shortly before Clito is due on stage to play the role of a lifetime. In explaining how she is well suited for the role, Clito (Clotilde) tells her story. After a happy childhood in Barcelona with a loving father, she met and marrried Hans, a German from Hamburg, moved to Germany and gave birth to a daughter, Iris. Shortly after, Hans starts an affair with a

younger woman, Helena, and he takes Iris with him on a skiing
holiday to the Alps to meet his lover. During the holiday the little
girl is killed and Hans repents. Clito, meanwhile, falls in love with
Helmut, a poet. Hans finds out two years later and she ends the
affair. She gives birth to twins (one of each sex) and, on her father's
death, decides to stay in Germany with her two German children.
When her mother is taken ill Clito returns to Barcelona and an old
friend persuades her to take part in a play.

The role she is asked to play is, of course, Clytemnestra in
Aeschylus's *Oresteia*. Her aim is to vindicate the much vilified
Clytemnestra in public. The analogy between her story and that
of the tragic heroine are clear. Not only does Clytemnestra's
husband Agamemnon attack Troy in a war which lasts two years
all for the sake of a woman, Helen, but in order to have favourable
winds he kills Clytemnestra's daughter Iphigenia. Clytemnestra
takes a lover and kills her husband when he returns. Then her two
twins, Electra and Orestes, kill her and denigrate her name for
posterity. The real Clito does not kill her husband, of course, nor
is she murdered by her twins; her story is not tragic in the classical
sense but simply disappointing. She vegetates in a life of relative
comfort. What is important, she tells the audience, is that her own
experiences enable her to sympathise with Clytemnestra, the
tragic queen; she feels 'authorized' to play the part. She can both
save herself and play at killing her husband; with fictitious revenge
she can enact the escape from a mundane destiny. Clito has no
sympathy for the much celebrated Electra (a hysterical woman in
her view) or for Orestes (a weak, manipulated man). She wants
to make Clytemnestra live, tell her version, and reclaim the justice
denied to her for so long. What seems a rather contrived example
of parallel lives works effectively mainly because the audience can
sympathise with the ordinary Mrs Mestres, and through her, with
Clytemnestra, the epitome of the wicked woman and spiteful wife
in patriarchal myth. Myth and history are again rewritten from a
woman-centred perspective and the everyday lives of women
today are given mythical, heroic dimensions.

The archetypal representation of woman focussed through the
*Odyssey* was important in *La hora violeta*. In the sections 'La hora
perdida' ('The Lost Hour') and 'La hora abierta' ('The Open
Hour') of that novel Natàlia reads the epic and casts herself as
Circe and Calypso as well as Penelope. In *Dime que me quieres* Roig
returns to the theme stating that when she read the *Odyssey* 'I was

also Ulysses and Achilles' (88). Roig, however, warns women readers not to confuse the mythical female figures of literature with the biographies of real women. That would be to read literature from a 'masculine perspective'. The identification with such archetypes 'has to be poetic . . . in the imaginary universe' (88). Bearing that in mind, she adds:

> My Clytemnestra is a woman whose husband goes to a war she does not understand, a mother who sees how her husband takes her daughter away to kill her in a sacrifice to the gods and sees that same man return from the battle with a young, intelligent lover. (88)

After all, Clytemnestra is a woman of the twentieth century. Roig goes further:

> Clytemnestra is not stupid and she imagines the story the other way round: if Menalaus had been kidnapped she would not have killed their son Orestes. The crime of Clytemnestra . . . is to want to act like a man, she wanted to decide her destiny. . . . My Clytemnestra has the courage Aristotle denied her. And she also knows how to cook. (89–90)

### *El cant de la joventut* [*El canto de la juventud*] (*The Song of Youth*)

One year before her death, Montserrat Roig published in Catalan and Spanish a second collection of short stories entitled *El canto de la juventud*, 1990 (*The Song of Youth*). Two of the eight stories, 'Mar' ('Sea'), first written in 1980 and revised in 1988, and 'Antes de que merezca el olvido' ('Before I deserve to be forgotten'), almost reach novella length and are divided into five and six parts respectively.[2] They are skilfully written, poignant, and moving models of the genre, and trace new directions Roig may have pursued had she lived longer. 'Mar', in particular, makes use of long, flowing unbroken sentences, not usually associated with Roig but with another writer from Barcelona, Esther Tusquets.[3]

2. 'El canto de la juventud' was first published in *El País*, 5 April 1988. 'Mar' was first published in *Triunfo*, 11, IX, 1981.
3. Tusquets's trilogy was published between 1978 (*El mismo mar de todos los veranos*) and 1980 (*Varada tras el último naufragio*) which were the dates of publication of the Spanish translations of *Tiempo de cerezas* and *La hora violeta* respectively.

The much shorter 'Canto de la juventud' is eerily prophetic in its portrayal of a woman dying of a long illness in hospital and is, in fact, dedicated to two doctors. Roig stated that she had written the stories shortly after her father's death and notes the sad 'feeling of absence' in them; she also said the book is a song to lost youth.[4] As in Roig's first collection of short fiction, several of these stories can be related to the published novels, for example, 'Madre, no entiendo a los salmones' ('Mother, I don't understand the salmon'), written in 1980, refers directly to a passage in *La hora violeta* and a conversation between Norma and her son. In his review of *El canto de la juventud* Fernando Valls writes: 'its pages show an evolution, germinating throughout the 1980s, from activity to contemplation . . . as in no other book the writer of fiction prevails over the journalist'. Valls underlines the overriding tone of disillusion and pessimism in the book; all the stories touch on the common themes of love, death, loss, memory, failure, and abandonment.[5]

The lyrical prose of 'El canto de la juventud', written in free indirect style, would appear to be a continuation of the final two pages of *Tiempo de cerezas* which describe an unknown character gradually waking up in the morning. In *Tiempo de cerezas* the character turns out to be the ailing and confused Joan in the old people's home. In 'El canto de la juventud' by the end of the first paragraph it is clear the protagonist is a woman. She is in hospital and she slowly wakes up in the early hours of the morning glad to find herself still alive. There are interesting stylistic and thematic similarities between this story and Rosa Montero's novel *La función Delta* (*The Delta Function*), published eight years previously. In both, an elderly woman (in Montero's novel her name is Lucía, in Roig's story it is Zelda) faces death in hospital with nostalgia, dread, and black humour. Both women, irritated by their nurses and their own immobility, are irascible yet sharp-witted. They dwell on memories of love and desire, musing on the varying intensities of emotion, feeling once again the spark of life in their lingering moments. In Roig's story the broad back of the young doctor in his white coat reminds the woman of an early passion,

4. See Rosa María Piñol, 'Entrevista con Montserrat Roig: La etapa de *L'hora violeta* ya queda para mi muy lejana', *La Vanguardia*, 7 October 1989.
5. Fernando Valls, 'Sobre *El canto de la juventud* de Montserrat Roig', *Insula*, 531, March 1991, p. 25.

the likes of which she has never experienced since. Zelda, engaged to be married to Lluís, is drinking an aperitif with her parents in a bar during the Civil War when she catches the eye of a tall, good-looking foreigner in a white shirt. She feels her 'legs turn to steel' (13); when she passes him to go to the toilet she 'feels as if she were naked' (15). He follows her and they embrace for a moment in the toilet; she feels dizzy, 'everthing was one thing, the beats of his heart, the white of his shirt, the white of the tiles, everything was one and infinite' (15). They arrange a meeting the next day on the hillside and, as they make love, he tells her he is returning to the Front that evening; she never sees him again. But the memory of that fleeting moment, when she digs her nails into his back tearing his shirt, is relived with such intensity in the hospital bed that Zelda tears the sheet exclaiming, 'I don't want to die' (17). In the story, the images, songs, and 'diabolical' (14) feelings of the past are relived with such vividness that they become more real than the tedious present. Passion is the stuff of life, and it is this memory which keeps Zelda alive. As in *La función Delta*, passion is clearly differentiated from marriage and love. Zelda looks at her withered hand and remembers how pretty it was in her youth:

> Before he went [to war], Lluís had kissed her hand, 'In three weeks you'll be my wife. I love you'. There were darker waters in the slate earth where the high vines grew. 'I want [desire] you', he [the stranger] had told her when they lay down near the vines. (17)

Like Montero's novel, this story foregrounds a woman's conscious response to old age and imminent death. In the woman's final assessment of her life, what defies nothingness and gives her life meaning are momentary flashes of passion and desire for a man. All else fades in comparison. The story skilfully weaves the past into present with the thread of memory from a feminine perspective, and the old adage 'love conquers death' is given a new, existential relevance in the contemporary world.

It could be argued, however, that the story 'Mar' completely contradicts this emphasis on heterosexual passion as the highpoint of a woman's life. Alternatively, the different kind of love articulated in this longer story could be read as supplementing heterosexuality. In any case, 'Mar' is central to an understanding of Roig's work. It recounts through flashback the 'romantic friendship' between two women (both married with children): the bohemian Mar, who had since been killed in a road accident, and the more reserved narrator. The focus on love between women and the flowing, lyrical prose make this a singular piece of writing:

> as Mar said, . . . we loved each other in another way, without going to bed, we 'fucked' each other, in their words, when we held hands and were lost contemplating the sea, sitting in the wet sand . . . lost in each other's thoughts in a silence that sometimes merged and sometimes flowed away, like silence usually is between two people who talk to each other without words, without scripts, without explanations or commentaries about what we saw or felt, watching the sea and thinking we had no body or perhaps only one body, or perhaps two bodies that had come across each other after wandering like idiots through an unknown galaxy. (42)

'Mar' is exceptional not only for its style (reminiscent of sections of *La hora violeta*), but also because it foregrounds the subject which Roig continually skirted in her fiction: the love and desire between two women. The plot is simple. Two years after her friend Mar's death, an anonymous author-narrator remembers the year they spent together and the unnameable experience they shared. The narrator, a middle-class socialist feminist and intellectual, married with children, has since separated from her husband, Ferran. Mar, also married with children, is more spontaneous, anarchic, and strongly critical of feminists and intellectuals. As an adolescent, after an affair with her best friend's father, she had been obliged to marry her cousin, Ernest, but could not consummate the marriage because of her husband's sexual phobias. By the time he was aroused she had taken a stream of male lovers. During the year the two women are together, Ernest finally leaves and is given legal custody of the children. Desperate, Mar asks the narrator to go away with her to 'the North', but the narrator is too afraid. Three days later Mar is killed in a (possibly suicidal) car accident.

The narrator remembers how she is filled with love and resentment while watching Mar's unconscious body in the hospital; 'she woke in me, I can say it now, the shoots of another kind of woman, of another kind of person, which I have buried again' (57). She realizes she has lost the opportunity to live differently, and that now she 'would have to pretend again . . . that I was what I was not' (43): affectionate and hysterical mother, intellectual, female lover, friend, and confident. What Mar offered was the missing key the narrator had been searching for all her life:

It was as if all the pieces of the jigsaw fell into place, as if each limb
of my body was alive, separate and joined to the rest, as if my mind
was linked to all the Universe. During that year I was not just who I
was, but who I could be. (70)

What does this relationship consist of? It is not erotic but
tremendously tender; the two women kiss only once. They spend
time together, embrace, hold hands, talk, walk, listen to music,
play games, have fun, and laugh. After stealing decorative plant-
pots one night Mar says to the narrator, 'Do you realize how we
make love? How two women can love each other in a way that's
different, still inexplicable, in another way, not like a man and a
woman?' (70). Again, the threads of the narrator's memories
weave the past to the present, and through her memories and
reflections a love is perceived that defeats words. Not once is the
word 'lesbian' used in the story, or any other label, to denote and
classify the relationship from the women's points of view. So Roig
returns and reworks that crucial absence in *La hora violeta*, the
relationship between Kati and Judit. The narrator talks around this
subject, but still refuses to define and classify:

> We understood each other, but the word describing what was born
> the day I first saw her has yet to be written . . . and I can't even invent
> one myself, despite the fact that in those days I devoured every book
> on feminism that came my way . . . On the other hand, it never
> ocurred to me to give a name to that time of silence, bustle and
> madness, to that time when the hours flowed together, continuously,
> when our intellectual friends looked at us disapprovingly, or frowned,
> what a nerve, you could read in their eyes when they looked at us
> with the gaze of someone unwittingly afraid . . . and it's just that there
> they are, always ready to define what can't be defined, needing to
> underline with a very thick pencil, that there's something going on
> between those two, always together, they've got something going.
> Their eyes said all this with a fairly poor vocabulary, they couldn't
> understand. (41–2)

Mar awakens in the narrator desires, impulses, and a 'magical
teluric strength', often described by men – she writes – as 'the lost
chain, the silent chain of grandmothers and great grandmothers
who buried complaints and pleasures without affidavits, behind
the closed walls of isolation' (48). Elsewhere the narrator describes
the relationship between the women as a 'string of concentric
movements' like in a 'spiral that pushed us further and further

on'; her relationship with her husband, by comparison, is static (50–1). After Mar's death the narrator returns uselessly to her role as 'femme savante', to 'reason and common sense', and to reading books 'which explain to me what I don't understand' (42). It is also interesting that the narrator can only relate to Mar in the first instance within the confines of masculine discourse of desire. She admires Mar, 'according to the rules, the only ones I had at hand . . . as if I were a man and she the mystery that men look for in women'. The narrator cannot conceive of love other than as a bargain between two antagonistic people. But this is an error, because Mar does not enter into the power game, 'she didn't allow herself to be dominated because she didn't dominate anyone. She hadn't broken with any "master" because she belonged to no one' (46). Mar is not vindictive, she does not hate men, she is just tired of the 'sorrow of the game' (69).

The kind of woman Mar represents is diametrically opposed to the typed socialist feminist the narrator is forced to impersonate. Mar has no plans, theories or political ideas. She lives for the day. She discovers her body, the locus of her power, by learning to look at herself outside the masculine gaze. She looks in the mirror not to see if she is ageing, or if she is attractive, but to 'give value to the shape of her body, the way she was made, she and no one else, she herself and not the images we see everyday in magazines and on television' (62). Above all, she looks at her own vagina and sees it not as 'a symbol of absence but as a promise of inner presence' (62). This leads the narrator to question her own political and feminist consciousness which she believes is no more than a reflection of bourgeois hypocrisy and cultural convention. She and her husband may well have moved to a dormitory town outside Barcelona to live amongst the 'most disinherited, the lumpen of lumpen' (49) but there was always a barrier between her and the locals with regard to money, ideas, and language. The narrator rescinds her former, progressive, feminist self and glimpses another way of being in response to her own desires and her body. She admits:

> it was useless for me to go on theorizing about the condition of women . . . in order to understand the damaging cultural and historical muddle that has distanced women from men, talking to local women about our castration and our dregs of resentment, it was useless because all this rhetoric did me no good. I had to use sleeping pills and I still cried every morning under the shower. (69)

What is now important is to experience a forceful woman-bonding, originating in drives, self-awareness, and knowledge of one's body, a bonding which slips language, rationality and thought-systems, whether they be Marxist or Freudian, which exists in its very living. The author-narrator glimpses something different, something new.

Several points need to be stressed: first, the love between the women is clearly transgressive, their behaviour is not accepted by the 'aggressive, anonymous mass' (71) or by close friends; second, it is unnameable; third, it offers a glimpse of another female-centred order ('what could be'); fourth, it is (yet again) an inside critique of socialism (of professing to love 'all humanity' without finding time to love one person properly) and yet it rejects radical feminist strategies. In fact, it rejects all feminist theory. The non-sexual love the women feel for each other defies categorization, theory, and labelling. The terms used by others to describe the relationship are euphemistic or derogatory, the relationship cannot as yet be expressed in words, it is 'what has to remain dark, an unexplored continent' (71). Roig refuses to use the word 'lesbian'; she refuses to identify. The other mode of being is outside the confines of male-defined rationality, heterosexuality, social institutions, power, and language. It is spontaneity, innocence, magic, intimacy; its source of strength is the female body. It escapes the symbolic order, 'the misery of established words, the scant originality of signs' (69), and feminist theory cannot cope with it. The whole story is an exercise in naming. When Mar asks the narrator to go away with her she refuses, and Mar apparently commits suicide. The narrator is unable to make the leap into the unknown, magical space, the 'rift' which opens at her feet. That she has to return to being what she is not suggests both an unrevealed essential identity that slips words and the impossibility of constructing a self without language. The narrator must renew her place in the signifying chain of language to survive. A new discursive space is cleared; it is elusive, but it reinstates sisterhood, the mother, and matrilineality as 'empowering concepts' (Gunew, 306); here unashamed love between women is 'telluric strength' (48). But, ultimately, it is powerlessness. Mar commits suicide because she loses custody of her children; as a mother and a lover she has no place in the symbolic order, she is considered mad.

This story could be read as a late shift by Roig towards

difference feminism. However, the story is dated twice: 1980, revised 1988. A retrospective view of Roig's work shows clearly that the theme of hidden love between women is at its very centre, buried by surrounding socio-historical narrative. It is gradually revealed throughout the 1980s, first tentatively in *Tiempo de cerezas*, then more clearly in *La hora violeta* in the continually deferred story of Judit Fléchier and Kati. This story, in many ways similar to that of 'Mar', is displaced to the time of Civil War. Judit is married with children, Kati is a promiscuous, socialite. The relationship is ambiguous, undefined. In *Tiempo de cerezas* Kati gives Judit a rose and they hold hands for a moment. In *La hora violeta* their story was to be the subject of the whole novel, but is relegated to the central chapter entitled 'La novela de la hora violeta'. Here the women meet, hold hands, discuss marriage, nothing more. But Judit refuses to leave her family and go away with Kati, who commits suicide. The most explicit declaration of eternal love is when Judit imagines a dead Kati speaking to her eleven years after her death, 'I will return, Judit . . . love of my life, love of my death' (163).

These two stories of love between women are fundamentally different in two related ways. One is embedded in layers of realist narrative and scattered throughout texts; the other breaks out as a fictional manifestation in itself. One associates women's liberation with future political change ('I'm sure', writes Judit to Joan, 'that if we win the war our lives will be very different. I'll work, Kati says that . . .', *Tiempo de cerezas* 163); the other dispenses with all such illusions. Like Judit, the narrator in 'Mar' must return to the 'convention of signs, of words' to live in society and effect change. As Janice Reynolds argues, 'the possibilities of female friendship are founded on vision' (Gunew, 342) and here the vision is the void in the text.[6]

---

6. This story could be read through the work of Monique Wittig. The narrator finds she can only relate to Mar as a man. There is no other position she can take, i.e. she is male-identified, alienated or marginal.

# Part II

## Rosa Montero: Women, Institutions and Thought Systems

# 4

## Sites of Resistance: the Narrative of the End of a Decade

osa Montero (born in Madrid, 1951) is one of Spain's leading investigative journalists and novelists. She has worked for the prestigious Spanish newspaper, *El País*, since 1977 and was chief editor of the Sunday supplement between 1980 and 1981. She has won several national awards for her journalism and interviews, including the Human Rights award in 1989. Rosa Montero has published six novels to date: *Crónica del desamor* 1979 [*Absent love. A Chronicle*, 1991] (*Chronicle of Unlove*); *La función Delta* 1981 [*The Delta Function*, 1991]; *Te trataré como a una reina* 1983 (*I'll Treat You Like a Queen*); *Amado amo* 1988 (*Beloved Master*), *Temblor* 1990 (*Trembling*), and *Bella y oscura* 1993 (*Beautiful and Dark*); plus a short novel for children entitled *El nido de los sueños* 1991 (*The Nest of Dreams*). She also published a short story, 'Paulo Pumilio', in a collection of short fiction written by women, and two volumes of interviews.[1] Her narrative is characterized by its diversity; although she always concentrates on women interacting with society, the situations and individual characters of each novel are quite different. Perhaps what relates her female protagonists to each other is the fact that they are all working women: journalists, television producers, nightclub singers, working mothers, even priestesses. And all the novels, except *Temblor* (a romance fantasy) are set in contemporary (or future) Spain. Montero's style, developed through journalism, is unpretentious, precise and effective. On the whole, she keeps to the conventions of the realist novel with metafictional inflections.

1. Ymelda Navajo, *Doce relatos de mujeres*, Madrid, 1982, pp. 68–93; *España para ti para siempre*, Madrid, 1976; *Cinco años de país*, Madrid, 1982. Montero has also written various scripts for the television programme 'Media naranja' screened in 1987, and a feature film script 'La vieja dama'.

What differentiates her narrative from that of the majority of her female contemporaries is its wit and humour. Montero has the uncanny ability to reproduce the idioms, ironies and exaggerations of everyday Madrid repartee and thus invest otherwise dull, run-of-the-mill and even desperate situations with sparkle and verve. Her earlier novels are concerned above all with women's rights articulated as a new literary topic, ordinary women's everyday experiences and activities. Montero aired women's common private problems in public. She raises a whole gamut of feminist issues for public debate: sexual politics, women's control of reproduction, feminine cultural myths and taboos, women in the workplace and before the law, male violence, and traditional family structures. Through her first novel, in particular, published in 1979, Montero brought pressure to bear on politicians for the implementation of the reforms arising from the new Spanish constitution, passed through parliament the previous year. This novel can be considered part of the general offensive by progressive women keen for change. Abortion, for example, which is a major theme in the novel, was not made legal (under very stringent conditions) until 1985. Montero rejects the concept of what she calls 'literatura militante', that is, propaganda – whether it be 'feminist, socialist or pacifist. Novels for me are like the dreams of Humanity: they speak of that which has no name . . . they are a way to knowledge, an inner adventure' ('Escribiendo en la luna', 7). She adds, however, 'if you are a feminist, as I consider myself, it is more than likely that the problem of sexism will appear in your books' and although she believes 'the world doesn't change because of novels' (7) it cannot be denied that her first novel was extremely important as the vehicle for a concerted feminist critique of Spanish society.

### Crónica del desamor (Chronicle of Unlove)

Montero describes her first book, Crónica del desamor, 1979, (an overnight success which went through five editions in its first year of publication, selling 75,000 copies in the first edition alone) as 'not a novel precisely' but rather 'a chronicle without pretensions, a quick look at the world which surrounds us, an approximation to the everyday problems we all meet up with' (on the book jacket). The novel is obviously intended for women readers.

Montero was originally commissioned to prepare a book of feminist interviews, but she preferred to write documentary narrative. The story of *Crónica* is set in the Madrid of the late 1970s during the uncertain transition period between dictatorship and democracy. As in Roig's novels, the climate is one of upheaval, disenchantment and confusion. The female protagonists, in their thirties and forties, find themselves in situations which not only force them to reconsider traditional ideas and values regarding women's role in society, but also to seriously question the apparently more progressive solutions resulting from feminist debate, the Women's Liberation Movement, and the sexual revolution. The women in the novel must assess and reshape their lifestyles despite the social changes resulting from the gradual disintegration of traditional institutions such as the family, largely instigated by their own quest for liberation. Above all, they need to find a new identity, a meaning and a purpose to life. As Roberto Manteiga suggests, 'more than a struggle for equality and independence, Montero's is a search for understanding. Women should not have to lose their identity as women to gain acceptance and recognition in today's society' (Manteiga, 115).

The title of the novel indicates that this is a day-to-day account of the unlove between men and women, of the misunderstanding and lack of communication between the sexes in the contemporary urban world. The novel could be thought to expose a 'male conspiracy', but none of the characters finds a formula for a satisfying long-term sexual relationship; they all (men and women, but primarily the latter) take refuge in their cliques of friends, cultivating a group rather than an individual identity. In the words of the narrator, to find these men and women 'all you have to do is follow the umbilical cord to five or six smelly, smoky well-known bars . . . small rooms stuffed with people stinking of semen, shady deals, blood and sick'. It is 'a reunion with the little group which is almost the mother's womb' (170). All the characters are unhappy; for women, relationships with men are invariably oppressive. What saves the novel from degenerating into an uninteresting, sometimes nauseating account of domestic tedium and despair is its humour and vivacity. Each chapter is structured as a series of short, interrelated snapshots, set in the present and the past, presented through various modes of narration. The snappy pace, quick changes of scene, the characters presented with bold strokes, and the plentiful action centering usually on domestic non-events suggest a film-script. Indeed, Montero includes various pages of scripted dialogue. An objective narrator follows closely the thoughts, movements, and conversations of several women like a camera's eye, but focalizes through one young woman in particular – Ana Antón – who holds the novel together. Ana is an unmarried journalist with a four-year-old child, Curro. Her relationship with the father, Juan, broke down soon after Curro's birth and since then she has not been able to establish a satisfying relationship with a man. She works hard, but on low pay because she has not been offered a permanent position. Her humdrum, everyday existence is lonely and dull with one element of excitement – an imagined romantic affair with the editor of the newspaper for which she works. Ana's dream comes true; she spends a night with Soto Amón (Ramses the pharaoh to his staff), only to realize that her smooth-talking, suave and apparently self-assured idol is as clumsy, predictable and as boringly egocentric as any other man. Worse still, he is not aware of it.

The skilful dexterity with which Montero presents this story is evident from the first pages. Chapter one covers twenty-four action-packed hours in Ana's mundane life. It shows her working late in the office one evening, then at home putting her son to bed, reminiscing on her past relationship with Juan, remembering a friend's comments on that relationship, thinking up two typical, hypothetical situations she has learned to expect from her men friends (a long-awaited telephone conversation and a rushed bedroom scene), a real telephone conversation (as she reads the newspaper) with an unknown man who rings her number by mistake and invites her for a drink, another telephone conversation with her friend Elena, and finally bed. The next day she hears shouts and cries from the flat below where she believes a woman is being beaten up; she meets Elena and Candela (Elena's sister) at the gynaecologist's, muses on the new breed of punk taxi driver, and, in the doctor's waiting room, considers Elena and her story, and then Candela and her experiences with several contraceptive methods including an ineffective IUD and an abortion in London; she remembers Teresa (Juan's sister) and Teresa's back-street abortion which nearly cost her her life and the surgeon's threat to denounce Teresa to the police. The scene of the conversation with the arrogant and incompetent gynaecologist, and the women's biting remarks on their way home, switches to show Ana at home that evening feeling lonely, her thoughts on

Curro's need for a father figure, her speculation about the next day which includes a dreaded interview with her supervisor to request a proper contract, and finally sleep. All this takes place in thirty pages of large print. The pace of physical and mental activity creating a tension bordering on the hysterical would seem particularly appropriate in a Pedro Almódovar film (*Women on the edge of a nervous breakdown* was released three years later in 1982). Similar, too, is the sharp and often black humour, sometimes used to make a serious political point sometimes more tenderly pathetic.

The novel opens with Ana's mental description of an office littered with empty plastic coffee cups: 'The coffee machine in the corridor has run out – the machine was installed by the firm, moved by managerial consideration of output, so that the staff could save themselves trips to the street and not waste precious minutes, seconds of work' (5). Here Ana thinks as a worker conscious of her rights. She waits all year (the duration of the novel) to be made a permanent member of staff, but is unsuccessful despite the fact that the newspaper relies heavily on her hard, poorly paid work. But Ana is also a mother, as this conversation with her young son reveals:

Daddy took me to the zoo, mum.
That's not your daddy, Curro, he's my daddy, so he's your grandad.
Aaah . . . So my daddy is Tato.
No, darling, Tato is my brother, and he's your uncle because grandad is his daddy too.
Aaah . . . (7)

The novel is full of jibes aimed both at the bulwarks of what was Franco's Spain and at the so-called progressive alternative. Neither political option offers solutions for women, particularly regarding what was the most debated feminist issue of the late 1970s in Spain: contraception and abortion. Contraception (other than by natural methods) was still not widely approved of and was banned by the Catholic church. Progressive doctors, however, prescribed the pill and other contraceptive methods without the necessary medical advice or care. Abortion, on the other hand, was still considered a criminal act. Those women who could afford to went to private clinics in London, set up especially for foreigners. Others did not have the choice. It is against this background that the visit to the gynaecologist in chapter one should be read. The theme of birth control was polemical in itself, even in 1979, and to be presented from a woman's dissenting point of view was still shocking for many readers. The scene opens with an obvious phallic representation: 'Because the gynaecologist was politically correct his surgery was on the outskirts of town, but – of course – in a brand new luxurious tower block, which rose up out of the surrounding cheap and substandard housing' (19). The doctor meets the three women with a 'smile of commiseration and disdain on his pink and childish lips'. He is 'sitting up straight in his seat and he rests the tips of his fingers on the edge of the great desk in his office, stretching them out in a gesture which he perhaps considers dignified and distant' (28). This picture of authority and control breaks down, however, when the unknowing doctor opens the box containing Elena's diaphragm:

> The man has opened it disagreeably, and the talcum powder has covered his desk, filling in the cracks, leaving a snow white sheet generously spread across his trousers and doctor's papers. . . . It's clearly the first time he has seen a diaphragm. It clearly nauseates him, he relates it, perhaps, like many men, to the hated condom. The pill, the coil, are women's problems. She takes them, she suffers them. The diaphragm, though, has more to do with the couple. Does it mean the man has to stop his passionate run-up so she can put in a plastic disc? How awful! Has he got to use spermicidal cream? What a disaster! The pill and the coil are so easy, they are methods men don't have to suffer . . .. He charged them a thousand pesetas each. (30)

Earlier in the chapter, after remembering Candela's experience of abortion ('. . . she went to London. She aborted hygenically, sterilizedly, internationally. She aborted with bitterness, like they all do, always') Ana thinks:

> If men gave birth, abortion would be legal by now all over the world from the beginning of time. What Pope, what Cardinal Benelli would dare to censor a right which their own bodies clamoured for? Politicians who could get pregnant wouldn't misinterpret their own needs, like they do now when they say abortion is just one more form of contraception demanded by guilty, unscrupulous women. And yet, these guardians of the genital order of others would not think twice about paying for an international scrape for their stray daughters while other women have to make do with illegal Spanish butchers. (21)

It could be said that this kind of diatribe sits uneasily in a novel, that the journalist brings her newspaper column to the work of fiction and crosses conventional genre demarcations between feminist propaganda and narrative fiction. Obviously, it is not Ana voicing her thoughts here, but the self-conscious narrator, the implied author. Montero, however, is doing no more than following the conventions of nineteeth-century realist narrative where documentary and fiction were mixed similarly. She writes fiction of debate.[2] It should also be remembered that the book was not conceived as a novel at all but as a chronicle. This gives the author plenty of scope to introduce topical and politically sensitive feminst themes, such as abortion and divorce, within a loose narrative framework. Other such hitherto taboo subjects raised in the course of the novel are: oral sex, orgasm, male prostitution, homosexuality, menstruation, male and female masturbation, and the constant sexual harassment endured by women in Spain – in the underground, the street, the cinema, in school, on the buses, and even in the civil service – against which they are obliged to wage 'guerrilla warfare' (159). More general social issues are of secondary importance but nevertheless form part of this ferociously acid social critique: cancer, senility, geriatrics, bomb threats, shanty towns, the indiscriminate use of smoke bombs by the police, female victims of police torture, food adulteration, and the treatment of psychiatric patients are all woven into the narrative. A controversial theme of a different nature, dealt with also by Montserrat Roig, is the incapacity of conventional left-wing political movements to recognize and act upon sexual discrimination within their own ranks. The former Communist militant, Juan, is not a sympathetic character. Police repression has broken him and he is totally selfish. He lives off Ana and his sister Teresa and shows no concern for their well-being. It is the women of the novel who continue the struggle for equality and social justice – at a public and a private level. When Ana met Juan,

2. Eunice D. Myers, 'The feminist message: propaganda and/or art. A study of two novels by Rosa Montero', in Roberto Manteiga et al (eds), *Feminine Concerns*, pp. 99–133.

Rosa Montero

It was the final phase of the Franco period, the executions, the death penalties, the antiterrorist law, the country sweated cold fear. Ana, struggling against her fears took part in the demonstrations [. . .] and when she returned home [. . .] Juan asked her how it had gone, and without waiting for an answer preached severely that the meeting had been suicidal, that you do it all wrong, the political situation needs, and then he would spin out slowly the theories of a veteran and broken militant. (22)

Ana's friend, Elena – formerly a member of the Spanish Communist Party for five years – is a good example of women continuing the political struggle during the post-Franco period outside traditional organizations such as the trade unions. She is one of the few participants in a demonstration of 5,000 people (small by Spanish standards) organized by the local Neighbourhood Association, but during the march she finds herself protesting more about (male) trade unionists who she feels are hijacking the meeting for their own ends. However, such political activity seems irrelevant to the kinds of problems faced by women in the Madrid of the late 1970s. Memories of how joining the Communist Party coincided with her desire to 'stop being a virgin' (49) and how difficult it was to find an obliging partner once she confessed her intention, make Elena (a non-tenured lecturer) review her current, stressful relationship to a (married) university lecturer. Somewhere along the line she has lost 'the most tender part of herself' – even the failure of her relationship hardly hurts. 'Elena lives unlove with melancholy, without tears, only with exhaustion, with the conviction that it is all irreversibly, definitely lost: it is the same exhaustion she felt when she left the Communist Party' (62). Elena realizes it will take an immense effort of willpower to defeat apathy, to feel again, to love a man, and also to love an ideal: the one necessarily involves the other.

The narrator focalizes exclusively through Elena in chapter three. Other characters foregrounded in this way are the middle-aged homosexual Cecilio (chapter six), Elena's sister Candela (chapter eleven), and El Zorro (chapter nine), who Ana knows through her schoolfriend, Olga. Cecilio, supposedly liberated like his female friends from stereotyped roles and sexual prejudice, is as unhappy as they are. He too finds love frustrating and disappointing. He spends his time in cafés among male prostitutes waiting for his young lover to correspond to his feelings: 'the long, painful wait of the homosexual is just the latest, most obvious symbol of the misencounter of all relationships, of the collapse of faith in the couple' (133). Candela is possibly the one character who seems to have achieved a goal in life; but this is only after she breaks up with Vicente, the (already married) father of her second child; her first partner, with whom she also had a child, threw himself out of a window. Candela is saved from humiliation and self-deprecation by her mother who appears to her in a dream. Her mother, screaming with laughter, tells her the parable of the handkerchief: a woman takes a dirty handkerchief, she puts it in hot water and detergent for a long while, then she throws away the water and rubs the handkerchief with soap, she changes the water and adds a few drops of bleach to make it white, she rinses it and adds blue to make it even cleaner, then softener to make it pleasant to touch, then she rinses it, she dries it in the sun, and when it is dry she irons it, with a little bit of water so that all the creases will disappear, then she folds it carefully and places it in the cupboard with the rest of the white linen where she has already put some mothballs and little sachets of herbs to make it smell good. And so, there is the handkerchief, clean, fragrant and folded. Along comes a man, picks it up without looking, blows his nose in it noisily and then throws it in the dirty linen basket. 'Hilarious, isn't it?', says her mother (226). Candela, the only character to be warned by her mother of the absurdity of women's servitude to men, resolves not to fall into the same trap. Candela moreover, is a psychologist. She believes Freud invented the castration complex to disguise men's womb envy, so she takes the decision to have a second child and to go it alone without a male partner. The novel does not portray mothering as oppressive; on the contrary, maternal power and the mother-child bond is one of the few edifying aspects of women's lives and compensates for female powerlessness. Even the childless Elena comes to see motherhood in a positive light. True to the tenets of the early Women's Movement she had previously considered maternal feelings the result of 'cultural deformation' (230), but now – in 1979 – she wonders if 'for a long time she has confused women's liberation with scorn for women themselves' (230). Elena realizes the significance of her body and her reproductive potential: 'she has discovered the pride of finding her own sex' (230). Self-questioning of this type has been interpreted by at least one critic as an indictment of

feminism.[3] It is more a case of a widening of horizons, an awareness
by women of the need to revalorize and appropriate their own
bodies and reproductive potential for themselves within the new
democratic context.

Not all the victims in the novel are women. The most desperate
character in this disillusioned crowd is el Zorro (the Fox). His story
is told in a bleak chapter which stands out from the others in as
much as Ana is not present, the narrative point of view and
perspective is entirely masculine, the setting (a sleazy bar) does
not change and, above all, there is no comic relief. El Zorro,
formerly the lawyer Antonio Abril, sinks into a world of despair,
crime, thuggery, violence, drug addiction, and attempted suicide;
he cuts his wrists in public for kicks and showers his shocked
onlookers with his blood. He has refused his only opportunity to
find happiness in a stable relationship with Olga who, devastated,
fled to India to find the meaning of life, and succumbed to drug
addiction. El Zorro, after searching for her in India unsuccessfully,
returns to Madrid a broken, lonely man without illusions: 'India
was burnt out, paradise on earth was burnt out, his last hopes,
burnt out' (198). The hellish, violent underworld he currently
inhabits functions in the novel as a threatening counterpoint to the
tedium of Ana's more domesticated, middle-class circle. For the
moment at least, she maintains a safe distance, but the dangers
represented by the libertarian violence of el Zorro are always
present.

The other characters – predominantly professionals – are
focalized through Ana: Ana María (a forty-year-old doctor who
keeps a dead bunch of roses sent to her by a 'beast' who
consistently lets her down); Pulga (married at nineteen to a man
who raped her on their first night and who now, in middle age,
mothers a series of young men); Julita (aged thirty-seven, whose
husband left her for a younger woman); Mercedes and Tomás
(progressive parents who give up their staid middle-class lifestyle
to set up a bar in Madrid and keep in touch with their wayward
children); Javier (Elena's married boyfriend – who finds he has
cancer); and José María (Ana's married boyfriend who finds their
ten-year extra-marital relationship has been one of mutual

3. Roberto Manteiga, 'The dilemma of the modern woman: a study of the female
characters in Rosa Montero's novels', in Robert Manteiga et al (eds), *Feminine
Concerns*, p. 115.

deception). All the characters articulate between them the collective malaise of post-Franco Madrid. They all participate in a great charade, a farce in which they pretend to be eternally young, fashionable, anti-establishment, self-reliant, interesting, and sociable individuals. Ana sees through the play-acting and comes to realize that the men and women around her are, like herself, lonely, vulnerable, disorientated, and in need of love and affection. The only immediate solution envisaged in the novel is to leave Madrid – the centre of urban depravity: Cecilio goes to Brazil, Ana María to England, and Julita to the countryside. The fragility of human relationships is just another symptom of the degenerate, tragi-comic simulacrum these postmodern characters together represent.

References to the theatre are numerous. From the scripted dialogue of the first chapter pointing explicitly to the theme of role-playing, the allusions accumulate until – at the end of the novel – it becomes clear that the analogy between modern life and carnivalesque play-acting is a prime structural and thematic device. One of the last scenes in the novel takes place in a restaurant where Ana tries, for the first time in ten years, to talk seriously to her lover José María. She feels ridiculous because 'the roles she has played for so long weigh her down, so that Ana feels naked speaking to José María without the help of smiles and laughter' (254). She finally sees the truth of their relationship; they have spent ten years pretending not to need each other. José María, despite the image he has projected to Ana, is an affectionate, insecure man:

> his strength is no more than an armour. And she, Ana, played the part of the hard, independent woman for years, and she played it so well that it made him afraid. Ana suddenly understands, like a flash, these ten years of misunderstandings and lies, they each made their respective puppets dance so well that they completely deceived one another. (258)

Ana learns to see the other's other self behind the well-mounted disguise. She tests her newfound insight on her boss Soto Amón and, unsurprisingly, is able to predict accurately his cliché-ridden conversation and ritualistic behaviour when he finally takes her to bed. However, to see behind the masks in such pantomimes does not provide the secret key to happiness. Despite the humour in the novel, the final picture is one verging on desolation. Perhaps there is nothing behind the façades after all? Perhaps men and women are no more than animated cardboard figures playing out their respective roles, reflecting their refracted images? Such is the drift of the tragic melodrama of chapter nine, set in the Toño bar and focalized through el Zorro. The majority of the individuals who make up the Toño bar in-crowd have lost their original names and the identities these denoted. They are designated in the underworld by 'apodos' or aliases: la Mora (Moor girl), Músculo (Muscle), el Gobernador (the Governor), el Turco (the Turk), el Bardo (the Bard), and so on. They do not know each other's proper names, as the example of Mito (Myth) 'a Guillermo Fernández, or López, or something like that' (174) indicates. In a conversation with el Zorro, Nuria describes her encounter with Olga in India:

> Olga's face melted in front of my eyes, and the glitter of the silver make-up turned into a mask, I can't explain it, as if it were all an illusion, and behind the flashes I suddenly saw her face kind of hanging in the air, dark, like . . . like a skull. (183)

El Zorro is aware that he too is caught up in his image of 'the wretched of the night' (189) and that this has prevented him from contemplating a stable interpersonal relationship seriously; he confuses commitment with conventionality, responsibility with tradition.

Play-acting is as insidious in private as in public. Ana accuses Gonzalo, an old friend with whom she has just spent the night, of attaching too much importance to orgasm. Like all Spanish men, she insists, he does not talk while making love because he is too intent on his 'empty gestures'; he is totally absorbed in achieving orgasm at all costs and at warding off the ghost of failure. And women, she thinks, are as much to blame. They insist on fake orgasms,

> frightened of not coming up to the standard imposed by a macho sexuality that these days enslaves both men and women. Frightened of ruining their image of a prototype lover, and so contributing to the repetitive theatrical show. We are so chained to our *roles* in this society, where we live through stereotypes. As Elena says in her essay 'Odds and Evens', there is a man's role and a woman's. An old person's role and a young person's. The father's role and the son's, the traditional woman's or the liberated woman's, the roles of the mad and the sane, the losers and winners. They are all rigid characters, empty, unreal: distorted reflections of people. (243)

And yet, the very fact that the female narrator can finally identify the source of contemporary malaise and become aware of how a loss of identity in a society undergoing profound change affects men as well as women, enables her to step outside the cabaret. Her realization that a new order of things will only come about through communication and understanding between the generations and the sexes, and that basic values such as love, compassion, sincerity, self-respect, and (above all) self-awareness are crucial at this critical juncture, enables her to step out of character. The discursive and historical reconstruction undertaken by Ana in the chronicle she starts to write and by the implied author in the novel *Crónica del desamor* leads to recognition, insight, and understanding. Better, Ana thinks, to have lost in this world-weary chess game of moves and counter-moves than never to have taken part at all; better to be searching for something, than (like Soto Amón) not searching at all. She faces up to one last disappointment however. Having never been to bed with a man who usually wears a tie, Ana relishes the moment when she will remove this item of clothing from Soto Amón's neck; but he takes it off himself 'in an automatic, well-rehearsed, self-sufficient gesture' (273). That powerful but cruel gesture, she thinks, 'could be a good start to that book which she is now sure she will write, it won't be the rancorous book of the Anas, but a sketch, a chronicle of everyday unlove, emphasized by the mediocrity of a silk knot undone in a tedious routine' (273).

*Crónica* is metafictional narrative, that is, it 'consciously and systematically centres on aspects of its own creation' (Alborg, 68). Ana writes a newspaper article on middle-aged Spanish men castrated by the sexual repression of the Franco regime. A fragment of the article, framed in quotation marks, is embedded in the narrative as journalism in fiction (86–7, 88–9).[4] At the beginning of the novel Ana muses on how she would like to write 'something', 'the book of the Anas, about all of them, and about her too, so different, so unique' (8–9). The metanarrative *Crónica* is the final product: Ana (the implied author and protagonist) starts her work at the end of the novel, so the novel recapitulates on the events leading to her decision to write. Alborg suggests

4. The substance of the article echoes leading Spanish feminist Lidia Falcón's bestseller, *El varón español a la búsqueda de su identidad* (*The Spanish Male in Search of his Identity*), Barcelona, 1986.

*Rosa Montero*

Montero uses metafiction to emphasize feminist issues, and – more importantly – to subvert conventional roles in life and traditional modes of representation (Alborg, 73). Women's life experiences, their reality, needs to be shown and told – but differently. This metafictional strategy, characteristic of the new realism, is intensified in Montero's second novel, *La función Delta*.

### La función Delta (The Delta Function)

*La función Delta*, 1981, is in many ways a continuation of Montero's first novel. Indeed, it even includes a *mise en abyme*, a film entitled *Crónica del desamor* with a plot similar to that of the novel of the same name. As Emilio de Miguel Martínez notes, the two novels share several themes: loneliness and isolation in an urban environment, lack of human communication, frustrated love relationships, disillusion, femininity and masculinity assumed as masquerades, the development of self-awareness, and a general disinterest in state politics, all focused from a feminine perspective. The Spanish critic wonders if *La función* answers the question posed in *Crónica*: what future does the postmodern world of the twenty-first century hold for women (de Miguel Martínez, 101)? The answer is not particularly uplifting. Women are as lonely and frustrated, and communication between the sexes as difficult as ever in the postmodern world. Death must still be faced with existential anguish or resignation but in an increasingly inhuman society. Death, euthanasia, disease, ageing, the biological decay of the mortal body, are all important issues. Despite this, romantic love is valued as humanity's only defence against death, the one thing that makes life worth living. The novel, then, is about the interdependence of love and death in the world of today and tomorrow. What distinguishes it from Montero's first book is the author's explicit intention to write a novel, the narrative techniques she uses to that effect with skill, and the resulting thematic condensation.[5]

As fictional autobiography *La función* develops two narrative threads both written in the first person by the same self-conscious narrator. This is a self-reflexive novel concerned with the problems

5. See Rosa Montero, interview with Antonio Monegal, 13 March 1985, Harvard University (property of the author).

of self-representation, writing and memory.[6] The dominant narrative is set in a hospital room in the year 2010 of the 'Contemporary Age'. It takes the form of a diary written by a sixty-year-old woman, Lucía, a film director by profession, who is dying of a brain tumour. She is unaware of this at first and thinks she is suffering from Menière's disease. Very little happens in the enclosed space of the hospital room. The monotonous routine of hospital life is broken only by the visits Lucía receives from her two nurses, the doctor, and her old friend, Ricardo. Yet, despite physical immobility and the discomfort of chemotherapy, Lucía's mind is surprisingly active, making the encroaching mental deterioration even more ironic and tragic. Her diary is dated from 12 September to 11 December, and there she records her thoughts on illness, age, love, the monotony of life, her conversations with Ricardo and, above all, her growing fear of death. As the illness affects her brain, her language becomes gradually less coherent, more confused, more poetic. Finally, Lucía is sent home to quietly die. The novel ends in a burst of lyricism, a eulogy to love and life, which Emilio de Miguel Martínez refers to as 'the orchestrated finale of a classical symphony' (90).[7]

The second narrative, embedded in the first, is provided by Lucía's memoirs written in a more matter-of-fact, objective style while she is in hospital. She attempts to recapture and understand her past, but in effect rewrites it to suit her retrospective projected self-image: the first words of the novel are 'I think I remember' (7). She shows her work to Ricardo who acts as reader and critic, contesting some of her versions of the past. The sequence the memoirs focus on covers one week in 1980, when she was thirty, a week which she remembers as a turning point in her career and personal relationships. Unlike the exceptionally static, main narrative thread, the seven flashback scenes (headed consecutively by the day of the week) are animated and dramatic. Lucía, in the prime of her life, is about to attend the first showing of her first (and, as it turns out, last) feature film entitled *Crónica del desamor*; she ends a passionate love affair with a married man, Hipólito,

6. Kathleen M. Glenn, 'Fictions of the self in *La función delta* and *Primera memoria*', in Sixto E. Torres and S. Carl King (eds), *Selected Proceedings of the Thirty-Ninth Annual Mountain Interstate Foreign Language Conference*, Clemson University, South Carolina, 1991, pp. 197–203.

7. C. Alborg also refers to the final scenes as ones of 'lyricism without clichés' in 'Cuatro narradores . . .', in R. Landeira (ed.), *Nuevos y novísimos*, p. 23.

and she decides to settle down with the more accommodating, companionable Miguel who remains with her until his death more than twenty years later. During that critical week, Lucía takes refuge from her emotional anxieties in her friend Ricardo's bed, but the hapless Ricardo becomes momentarily impotent and they cannot have sex.

It is, of course, the same Ricardo who visits Lucía assiduously when she is on her death bed, who entertains, distracts, and comforts her, who acts as interlocutor and who enables her, therefore, to represent and analyse her self and her past. He is her sole surviving suitor. The climax of the novel is marked by Ricardo, after waiting for thirty years, finally makes love to Lucía in her hospital bed. From then on, as the novel and Lucía's life come to a close, the two narrative threads merge together as the past and present become one in the confused Lucía's mind. This span through time, the transitions from past to present, memoirs to diary, is signalled in the text by the figure of a decrepit flyover with which Lucía identifies. It has aged alongside Lucía and is about to collapse:

> It was always badly built that bridge, now with the passing years and the gradual deterioration of the city, the bridge is becoming a ruin . . . No one dares to cross it any more, and there it is, useless, forlorn, remembering past glories. Poor bridge, I feel you will only outlive me for a short time. (354)

Lucía projects her human mortality onto the concrete construction and on the city as a whole. As far as she is concerned, when she dies the world comes to an end (355). This beautifully written story, then, is moving, poignant and strangely hopeful. In the face of death and decrepitude there is memory, compassion, admiration, and humour; above all, there is love and desire.

The impact of the structure which continuously juxtaposes past and present is extremely effective. The novel catapults the implied thirty-year-old female reader of 1980 (presumably a liberated, independent professional like the young Lucía) into grim old age. The intervening thirty years are eliminated. The reader, too, in the prime of her life, is forced to confront death – which is exactly what Lucía wishes she had done in order to have made more of her time. In hospital, Lucía suddenly finds herself facing death as had the elderly Doña Maruja when Lucía was thirty. Lucía recounts in her memoirs how Doña Maruja (aged 67), tired of living, having outlived her role as mother and wife, and afraid of the pain of arthritis, calmly and repeatedly tries to kill herself. She asks a young and appalled Lucía to help her. Thirty years later, the moribund Lucía is to the reader what Doña Maruja was to the young Lucía. In fact, the novel opens with Lucía recalling Doña Maruja's request to be helped to die, 'I have done everything I had to do in life' she says. Clearly, Lucía (nor, presumably, the implied reader) share these sentiments. Towards the end of the novel objective time is annulled completely as the protagonist's past and the reader's possible future merge into a realistic and yet speculative narrative present.

One reading of the novel would stress the importance of the traditional lyrical themes *tempus fugit* and *carpe diem*, each moment of life should be savoured, particularly moments of love shared with others. But reading from a feminist perspective is more problematical. Lucía is attempting to create an autobiographical narrative from her recalled life experiences and to do this she establishes a developmental pattern, a series of connections, which are fundamentally flawed given the nature of memory. Her subjectivity is produced by this process of identity formation, cast retrospectively on a series of multiple selves. As Kathleen Glenn indicates, 'It is clear that Lucía is a master (mistress) of self invention. Her writing is a rewriting, her reading of experience is a misreading' (Glenn, 1991, 200). However, Lucía's writings reveal that this identity depends on how she is perceived by men. What gives Lucía's life meaning and gives her a sense of self is her interaction with men, suggesting that feminine identity is the effect of heterosexual desire. Paradoxically, as we shall see, according to Ricardo, Lucía has a greater sense of personal worth in a sexist situation (with Hipólito). She refutes this claiming that the effect of passion is a dissolving of the self into the other.

Three apparent dichotomies are set up and deconstructed to enable a playing out of these issues which puzzle the self-conscious author-narrator-protagonist. These are: passion (eros)/companionship (agape); fiction/reality; the individual/society. The workings of heterosexual relationships, considered from a predominantly feminine perspective, are at the crux of the novel; they baffle Lucía and motivate her diary-memoirs. Lucía asks herself constantly what love is and why it is so important in life. Analysing her own experiences, she divides love into two irreducible categories; one involves desire and romance, the other comfort and protection. This is what Hipólito and Miguel represent respectively in what is almost a feminine version of the angel/whore (angel/toyboy?) opposition. Ricardo, however, disputes the binary classification – which excludes his own relationship with Lucía – arguing, at first, that only desire is real love and, later, that desire is not love at all. According to Ricardo, Hipólito did not love Lucía, Miguel did. He deconstructs Lucía's false division, 'every kind of companionship-love has moments of passion and vice versa' and he accuses Lucía of 'artificially classifying unclassifiable things' (212). The interlocutory role Ricardo plays is extremely important as a structuring device in the novel. He counters Lucía's subjective, feminine interpretation of her past relationships from a, possibly, more objective, masculine point of view. But Ricardo is not only an observer of past events, he is also an imaginative story-teller himself and keeps Lucía entertained with extravagant tales the truth of which he subsequently denies. Neither he nor Lucía are reliable narrators, and as first-person narrators their point of view is necessarily limited. This way the difficult question of fiction and reality and the very authorship of the so-called 'auto' biography itself is raised.

Ricardo's comment on Lucía's first autobiographical piece is, 'It's alright as a novel, but as memoirs it's a fraud. Everything you're telling is a lie . . . a distortion of reality' (51). The difference between Lucía and himself, according to Ricardo, is that she writes (autobiography) in order to be believed while he consciously tells tall stories or lies (fiction). Presumably, authorial intention is what differentiates the genres. Lucía listens to Ricardo's advice, begrudgingly, and writes her memoirs accordingly. For example, when Ricardo complains he is hardly included in one episode, Lucía writes him in. At another point, he questions her idealized description of Miguel and reminds her how she was bored with Miguel, took up various lovers, and was on the point of leaving (327). However, Ricardo is very jealous of both Hipólito and Miguel and wants to tarnish Lucia's representation of them both. Whatever Lucía's intentions as an author may have been, in the final text Hipólito certainly comes across as a pathetic heel, Miguel as a cuddly bear father-figure, and Ricardo as the tender-hearted, long-suffering saint. Is the reader to believe Lucía's account of her own experiences, despite her faltering memory, or Ricardo's biased account as witness and observer? Are the memoirs coauthored? Ultimately, of course, the whole novel is presented as Lucía's diary-autobiography and it is she who inserts the conversations with Ricardo. She is the implied author, and although the verisimilitude on which her account depends is undermined by these metafictional strategies, the common-sense, masculine, approach of Ricardo does have the effect of anchoring the novel in reality.

All this raises the question of the reliability of memory and the inevitable fictionalization of the story of a life. On various occasions life is likened to a novel or a film; Hipólito tells Lucía he cannot get past the prologue of his life-story while she accuses him of considering her a serialized novel (23). Ricardo disputes the polarization Lucía draws in her memoirs between the two men in her life: 'Life is NOT like that. Life is not black and white, it's not made up of traitors and heroes, according to your memoirs Hipólito is completely perverse and Miguel is the only good one around' (161). Lucía sees herself as 'a protagonist of a film in the mind' (61), no doubt, one of her own. This self-reflexive narrative, drawing attention to the way it is written, distances the so-called objective reality of history and privileges feminine subjectivity, woman-centred experience and memory. But – as we have seen – the feminine version is continually called to account by the narratee Ricardo, who reads as a man in the text.

What, then, is love between a man and a woman, and why is it so important? The novel presents (tenuously) the views of a man (Ricardo) and a woman (Lucía) but always mediated by Lucía and by her representation of an argumentative and jealous Ricardo. For Lucía, love is important because it functions as an ideology or a religion, it is 'the only sufficient justification for life' (10). However, she feels constrained by the traditional one-to-one heterosexual relationship and declares herself 'monoandrous at heart and polyandrous in practice' (17). She also identifies a tendency in herself to either love two men very much or not to love at all. It was as if 'destiny had forced on me this fatal duality, this schizophrenia, two loves or none' (17). The young nurse, María by Day, feels similarly (41). Lucía suggests love may be a momentary flash: 'There are moments when I think I love someone, love him intensely, and within an hour I realize I don't love him at all, I don't feel anything for him' (117). Miguel, a mathematician, has a scientific explanation for fluctuating desire; it is the Delta function, 'a function that describes discontinuous phenomena of great intensity but brief duration . . . phenomena whose intensity tends towards the infinite and whose duration towards zero' (118). Hence, the disappointment when 'the pantomime of mad love' (9) does not work out. In fact, the novel shows a love that defies mathematical formulae; Ricardo's love and passion for Lucía slowly burns for thirty years. Whatever is signified by the word 'love' cannot be reduced to an essential substance, yet its effects are great. Love can communicate transcendence and intimations of immortality. It can defeat time as Lucía experiences with Ricardo: 'under the wrinkles I discovered the same Ricardo of thirty years ago, conserved intact for me' (280).

In the crucial week of 1980, torn between Hipólito and Miguel, Lucía asks Ricardo if he would rather be a lover or a companion. He replies a lover; Lucía chooses companionship. Her reasoning is that passion belongs to novels of romance, while everyday love depends on tenderness. 'I don't know if you realize this', quips Ricardo, 'but you've just invented the conventional marriage' (82). Thirty years later the discussion continues. Lucía still insists on dividing love into two types and is ambivalent about both. On the one hand,

> You give everything, completely and stupidly, to passion, even your own life; your hours, your days, your minutes seem empty without it, they don't deserve to be lived. It's a repelling and sickly obsession. In passion you are possessed by another self infinitely more stupid than your real self which is left behind in the furthest recess of your consciousness. From back there, a prisoner in your silly, foolish love personality, your real 'self' moans desperately, 'Don't you realize you're behaving ridiculously? Don't you realize it's no good for you, it's not clever, it's not useful, it's not dignified to act like that?. (230)

On the other hand, companionship is thoughtfulness, care and protection. Thus Lucía quizzes the dialectic love/aggression in humanist discourse and human relationships. Ricardo, having read the latest instalment of Lucía's life-story, interprets her self-imposed categories differently. He believes passion involves the risk and struggle of the independent woman wanting to be a person, to exist in her own right. Companionship leads a woman to depend on another. In Ricardo's analysis, in the role of passionate lover Lucía assumes traditional masculine attributes (she is active, sure, and free) while as a companion she plays the passive feminine role of needing protection and help. Ricardo adds:

> Really, this absurd problem . . . is no more than a sublimation of your own identity problem as a woman: between the independent woman you wanted to be and believed you were, and the 'someone's wife' woman which is inside you and who you were educated to be. (213)

When Lucía went to live with Miguel, he says, she gave up the fight. She was smothered by 'old feminine' customs because 'what you call everyday love is, in fact, nothing more than fear', 'you have become more and more conventional with every passing year' (215). Of course, Lucía hotly disputes this and it leads to a furious argument with Ricardo. But the memoirs seem to bear out Ricardo's view. Ricardo's analysis of Lucía echoes Freud's concept of narcissism, the love of one's self-image, which in its adult stage involves misrecognition in the other, the love-object, of what the subject imagines or wishes to be. With regards to libidinal energy, Lucía invested highly in Hipólito, arguably, therefore, she loses a part of her narcissism and self-respect when he leaves her. With Miguel, this is not the case. But Lucía does seem to revert to a child-like state with Miguel as is indicated by the numerous diminutives (Miguelito, chiquitita [little girl], bobita [silly little girl]) which pepper their dialogue. By settling down with one partner, then, was Lucía strengthening or blurring her sense of self?

Paradoxically, Lucía recounts in her memoirs a conversation with Ricardo thirty years earlier on the same subject (which he, of course, refutes). At that point, a romantic Ricardo argued that the only form of true love was passion, desire endlessly deferred, it is 'the creative impulse' and without it there would be no art or genius (190). But passion is dangerous and 'antisocial because it leads to loneliness and marginalization. It is always transgressive. The more it is prohibited, the least honourable and the more impossible it is, the more . . . intense it becomes' (191). On that occasion Lucía agreed with him, passion 'is intellectual, you invent it, you imagine it . . . only you yourself suffer and feel pleasure, it's a private love'; everyday love is what leads to a commitment with others. The problematic of the individual in society is thus introduced. According to Lucía, it is the commitment she recognizes in Miguel, her power to control his attention, and Miguel's acknowledgement of her femininity as something more than a sexual object (he calculates she is suffering from painful periods and brings round food and drink for dinner), which makes him her object-choice. Yet Lucía counters this rationale by making a love scene between herself and Miguel the most erotic in the novel. Moreover, thirty years later Ricardo offers Lucía both unshakeable friendship (philia) and passion (eros); arguably there is nothing more transgressive and prohibited than making love to an old lady in her hospital bed. All this bears out Ricardo's critique of Lucía's false binary classification. He incarnates the deconstruction of the opposition passion/companionship. His position represents, rather, a continuum, a process of communication between man and woman which leads to the mutual construction of identity; it is a matter of which end of the spectrum between affection and passion is valued more highly at a given moment, and what image is being both projected by the multifaceted self and reflected by the mutlifaceted other. So, does settling down with one partner mean a woman is giving in to convention? Certain doubts on Lucía's part, possibly relating to the unconscious in view of her mental state, are suggested by the drawn-out ending of her first (and last) film, *Crónica del desamor*. Unlike the relatively optimistic ending of the novel of the same name (Ana working towards self-knowledge and about to write her book), the film – according to Lucía's faulty memory – ends thus: Ana, dissatisfied with Soto Amón, leaves his country house and drowns herself in a nearby lake. Such a melodramatic finale seems totally out of character with the rest of the film and may well be a retrospective projection by an elderly Lucía. Was this the point in her life when she capitulated, gave in, killed herself off?

The novel offers another reading concerning the thorny question of love from a woman's point of view. At the end of the novel, the confused Lucía faces the darkness of death, the horror of self-dissolution, the absurdity of life: 'It has taken me so many years to construct myself as I am', she says, recalling the bridge metaphor, 'and now it will all disappear, it will disintegrate without trace' (339). In the clutches of fear she remembers the love and protection her mother gave her when, as a child, she was afraid of the dark: 'someone holds me and strokes me, I recognize my mother . . . What deep calm, what intense relief' (343). Sent home, finally, from hospital, Lucía fearfully awaits Ricardo's return from the shops for the same potection her mother gave her; she doesn't want to die alone. As she waits, her thoughts turn to the men in whom she has searched for a mother substitute. She mixes up their names and personalities and they become, metonymically, one male love object which has proven to be, somehow, unsatisfactory: 'Poor Lucía', she tells herself, 'no one has ever loved you as you want them to' (367). Her final words are 'Come here, I'll tell him, come here, my friend, my beloved, hurry because I'm beginning to be afraid of the dark' (369). Montero seems to be indicating that no heterosexual relationship can restore the primary, irreplaceable female, mother-daughter bond. Lucía's search for connection, for symbiotic closeness, is doomed to failure if restricted to the subject-object power relations of patriarchy.

Solitude, unconnectedness, is something Lucía cannot abide: 'I was incapable of being satisfied with my space, it suffocated me.' She wonders if this has anything to do with 'centuries of feminine education' that have robbed her of her 'integrity . . ., peace, . . .. completeness' (62) and she envies men who seem to be able to enjoy 'intense inner adventures'. Yet the society she lives in encourages individualism. For example, a new chain of restaurants has opened for singles where each table is provided with a video monitor so customers can take refuge in 'shared solitude' (70). It is this 'curse of the woman-as-partner, the woman-as-lack, the woman-as-support and supported' which makes Lucía seek out relationships with men, thus bridging the gap between the narcissistic, alienated individual and society. Ultimately, a different order is glimpsed in *La función*, although Montero doesn't follow it through. The decision of Rosa (Lucía's friend) to opt out of unfulfilling heterosexual relationships and at the same time not to resign herself to solitude, in other words, to live with a group of women, at first shocked and repelled the young Lucía: 'I found her feminine group rather repugnant, remembering those disgraceful little cliques of spinsters weeping the absence of the male' (63). However, in old age she recognizes the validity of Rosa's alternative.'There must be another way of relating to people, other better ways of living' (357), Rosa had told her years ago. Rosa explained that she got on better with women, which she found perfectly natural. When Lucía disputed this Rosa accused her of wanting to be a man: 'you feel very modern and liberated and you're ashamed of your sex, can't you see it's a trap?' (63). Now, in 2010, Rosa writes to Lucía, 'Yes, Lucía, I'm quite happy. Life here is very simple and I feel surrounded and protected by my people' (359). But although she is sheltered in the womb of a women's collective Rosa is not entirely happy either; at times she feels the melancholy of not having a man at her side, 'of not growing old with a companion, with the companion who is just like you and knows you to the bone. You know, the ideal future I always wanted. But that, dear Lucía, is just a dream' (359). This destabilizing and questioning of heterosexuality, on which the novel is based, is continued in the enigmatic figure of the secondary character, the janitor-transvestite Tadeo, who similarly shocks the young Lucía (244).

The novel thus cannily undermines time and reality in the world as we (and Lucía) know it and, paradoxically, leaves room for hope. This is achieved by establishing one opposition which remains intact and illuminates the death/love theme: it is the opposition body/spirit, or contingency/transcendence. As Lucía intuited in her early days,

> with passion we try to deceive death, we try to reach the keenness of life, those intense moments when you think you're eternal. With companionship you try to conquer death, but without deception, you face its existence with the help of another person. (137–8)

La función Delta is a novel of science fiction. It is full of allusions to science and medicine, in particular to biology (the knowledge of the physical life of humans, animals and plants): Doña Maruja's 'homozygotic blood' (16), the doctor's long explanations of Menière's disease, the description of Miguel's stroke, thoughts on menstruation, the menopause, brain tumours, and so on. Body matter lives and dies; it is mortal. However, humanity can transcend the contingent in moments of epiphany or revelation, in glimpses of eternity. This is a theme Montero returns to in all her later novels. In La función Lucía experiences such moments with Hipólito, 'violent, sharp moments, extraordinary moments of brilliance when I felt eternal, filled with life, compensated'. She is transported to a magical space. Again, she remembers as a child seeing an immense mountain range, seeing 'the interminable extension of the universe', sensing 'for the first time the terrifying dimensions of the eternal' (360). In fact, she makes films not to communicate with people, but 'to treasure moments of brilliance, to take hold of intensity' (115). Sadly, after such fascination there is the inevitable return to monotonous routine, but these brief moments of magical, spiritual transcendence – symbolized by the

Delta function – defy mortality and postmodern fragmentation. Additionally, to be both the subject of transcendence and the agent of desire, like Lucía, is important for woman, traditionally culturally bound to nature, the body, and immanence.

This is a science fiction novel in another way. It takes place against a backdrop reminiscent of Orwell's *1984*. The unnamed city where it is set is part of a violent, oppressive, highly organized 'police super-state' (166) which, paradoxically, thrives on microelectronic 'communication' networks controlled by a Western Information Bureau. A shocking scene describes how a bearded man is accosted on a café terrace in mid-afternoon by police. His stomach is split open and he is knifed to death while the café clientele, including the young Lucía, attempt to ignore what is going on. 'The city is going under, Lucía, the world we knew is coming to an end' (166), Ricardo warns years later. He and Lucía are non-conformists, merely tolerated by the system because they belong to another generation. Although neither Lucía nor Ricardo takes part in political activity, their disquisitions on love can be read as highly subversive. The personal cannot but impinge on the political and private love provides a cell of resistance. Yet, by the same token, private love is completely ineffective in state politics.

*La función Delta*, then, unlike Montero's first novel, is inward-looking. It foregrounds a hesitant female self-awareness and fluid interpersonal relations and it plumbs the depths of the quagmire of heterosexual romance from a feminine perspective. Nevertheless, a sense of the social is always present, as a threat rather than a propitious arena for the process of identity formation. In this respect it is recognizably an end-of-the-decade work. The novel envisages the emergence of a new social order, a dystopia, which – in the insecure years of the 'transition' – betrays fears that a new, technically advanced Spain might promote egocentricity to the extent that all human relationships are thwarted. Thus the concern is fundamentally humanist. But clearly the Spain in the offing would also pose different problems for women and demand new approaches from women writers of fiction.

# 5

## Inner Spaces and Power Lines: the Narrative of the 1980s

etween the publication of Montero's second and third novels much had changed in Spain. The transition was over; a military coup was thwarted in 1981 and a socialist government elected to power in 1982 under the premiership of Felipe González. The feminist movement was fizzling out. Montero, on the other hand, was now recognized as one of the country's leading journalists and a successful novelist. Her first two novels had been realist and semi-autobiographical. When she came to think about her next one she realised 'I needed more space, more imagination. To get out of the domestic walls, which I had transposed to my novels. To invent worlds that did not exist' ('Escribiendo en la luna', 10). In her following two novels Montero engaged in a scathing criticism of journalistic practice and newspaper management in Spain, as she had done in *Crónica*. At the same time, as Joan L. Brown indicates, 'a gradual rejection of the conventions of journalism in favour of novelistic ambiguity and invention' (Brown, 254) reinforces her offensive.

Before examining her third novel, *Te trataré como a una reina* (*I'll treat you like a queen*), 1983, a brief commentary of the short story 'Paulo Pumilio' would be appropriate. This story was published in a collection of short fiction, *Doce relatos de mujeres* (*Twelve stories by women*) in 1982 and it previews, in many ways, Montero's later narrative – in particular *Te trataré como una reina* and *Bella y oscura* (1993). This strange, allegorical tale, not one to be expected in a collection of women's fiction, is both anti-Francoist and feminist. It takes the form of the confession of Pablo Torres ('Towers'), who is jailed for murder and writes his story for the magazine *There's a Murderer On the Loose.*[1] On one level, the story clearly parodies Camilo José Cela's *Pascual Duarte's Family* (1967 [1944]), but there is an important difference. While in Cela's novel Pascual's murders can be attributed to his character, to individual psychological motives or social deprivation, Pablo's reasons for murdering his former hero are more insidious and socially threatening. Deformed in body and mind, Pablo represents a collective way of thinking which is twisted and has strong Fascist overtones. He perceives himself as a misunderstood hero living in times of vulgar mediocrity but the hyperbolic quality of his confession, a bombastic 'epic', reveals him as an egocentric and pathetic 42-year-old man with delusions of grandeur. Such a reading is made possible, despite the narrator's intentions, by the yawning gap separating his concept of himself and of reality and the implied reader's more common-sense perceptions.

The story is political in as much as it is a strong indictment of Francoist rhetoric and anachronistic values. Pablo is raised by a Civil Guard in an ambience of 'military glory'. He wants to join the force for a 'brilliantly heroic career' and feels a deep 'nostalgia for the past I had never lived' (70). Unfortunately, Pablo is very short (less than a metre high) and has bandy legs; he is not accepted into the Civil Guard and enters the employment of a priest until he is twenty-eight years old. The priest dies leaving Pablo a book on which he is to model his life. It is Plutarch's *Parallel Lives* with a prologue witten by the priest 'where he emphasizes the parallels between the glorious feats of valour narrated by Plutarch and the heroism of our own National Crusade . . . this has been my ethical and human guide, my bedside Bible, the compass in my life' (73). Pablo discovers he is homosexual and is proud of the fact:

> homosexuals were, in the Ancient world, all the heroes, geniuses, saints . . . homosexuality is the natural result of extreme sensitivity and delicacy . . . In the past I would have been a warrior of the legendary Sacred Cohort . . . Plutarch would have included me among his golden biographies: Paulus Turris Pumilio, four times consul . . . – the word 'pumilio' means in Latin 'small man' . . . homosexuality in the Ancient world was natural and understandable, because what

---

1. The story also brings to mind Ernesto Sábato's novel *El túnel* (*The Tunnel*) where the imprisoned murderer-protagonist, Pablo Castel (Castle) also writes his confession.

could be a better and more deserving object of passion than a powerful warrior? (76)

With such an education, based on the tenets of the Altar and the Sword, imbued in the Graeco–Roman classics, our hero sets out in the world to make a living and takes up with a pair of magicians – the handsome Gran Alí and his overweight and weepy woman, Asunción.

From that point on, the story centres on the oppressive, violent world of sleazy nightclubs predominant in *Te trataré* and *Bella y oscura*. The magician Gran Alí is a forerunner of Máximo or Segundo in *Bella y oscura*; Asunción reminds the reader of Antonia or Bella in *Te trataré*, Pumilio himself of Poquito, and the club Jawai of the Desiré. Even the false dagger of Montero's most recent novel first appears in the story. The plot of 'Paulo Pumilio' unfolds dramatically. Pablo adores his master, Gran Alí, and despises the woman, Asunción, until one day Gran Alí disappears with a pretty mulatta. Pablo patiently awaits his master's return. Five years later his loyalty is rewarded but Gran Alí returns a broken, fat and balding man. Pablo cannot bear the disillusion and kills him with a dagger. With the money earned from the magazine with his story he plans to bribe the jailer to bring him arsenic and thus he will commit suicide in true stoical fashion; his heroic name – Paulus Turris Pumilio will go down in history.

Throughout the story, through the figure of Pablo and, more importantly, Gran Alí, Montero cleverly conflates the classical values of Greece and Rome (purportedly the basis of Western humanism and civilization) with militarism, sadism, masochism, misogyny, violence, racism and authoritarianism. Gran Alí (real name Juan) might well be beautiful and upright, a Nietzchean superman, but he is cowardly and cruel; he repeatedly beats Asunción and Pablo with his belt, and on one occasion breaks Pablo's back with a stick. But while Asunción sinks into drunken stupor, Pablo (masochistically self-cast as a slave) admires his master for this harsh treatment which he perceives as Spartan-like training. Gran Alí's verbal cruelty is interpreted by Pablo as 'divine disdain' (78) and his silences as stoical control. He was, admits Pablo, 'the nearest thing to a god I have ever known'. Pablo challenges the uncomprehending reader, 'What do you know of Alí's greatness when he imposed his strict laws: his ferocious pride was the only value which ordered are ruinous world' (81).

The most disturbing aspect of the story, however, is the physical and verbal abuse perpetrated on Asunción and the narrator's overwhelming misogyny. Asunción is described throughout as a grotesque 'worm', a lower form of life. Even when she weeps for the injured Pablo she is decribed by him as a 'disgusting remnant of humanity' (78) and he is tempted to kill her. Reading between the lines of Pablo's biased account, it is obvious that Asunción has been reduced to the state of miserable victim by the manic sadist Gran Alí. Once he leaves her and she starts a relationship with a North American Vietnam veteran, Ted (described by Pablo as a 'eunuch'), she gives up alcohol and pulls herself together. The story shows, therefore, that the so-called humanist, patri- archal values of the West are not only flawed by militaristic authoritarianism disguised as masculinist 'honour' and 'order', but are also 'macho' and violently gynophobic. Yet, just as the master needs a slave on whom to exercise his power, so too the man needs the woman over whom to exert authority. When Gran Alí returns to Asunción she strikes back and defends herself; he is accosted by the ill 'eunuch', and his aura of power crumbles. He is finally killed off by his stupified slave who is dumbfounded by the turn of events: 'I said nothing, troubled by such a subversion of values, witnessing such an apocalypse' (89). The masochistic, misogynistic slave, now without a master, has no reason to live and will commit suicide. In a feminist reading of the story the values of Western patriarchal culture, in particular those of Franco's Spain, are successfully exaggerated, ridiculed and exposed. There is only one worrying feature of 'Pablo Pumilio', and that is what could be read as a latent homophobia; in the character of Pablo homosexuality is associated with sado- masochism, classical mores and misogyny. Only in *Temblor* (1990) would Montero again question the social construction of sexual identity in this way.

### *Te trataré como a una reina* (I'll treat you like a queen)

*Te trataré como a una reina* was published in 1983 and went through seven editions in less than a year. It is a realist novel, written in the suspense genre, and incorporating elements of popular culture. The novel parodies sleuth fiction and popular romance from a feminist point of view, clearly engaging with feminist and other controversial social issues, such as ageism, media manipulation, police corruption, and drug addiction. Described as a 'richly atmospheric mystery novel' (Brown, 248), 'a black farce, a sentimental tragedy' (on the book jacket), or by Montero as 'a bolero, a grotesque melodrama',[2] *Te trataré* is certainly humorous, at times hilarious, and yet deadly serious. It does not involve the kind of ambitious metaphysical and psychological enquiry Montero broached in *La función Delta*, which she would pursue in the late 1980s and 1990s, although it does question the nature of reality. The novel suggests that patterns of collective thought (in this case, popular and romantic) impose a particular (pernicious) concept of reality on men and women alike.

*Te trataré* also demonstrates Montero's virtuosity with language and her narrative skills. Several types of narration, language registers, and discourses – ranging from song lyrics and lyrical poetry to journalism – are juxtaposed to create a postmodern collage which breaks down arbitrary divisions between high and popular culture, factual discourse and fiction. A strong plot developed through twenty-eight short chapters, a newspaper report, and three taped monologues provoke the kind of tension expected from this popular genre. In addition, for the first time, Montero writes a novel which is not self-referential in any way. She engages with a world of which she has no direct experience, working from a scene she once witnessed in Seville: an overweight woman, with eyes caked in mascara, hair dyed blonde, sings romantic songs and plays an electric keyboard in a cabaret. Unlike the majority of Montero's and Roig's female characters, the women in this novel do not belong to the young, professional middle classes. They are not liberated and have little idea of what liberation means; they are trapped in a dominant patriarchal culture and language which popularizes the romantic myths through which they project their own identities. These women are destroyed partly by the men around them, who are violent, selfish and cowardly, but partly also by their own impossible romantic fantasies. Montero explains how she hit on the idea of a female failure:

2. See Rosa Montero interview with Antonio Monegal, 13 March 1985 (property of the author), p. 11.

When I started to think about my third novel the only thing I knew was that I wanted to write a story about failure. I imagined a character aged about 45 or 50 who had failed in life completely; and without meaning to, during several months I thought of that character as masculine, for the simple reason that all the literary models of failure I had were always men: traditionally, the capacity for failure in women was not recognised because neither did women have the capacity for triumph. The only typically feminine failure in a machista society is to be left a spinster ... For several months, without knowing, I was trapped in sexist conventions. Until one day, I don't know why, I saw the light, 'And why not a woman?', I thought. ('Escribiendo en la luna', 11–12)

In *Te trataré* an anonymous narrator tells the love stories of two very ordinary women in their mid-forties who have both grown up in Franco's Spain: Isabel López, alias Bella Isa (a middle-aged, disillusioned nightclub singer) and her unfulfilled relationship with Poco, the decrepit father of the nightclub owner; and Antonia, a lower middle-class spinster, and her sexual relationship with Damián, an ungainly man twenty-three years younger than her. These tragicomic liaisons of middle-aged women are made the subject of literary interest and intrigue. *Te trataré* opens with an extract from a tabloid newspaper, *El Criminal* (modelled, no doubt, on the real-life Madrid broadsheet, *El Caso*) written by a certain Paco Mancebo (Young Man) who reports on 'The strange case of the smoking murderess'. The exact reference of this piece (18 September, 1982. Number 356, II series) and its formal, semi-legal language, suggests this is factual reportage, albeit from the sensationalist press, and that the details are to be taken as historically true. The veracity of the report, however, is subverted by Mancebo's numerous abusive expletives and evident bias. The account is of a 'strange and savage event' in which the 'murderess' Isabel López, alias Bella, attacks a certain respectable gentleman, don Antonio Ortiz (about to be married to a 'beautiful and honourable young girl'), in his flat. According to a witness, Bella (described as a 'homicidal beast') engages in abnormal behaviour. First, she breaks up the flat, then empties out the contents of several bottles of perfume all over the floor, then she sits on her victim while smoking a packet of cigarettes, blowing the smoke in his face, and finally she picks him up and throws him out of the fourth floor window. Isabel López is decribed as a dirty-mouthed demon without moral principles. 'She was taller and much more corpulent than the unfortunate victim [. . .] which shows that the weaker sex is not always weak' (10), writes the seemingly objective Paco Mancebo. Immediately, the reader wants to know what went on; female readers in particular suspect Mancebo's unlikely version. Three transcripts of taped interviews on which Mancebo bases his report are later included in the novel. The people interviewed are all men. Despite the fact that two of the men are secondary characters with little information, only their words are given credence and authority. Women's versions do not count; they are marginalized from dominant discourse. The purpose of the novel, then, is to present a more complete, woman-centred account of events, a 'corrective' in Kathleen Glenn's words (Glenn, 1987, 91). The female characters are allowed to speak for themselves, usually in direct dialogue, but also through dreams and letters. The textual collage is overseen by an omniscient implied author/narrator who, presumably more objective than Paco Mancebo, presents the 'real' version through third-person narrative and free indirect style. At times, however, the narrator is invisible and the reader has to decide who is speaking (Chapters 3, 24, 26) or who is being described (Chapters 4, 11, 20, 21). There are also several cases of mistaken or confused identity. In other words, the reader has to work to put the jigsaw pieces together, as in all crime thrillers. Moreover, it is not really a question of 'who did it?' – the reader knows this from the start and frequent prolepsis brings the denouement forward. The question is how and why? What possible motives could Isabel López have had for her alleged brutal behaviour?

As it turns out, Bella did not murder 'don' Antonio (Antonia's brother). She certainly threw him out of the window, but he did not die. In fact he is well enough to give his own outraged version of events towards the end of the novel, in the third transcribed account given to Paco Mancebo. However, having read the novel, the reader now knows the 'truth' and Antonio's declaration only underlines his crass insensitivity. He is not 'respectable', neither is Vanessa, the woman he was about to marry, 'honourable'. He wrongly believes Bella resented his impending marriage. The 'truth', as presented in the novel, is rather more complex and involves various frustrated affairs of the heart. Bella romantically idealizes the down-and-out Vicente Menéndez (alias Poco) who has been living in the club for three months; she has no idea he is the club owner's father. Poco romantically idealizes the sexy, eighteen-year-old Juana Castillo (alias Vanessa) who works in the club. Vanessa idealizes Antonio who she believes is a gentleman and who is really a sexual pervert. Antonio, tired of sleeping around with airline pilots' wives and afraid of impotency, asks Vanessa to marry him. Poco finds out, beats up Vanessa, then (it seems) commits suicide by throwing himself in front of an underground train. Bella is devastated by Poco's death, but it's not for this reason alone she throws Antonio out of the window. It has to do with the relationship Antonio's sister, Antonia, has with Damián. This incongruent affair – based on maternal feelings – is the only one which involves mutual respect and innocent love. Antonio sends Damián away and the broken-hearted Antonia runs weeping to Bella, who immediately goes round to Antonio's flat and commits the crime. In taking her revenge on Antonio, Bella – acting as a veritable she-devil – is venting her fury on all men and on the society which Antonio represents: an exploitative, machista, sexually obsessed, hypocritical, selfish, unloving society run by men for men. Hers is the only example of active female resistance and rebellion against male dominance in the novel. Bella refuses to become yet another compliant victim.

In a patriarchal system such as this, the men of the decadent middle classes (Antonio) collude with the media (Paco Mancebo) and the police (Inspector García) to manipulate and dominate women. In the novel women are used and physically abused by a conspiracy of men at all social levels, from the most refined to the criminal. Montero gives an inside woman's point of view through Bella (the independent, strong-minded, working woman) and Antonia (the much dominated, weaker, spinster). Both eventually lose out in the system, as does the naive Vanessa. Ironically, the feminine attributes of these mature women (maternal feelings, care, compassion, and solidarity) are subordinated to the repugnant, farcical perversions of an aggressive, masculine economy. Women are rendered powerless by the laws and prohibitions of patriarchy: Bella is imprisoned, and Antonia – having freed herself from the repression of the Church – cannot show affection to her young lover in public without being accused of indecency.

Men abuse their positions of self-appointed authority particularly in the home or other enclosed spaces. Antonia cowers under her brother's high-handed, sadistic arrogance. Although she waits on him hand and foot in her own flat, he considers her inferior. Both she and her furniture are in 'solid bad taste' manifesting 'a vulgarity that wounded his sensibility' (69). The more submissive she is, the more he hates her. His continual criticism makes Antonia feel worthless and, like Mancebo, he twists reality so he is perceived as the victim and she the guilty party. On one occasion, after reducing her to tears, he laments, 'All I want is some understanding, that's all, but the lady has to start crying, all she can come up with is a hysterical tantrum' (75). Antonia, of course, apologizes and blames the menopause. The fact that Antonia is banned from having an affair with Damián (because he is younger than her) by Antonio who not only sleeps with other men's wives on a regular basis but is also planning to marry eighteen-year-old Vanessa, shows the double standards of a patriarchal society to the full. Antonia (aged forty-four) and Antonio (aged forty-nine) may share the same name, and may be almost the same age, but their lives are radically different because one set of rules applies to men and another to women.

What comes across with force in the novel is Bella's character which is quite unlike that of the Isabel López described in the opening pages by Mancebo. Bella's resolution contrasts strongly with Antonia's passiveness. She is fair-minded, thoughtful, quick witted, and brave. The incident when she faces two thugs wielding knives to save Vanessa is particularly telling. Nevertheless, she is afraid of men because she does not understand them. It was an 'inexplicable fear. A fear which had grown through life. They were such brutes, so incomprehensible. So cruel. They were like children, but children capable of killing' (78). Towards the end of the novel, before she sets out to defenestrate Antonio, Bella finally perceives in a moment of revelation what she has never seen before; how she and all her sex have been oppressed by men. She feels an 'extraordinary calm', a 'strange lucidity', which enables her to be conscious 'of a thousand details at once, as if reality had lost its continuity and had broken up into the fragments of which it was made' (234). She sees through the apparent coherence of a masculine defined reality. The fragments otherwise hidden from view are the series of affronts and deceptions Bella has experienced because of men. For example, when (after Poco's death and desperate for comfort) she sleeps with one of the young delinquents who frequent the club, the next morning he asks her for payment; 'I've treated you well, haven't I?', he asks ironically (223). Bella feels suddenly 'ridiculous, fat and naked' but 'calm, very calm. Frozen with calm' (223). Or when Bella finds out that the letter of invitation to Cuba Poco had shown her, and on which she had built her hopes of singing in the Tropicana, had been written in 1954. Or one man's remarks on the smallpox innoculation scar on her arm, 'all you heifers need a brand to show who you belong to when you escape' (28). Bella realizes she has no chance of a meaningful life in a society where her body is merely an object of exchange or possession.

Indeed, power, which becomes increasingly important in Montero's work, assumes prime significance in this novel. Old Benigno, Antonio's subordinate, is treated atrociously by Antonio within the enclosed space of the small office:

> Antonio was convinced that his superiority over Benigno was evident . . . but he was also convinced the secretary didn't understand this, and that if a superior doesn't know what to order an inferior to do, then the very reason for the existence of hierarchy would go to the devil. (49)

Antonio – insecure and jealous, overlooked in the promotion list – can be compared to the neurotic César in *Amado amo*. As in *Crónica* and, later, *Amado amo*, the world of *Te trataré* is one of interior spaces which, like Antonio's workplace, are generally in permanent semi-darkness. In such private spaces power relations are traced in their most insidious form. From the nightclub itself (ironically named Desiré), to the various flats and bedrooms belonging to Antonia, Vanessa, and Bella, from Antonio's dimly lit office, to the hotel room, relations of power are played out. They usually involve men and women, and the women generally lose; but power can be exercised just as unfairly between men. Bella, representing sisterhood, supports Vanessa and Antonia, but Antonio persecutes Benigno and Damián. The only lengthy scenes which take place in the exterior are those involving the lovers Antonia and Damián who meet on the wasteland and in the park; a parodic concession to the pastoral settings associated with true love. The interiors are continually threatened from outside by a bleak, dangerous underworld of criminals, thugs, and drug addicts. Violence interrupts shockingly when a cat is set on fire and thrown into the club as Bella's dreams of Cuba, a prelude of how she, like the witches of old, will be persecuted; Poco squashes a helpless cockroach to death when Vanessa insults him, a prelude to when he later beats Vanessa senseless. The club, once a bar for prostitutes, is 'a frontier club, in a frontier district' (32), on the boundaries of respectability. Mediating between the underworld and the world of law and order is police inspector García, a sex-starved creep. In fact, although not apparent at first, García is one of the main characters of the novel because the plot would be quite different without his lurking presence. He is another factor in the power game. He turns a blind eye to Antonio's bribing of an airline employee to acquire information on airline pilots' wives; he denounces the activities of Antonia and Damián to her brother; he traces Bella after the 'crime'. Again, as in *La función Delta*, the forces of patriarchal 'law' and 'order' come under criticism.

The novel is extremely pessimistic, almost deterministic; there is no way out for women. There is no 'Mills and Boon' happy ending; women cannot escape the legacy of the gender roles foisted on them in Franco's Spain. At the end of the story Bella is in prison and Vanessa seriously ill in hospital. The one person who seems to have learned something and mustered up enough courage to make the break from her former life is the victimized Antonia. Despite great trepidation, she packs her bags and embarks on the adventure of a lifetime, to get onto the first train leaving the station no matter where it is bound for, 'Quickly, very quickly, on her way to an unknown destination, towards novelty, towards life. She had done it. She had been able to do it' (245). In a final ironical twist, she realizes she has boarded the same train she has been catching regularly for twenty years taking her back to her landlocked village and her elderly mother. The dry, inner plains of Spain offer no relief for Bella either. She, too, realizes she will never be able to sail away on the ships of her childhood dreams: 'how sad they were [the ships], hooting in search of the water between the stones' (113). It is this unbridgeable gap between sordid reality on the one hand and self-created dreams, desire, and romance on the other which informs the narrative. Far-away Cuba, home of the bolero, becomes a mythical, unreachable space contrasted repeatedly with its own dilapidated representation in the club: 'the only palm trees are made of cardboard. The only mulattas are the ones with straw skirts drawn on the wall. The only tropical beach is the one on the faded, flaking sea in the Desiré' (85). 'Here the palm trees were of cardboard and the seas neon lights and everything was a reflection of a reflection. But there, beaches were beaches, success success, and love love' (115).

The boleros Bella sings are a constant, pernicious reminder of unattainable ideals.³ In the words of Tony Evora, 'the memory of a good bolero outlives the amorous adventure which accompanied it. A genuine bolero is the expression of an authentic poet who is not afraid of sentimentality ... perhaps that is why everyone can share the bolero without feeling ashamed' (Evora, ii). It is on the basis of sentimental bolero lyrics that Bella constructs her dream-fictions; her idealized image of Poco, for example, is countered by a more realistic appraisal of the man by his son. After singing 'I need a heart to keep me company, that feels everything I feel ... That loves me truly, who loves me as I love him, who gives his life for me completely, I want a heart to stay with meeeeeeee ...' (31), Bella assumes the conservative ideology these words subsume and muses: 'The world is not meant for women on their own ... whatever those feminists say.' Yet she has the common sense, founded on experience, to remember why she had been a long time without a man: because a man might walk you home after work, but 'who's going to defend you from your man. Better to be alone than keep bad company' (31). Love, according to the bolero songs, is 'An unease, an anxiety ... To feel my heart beating desperately for you ...' (37). Clearly, the ideology informing the myths and discourse of sentimental romanticism needs debunking, primarily because uneducated women such as Bella and Antonia have no alternative discourse of which they can avail themselves to verbalize their feelings and their sexuality. Their role models are film stars and the glamorous singers of popular culture (Eydie Gorme, Elena Burke, Bo Derek). Likewise men, such as Antonio, are caught up in the Don Juan myth; he believes 'love could only exist ... wrapped up in its own lies, isolated from reality and its context' (74). In fact, the greatest victim in the novel is a man, Poco, who lives in a romanticized past. His dream of taking Vanessa to Cuba is a nostalgic desire to recuperate lost illusions, to be a big-time singer in the famous Tropicana club. He loved a woman but she let him down. Vanessa, who reminds him of this woman, also rejects him, hence his despair and suicide. Bella shares Poco's dreams of love and also longs to escape her banal reality. She does so through the songs she sings and her

3. Concha Alborg points out that the bolero dance, where a man and a woman dance together closely and swop partners, is the structuring pattern of the novel. Most chapters involve the interaction of two characters (Alborg, 1988, p. 72). Joan L. Brown refers to the bolero as 'a metaphor for characters' liaisons' (Brown, p. 250).

daydreams of accompanying him to Havana. However, the novel dispels any illusions of escape, or romantic flights of fantasy. Roberto Manteiga points out that Bella's bolero lyrics repeat the questions posed by Lucía in *La función*: what is love, how do we cope with loneliness? But Bella's formulation lacks the intellectual packaging and the theoretical discourse needed for understanding (Manteiga, 118). Consciousness-raising and popular, sentimental romance would seem to be antithetical.

Popular culture is thus incorporated intertextually into the realist novel via the bolero lyrics, the sensationalist press articles, the cliché-ridden conversations, and even a brief reference to Spanish Romantic poetry, Gustavo Adolfo Bécquer's collection of *Rimas [Rhymes]*.[4] The relationship between the discursive practice of popular romance which stresses women's dependence on men, and everyday reality is parodic. In *Te trataré*, women do not need men and, indeed, would be better off without them. As Elena Gascón Vera points out, in a phallocentric culture such as this women cannot be independent and successful, and expect to enjoy a satisfying relationship. Society makes autonomous women feel odd, isolated, alone – hence the importance of the theme of loneliness in all Montero's work (Gascón Vera, 1987, 63). The ironic title of the novel, the text of which shows women being treated heinously, is taken from the title of a bolero which reads:

> I have so many gifts for you, of tender love and compassion, so many I know not how to give them all, or tell you of my passion, impossible to explain my desire for you, what my soul longs for, that's why in my madness I can only swear, I will treat you like a queen. (178)

Caught up in this rhetoric of pretentious affectation and kitsch men and women are trapped by language and cultural codes. Women 'have to be treated like queens. They're romantic', Antonio tells Inspector García (without a hint of cynicism) (100). He is referring to the airline pilot's wife he deceived and who subsequently left her husband; 'I'll treat you like a queen', says Poco to Vanessa, before almost beating her to death (207).

The characters who suffer most from these delusions, Bella,

---

4. Manuel Domínguez writes, 'the popular roots and sentimentality of the bolero, [are] exactly the same as the 'copla' [ballad] in Spain . . .', 'Bolero. Golpe bajo al corazón', *Cambio 16*, 19 April 1993, 80. Rosa Montero's critique of popular culture can be usefully compared with that of the Argentinian author Manuel Puig whose approach is similar, in his early novels in particular.

Poco, and Vanessa, have all adopted supposedly more glamorous names or aliases to fit their pseudo double identities. Paradoxically, the female characters tend to degrade their own self images. Bella believes she is fat and ugly until she is transformed by her glamorous dress and chic South American accent, yet Antonia thinks Bella is pretty. Antonia, too, thinks she is unattractive, 'her face was too round and her features too small. The ugliest part was her nose' (20), but the army officer says she is good-looking (168). Antonio, too, is terrified of not being able to fulfil the virile image he projects and of not meeting Vanessa's sexual demands. In response, Antonio creates a whole alternative world for himself. He isolates himself from reality in an ordered space (his flat) which no one is allowed to visit and where he attempts to discover the ethereal in the form of an as yet unknown perfume. His narcissistic order, an attempt to recreate the harmony he experienced as a child with his mother, seems perfect; 'his domestic universe . . . was converted into the only existing reality, a perfect reality, without a trace of disorder' (185). In some ways Antonio represents human efforts to defeat contingency and to transcend reality through the aesthetic. But there is one flaw in Antonio's perfect order; it depends on the subjugation of women. Hence, the significance of Bella's rebellion when she destroys yet another male-defined version of artificial paradise. Antonio, moreover, suffers from castration anxiety. His nose is an obvious phallic symbol; when he smells perfumes he experiences orgasmic pleasure. He is finally castrated by Bella who causes him to lose his hypersensitive sense of smell and his ensuing lament is – as ever – couched in romantic rhetoric; it is 'a castration . . . my sense of smell was my gift, my art, my reason for being, my life. Without my nose I am nothing, I am no one' (239). All the characters, then, construct their identities from stereoptypical romantic fictions. Note how, in her letters to her mother, Antonia 'rewrites' her affair with Damián to suit romantic conventions, or how Antonio 'rewrites' his sordid encounters with married women in his diary as if it were a Hollywood script. The characters are trapped in a 'phallocentric fallacy' of male omnipotence; the women wait for Prince Charming to resolve their situation, the men have to be the Prince. It is even more ironic, then, that in this novel the longed for 'symbols of support' should be such unattractive, disgusting men (Gascón Vera, 71–2).

Within the framework of a critique of patriarchal relations and of popular romance, the novel presents several themes normally considered too inane or taboo for literature. The daily tedium of many women's lives becomes a literary topic. However, the boring monotony of Antonia's life,

> the clothes were ironed, the cupboards tidied, the pans cleaned and dried, and the previous evening she had gone over all Antonio's shirt buttons, and raised the hems of her summer suits because the fashion was short skirts. So, she had nothing to do and the afternoon threatened to never end, (14)

is broken by fantasies of rape accompanied by strenuous masturbation with a felt dog:

> She turned the photograph of her brother Antonio, who looked at her ferociously from the bedside table, towards the wall (she left the photograph of her mother as it was because the poor thing was almost blind) and grabbed Lulú, the felt dog . . . She leaned back slowly . . . closed her eyes and felt all sweat and all flesh. (22)

Such sessions are followed, inevitably, by guilt. The voyeurism provoked in this scene, offering an inside peek at a spinster's private life, is reflected in the figure of a (literally) cross-eyed Damián spying on Antonia through the open window. Similarly, Inspector García is portrayed masturbating against a tree when he spies on Antonia and Damián rolling together in the park.

There are several pointers to the directions Montero would take in her future work. One has already been mentioned. Power relations, hierarchies, enclosed spaces, and institutions would be explored further in *Amado amo*. A second metaphysical and ontological direction, involving the nature of reality and the construction of (feminine) identity, would have to wait until the publication of *Temblor* to become of primary significance, but is clearly present in *Te trataré*. After the great deception of Poco's death, after the destruction of illusion and delusion, Bella can now see reality as it is; in her toilet floor, for example, where she notices a pattern for the first time. She tries to remember, unsuccessfully, the house were she grew up which had since been demolished. The realization that the existence of her family house (of her childhood and her self) remains only in her own mind and memory causes her to panic:

> Fear, fear of having forgotten, fear of not being able to recuperate what was, an almost physical pain faced with the absence of what one was.

As if suddenly she knew she was an orphan, a complete orphan . . .
an orphan of herself, her past, her history. (230)

What was the colour of the tiles in the room where she used to
play?, she asks herself. But she cannot remember, 'And Bella knew
that this unanswerable question was the only, the greatest, enigma
of her life' (231). It is only after recuperating and assuming this
awareness of self in history, of seeing reality without rose-tinted
spectacles, that Bella is able to take revenge on patriarchy. This
reading, however, does not correspond to Montero's claim, in an
interview, that Bella never does see the reasons for her oppression
clearly. None of the characters learn; 'this is a melodrama because
[the characters] carry on believing the most stupidly beautiful
things' (Monegal interview, 11).

*Te trataré* questions authorized, masculinist interpretations of
reality and, as Kathleen Glenn perceptively shows, women as
consumers of the male produced texts (songs, poems, films) which
project these patriarchal myths. Men do not 'read' (understand)
women; similarly, women 'misread' (romanticize) men because of
their deficient education and cultural conditioning (Glenn, 1987,
191–9). Montero also shows how the women's movement fails to
reach women who are not youngish, middle-class, professionals,
how it even fails to address their problems. These women, after
having lived through the thirty-five years under Franco, are
suddenly faced with a socialist Spain in which women's rights are
very much on the agenda. Their adaptation to society's shifting
attitudes towards women, sexuality, and gender is difficult, if not
impossible. As Montero said herself, 'The group that's really
marginalized is the one that's not even aware of its marginal
status' (quoted in Brown, 250). In her fourth novel, Montero
explores the effects of women's rapidly changing role in society
on Spanish men and men's equally difficult process of adaptation.

### Amado Amo (Beloved Master)

By the late 1980s the policies of the socialist government, which
had been so promising, had fallen short of many women's
expectations. On the other hand, the undeniable improvement of
women's situation had defused the whole feminist issue which
lost the urgency it had ten years earlier. Women were perceived
by many to have achieved what they wanted. In an interview in

Rosa Montero

1988, in reply to a question, Montero sustained that Spanish men were now fearful of women's increasing participation in politics and society. She believed many men of her generation, between the ages of thirty and forty, feel 'threatened and accuse particular women of being aggressive . . . Fear degrades . . . men have lost the concept of what they are'.[5] *Amado amo*, published that same year, follows through these ideas. Public demand for an airing of the effect of feminism on men was high; the novel went through six editions in twelve months.

*Amado amo* is a deceptively simple novel; it is entertaining and easily read, yet it prods deeply into the dark recesses of the power games in which contemporary man and woman are inextricably enmeshed. The protagonist is a man in his mid-forties, César Miranda (Caesar the Marvellous); he is an artist and previously art director of a Madrid-based advertising company recently bought out by the Americans and renamed 'Golden Line'. César joined the firm when it was still under Spanish (Basque) ownership; he became important in the 1960s' Pop Art scene (one of his paintings was hung in the Museum of Contemporary Art) and he was quickly promoted to a senior post. But César lacks the necessary ambition to remain on top, and he is lazy. After resigning his post as director so as to spend more time on design, despite the fact that he is still a company executive on full pay, his position in the firm gradually declines. For over a year before the action in the novel takes place a younger, exceedingly ambitious man (Nacho), whom César originally introduced to the firm, has ruthlessly undermined César's position even further. Aware of his precarious situation in the company, César slips into depression and anxiety, aggravating matters by avoiding the firm altogether and wallowing in apathetic self-pity.

The novel starts in 'media res' with this past history presented through frequent flashbacks told in the third person by an anonymous narrator but focalized through César. Stream-of-consciousness techniques blend with free indirect style narration resulting in the story being perceived solely from César's point of view, through his memories, while at the same time the presence of the generally unsympathetic narrator tinges the account with irony. Montero points out that there is no dialogue in the novel because the narration is a delirium, 'the narration enters and

5. Sebastián Moreno, 'Entrevista. Rosa Montero', *Tribuna*, 25 July 1988, p. 59.

leaves the head of the protagonist and his delirium. You don't know to what extent it is a delirium and to what extent it is an objective narration in third person . . . That's why there are no dialogues; it is a "torrent" of words' (Glenn, 1990, 282).

The plot is straightforward. César, convinced he faces immediate demotion and shaken by a colleague's suicide, saves his skin by selling out his girlfriend, Paula, to the company. The reprieve offered by his superiors involves him signing a document testifying to the 'subversive' activities of his girlfriend, who – furious at being repeatedly passed over in the promotions list after years of service – has sent incriminating evidence of the company's underhand practices to the press. César, of course, signs. Even if he is a victim of the system, a man can always find a scapegoat in a woman. Thus, although feminist issues are not immediately apparent in this novel, which has more to do with the identity crisis of a persecuted male in the age of women's liberation, in the final pages the reader realizes with horror the full extent and nature of women's subjugation by men in the postmodern world.

The company, in its new open-plan building, functions as a microcosm and represents the post-industrial, transnational, capitalist world. It is patriarchal, highly competitive, totally unjust, and clearly inhuman. Structured into hierarchies of power, from the absent owners (in Los Angeles), through the Anglo–American directors such as Smith and Morton, the Spanish directors Quebrada and Matías (both drawn from the original Spanish company ironically named 'Rumbo'[Direction]), and the various echelons of Spanish employees such as Pepe, to, finally, secretaries like Conchita, at the bottom of the pile, the firm promotes, appoints, demotes or dismisses up and down this vertical axis according to unknown criteria. The rise and fall of any individual employee is apparently determined by mysterious influences: by rumours, hearsay, and information from unknown sources. More frequently there is no reason at all:

> On what basis the firm meted out its justice was a complete secret. You never knew if you had done something good or bad, but only if someone was in a state of grace or disgrace; mortifying or beatific states that the employees had to guess at by means of small revelations and signs, indications such as a smile from Morton during a 'brainstorming', Miguel stopping to tell you a joke in the corridor, or Quesada asking after your child's health, a very good sign this one even if you didn't have any children. (86–7)

Once a year, like an angry god, the company effects drastic changes. Imminent changes in the status of a person – particularly if it is for the worse – are communicated indirectly by innuendo, by a certain word, a look, or a gesture. Any occurence whatsoever can suddenly be invested with insidious meaning. All the characters, including the Spanish directors (but not, it would seem, the Anglo–Americans) are pawns in this game. They are all adept at reading the signs, but are at a loss at how to interpret them because the dominant dogma is foreign and, apparently, arbitrary. As in *Te trataré*, misreading can be fatal. Gleaning knowledge is essential because this is 'a world where knowledge is power, not to know was exile' (93). Every worker is susceptible and vulnerable to the whims of the power-brokers. Even Matías, a former director, commits suicide during the novel by drinking a bottle of bleach. The demise of César's fellow director is an ever-present reminder of his own incipient fate and only increases his despondency. But the shock does enable César to analyse his situation and that of his colleagues; despite his panic, he is fully aware who is to blame and in voicing his knowledge informs the reader.

Collective paranoia, he decides, is deliberately created by the US-based company to keep the staff on tenterhooks, to foster insecurity, and to increase productivity. He reads in a US management manual 'there was nothing worse for a firm . . . than to have its employees feel safe in their jobs' (89). The ferocious aggression of the more competitive workers, disguised under a veneer of civility, and the utter despair of their victims, is ultimately explained by greed and fear; greed for power and fear of losing not only a job, but also self-confidence and self-identity. César wonders: 'Why should he care so much about Morton's opinion of him? Why should the bosses control not only their subordinates' work but also their degree of self-esteem?' He knows the answer: 'the bosses were gods in an atheist world, the absolute kings of a republican society. . . . The bosses were the dictators of democracy' (39). César is caught up in this micropolitical theocracy against his will. He does not have the strength of character nor the ideology to escape from or break it. His failing is his own egotism, selfishness, lack of compassion for others, and lack of solidarity. César sells his soul to the company, betraying Paula, the one person who trusted him and was genuinely interested in helping him. He does so despite his misgivings and despite his full awareness of the nature of the power struggle in which he is trapped: it is

> a spider's web whose innumerable threads were intertwined, hierarchically, geometrically, joined by the intangible substance of Power, the fine web of domination. And there was no choice, you could only be the spider's thread or a trapped and kicking fly. (147)

The advertising company repesents capitalist power structures and men's (not women's) collusion with them. The system depends not so much on authority, which suggests a legal or consensual framework for the authorization of the execution of power, but more on ubiquitous power relations (ensuring the compliance or obedience of a person by dint of will) at all levels of public and private life. This propagates fawning sycophancy, over-praise, lies, deceit, mutual betrayal and humiliation. In a Foulcauldian sense the firm functions through power-knowledge, that is, gathering knowledge about its employees and exercising power over them.[6]

Furthermore, by making the company US-based, the novel effects a strong indictment of the effects of dollar imperialism on individual lives in Spain. Multinational mergers inherent in current globalizing strategies were a common feature of the high-tech, post-industrial Spain of the 1980s, as elsewhere in Europe. Montero points to the insidious and damaging social and psychological effects of an alienating, foreign ethos on the lives of men and women in a subaltern economy. In the Spanish commercial world firms had 'passed from the most ancient feudalism to the most advanced capitalism overnight, missing out a handful of intermediate social systems. César, in particular, would have liked an Enlightenment' (150).

That this is specifically a North American ethos is made clear by Clara in Chapter Nine when she explains what she sees as the origins of US competitiveness and aggression. She refers to the 1889 land run in Oklahoma when an extension of land, taken from the Indians, was allotted to the settlers on the basis of first come, first served. At twelve o'clock on the dot, tens of thousands of starving men, women and children ran and fought to possess a piece of land. Plots were gained not 'by those who were the most honest, the most intelligent, or even the quickest; but the strongest,

---

6. M. Foucault, *Discipline and Punish, the Birth of the Prison*, 1977, pp. 304–5.

cruellest, most selfish and inhumane. These were the ones who triumphed'. Clara adds that the episode was not simply a mistake, but calculated by a perverse desire to construct a society on such a basis (197).

Montero also points to another type of inequality addressed throughout twentieth-century Spanish history but apparently irrelevant or forgotten in the Americanized world of 'Golden Line'. Class consciousness, clearly present in the memories of César whose childhood was overshadowed by the Spanish Civil War, formed the basis of political consciousness and militant activity in Spain until the election of the Socialists in 1982. From then on it was of less importance. Montero reinstates the significance of class origins, interwined inevitably with personal histories, in César's own analysis of the relationship between him and Nacho – the young usurper of his position in the firm. César's father, with a good job before the war, fought on the wrong (Republican) side. He was released from prison in 1941–2, an ill and defeated man. César remembers only a poor, squalid home and a resigned, downtrodden mother who, nevertheless, encourages her son's love of decoration and colouring. He compares his early life to that of Nacho, who belongs to the Basque haute-bourgeoisie, in animalistic terms: Nacho is a pedigree dog; César a mongrel. Nacho's marriage to Tessa, a blonde, Anda-lusian aristocrat, is typical of the cementing relationships of the traditional oligarchy in Spain: 'nobles with nobles, names with names, fortunes with fortunes. Or perhaps, names with fortunes, or vice versa. But he, César, didn't have one or the other' (54). So, while César was forced to work his way up in the advertising agency in an autocratic Spain isolated from mainstream European art innovations, Nacho was studying architecture, travelling abroad, working in the USA and Germany: 'It wasn't fair. It wasn't fair. It wasn't fair' (67). This sense of not belonging to the dominant élites (Morton, too, is an English aristocrat, p. 27) comes out in César's unease when invited to a party at Nacho's house. On the surface, dressed impeccably, he looks as good as any of his well-heeled colleagues. But his underlying insecurities are sniffed out by the family's dog (a pedigree teckel, of course) who insists on masturbating against his trouser legs. However, although César is perfectly aware of the injustices of the class system, he does not formulate this consciousness into class-based politics or collective action. Even if he had done so he would have had no means of channelling his discontent in a US-based firm where collective action of any kind is actively discouraged. The only person involved in some kind of improvement of the workers' conditions in 'Golden Line' is Paula and she faces dismissal thanks to César. Ultimately, César has assimilated the company's way of thinking. Throughout the novel he succeeds in building up his self-esteem only by making others (Pepe, Matías, Paula) look small. In the final analysis, he is no better than his superiors.

The one group of people from whom César feels no threat is women. He uses women (a mother, a lover, a friend) in times of crisis to boost his ego, to give him support, understanding and self-confidence. Not surprisingly, he has no truck with feminist ideas. He might be badly off, Paula tells him, but women get nowhere in the company. César recognizes the truth of her statement,

> but somehow, he thought to himself, it was different in her case, none of this mattered for women, she could never understand the drama he was living through. After all, if Paula hadn't been promoted, it wasn't such a great injustice. Women lacked ambition. (67)

Paula only annoys him with her 'boring feminism' (48). César suffers from womb envy. He resents the fact that 'no woman had wanted to get pregnant with his seed' (23). He would have liked to have had a family, he thinks, but only because this might have furthered his career. He refers to the 'female dictatorship of motherhood' as 'an abusive and repugnant power' from which he feels excluded:

> There they were, deciding like tyrants who they wished to breed with and who they would condemn to everlasting sterility. Women, the owners of blood, the makers of bodies, the pitiless monarchs of life. He could never forgive women their power to be mothers. (23)

Here Montero not only indicates men's lack of understanding of sexual discrimination, even when they face victimization themselves, and their failure to join forces with women in a common struggle for equal rights; she also explores once again the slippery ground of heterosexual relationships, underlining the lack of communication or mutual comprehension between the sexes. The blame is put firmly on male egotism, selfishness, and insecurity. During the novel César is shown with three sexual partners: his former girlfriend, Clara; his current one, Paula; and a young female interviewer he ends up sleeping with. His relationship with his mother is also of great importance. The encounter with the young girl is totally vacuous; César feels like a pervert, he could be the girl's father. Exhausted by an hour of post-coital chat he puts a sleeping pill in the girl's hot chocolate and watches her sleep. It is then that he realizes he can only relate to women when they are asleep, as was the case during his three-year relationship with Clara. When she was asleep, Clara 'Sleeping Beauty' was fragile and needed protection; but once awake 'they [had] looked at each other from the opposite extremes of a astral void' (102). Similarly, he remembers once, when he was ill, he realized

> like a shock-wave that at last he had found his place in space, his moment in eternity, to be flat on his back in bed full of sickness but with Clara's hand on his cheek. It was a flash of lucidity that lasted only a moment. (112)

In other words, moments of tenderness and love between a man and a woman can only result from the incapacitation or subordination of one of them. Love, it seems, belongs to the subconscious, to the world of dreams. Hence the predomination of fairy-tale motifs in Chapter 5, motifs which are constantly undermined and ridiculed. When César administers the sleeping pill to the unsuspecting girl he likens her to Little Red Riding Hood and Snow White, and himself to the evil wolf and the wicked step-mother. It is no surprise that the waste disposal truck which passes by in the early hours of the morning 'chewed up crap just outside his window with a tremendous noise, as punctual as the lark in Romeo and Juliet, but adapted to the trash of modern times' (117). César has lost any romantic ideals he may have had. Clara leaves him; he makes no effort to stop her, although the reader suspects he loved her, and his life enters its current five-year period of crisis. César turns to Paula on the rebound.

Montero leaves sufficient ambiguity in César's one-sided accounts of these relationships for the (female) reader to be able to reconstruct the woman's point of view. If in the case of Clara the reader cannot help but feel some measure of sympathy for César because, although he is lazy and selfish, Clara admits to having a low libido making their sexual relations tense, in Paula's case he is less defensible. She looks after him, finds him a flat, furnishes it for him, and yet after five years has only won the right to leave her toothbrush there (120). He believes their relationship was the result of a 'chance, momentary union of lonely people' (110) but the reader suspects the real reason for the unhappiness in this affair; César is 'afraid she might want to start something' (110). His interest is rekindled, however, when he thinks Paula is having an affair with Nacho. He is plunged into despair when she does not respond immediately to his sexual demands being, at that particular moment, more interested in denouncing the malpractice of 'Golden Line'. César only wants Paula in order to relieve his existential anguish; he is acutely aware of 'the knot of anxiety in his stomach which he tried to push down to his penis' (175). Panic-struck, he even asks Paula to marry him.

The point is, although César, whose forte is certainly not self-criticism, feels everyone has betrayed him – and with respect to his male colleagues it seems, he is quite right – the person who in the end loses out on his behalf is a woman. César justifies his dirty dealings with the firm in the final, shockingly unjust, words of the novel: 'after all Paula betrayed me first' (208). It could be said that César has been 'zugswanged' (forced into playing a losing move) by the firm; but women lose out more. Women are not only the victims of transnational capitalism but also of more deeply entrenched patriarchal formations and attitudes within that market economy. Other female characters in the novel are glimpsed as perfect wives, objects of domestic decoration, or downtrodden secretaries. Today's thrusting, consumer society destroys men and women alike but, in the final instance, woman is man's scapegoat in the power games of public and private life.

There is only one moment of deeply-felt, human communication in this novel; it stands out with lyrical beauty from the surrounding dross. It is not César's flash of recognition when he realizes the impossible nature of his love relationship with Clara, but a much more emotive scene in which he visits his dying mother in hospital. César remembers this moment in the midst of a panic attack when, he believes, he has been betrayed; he returns to the memory of his mother for hope, faith, courage, and confidence in himself. His relationship with his mother had not been easy. During his early childhood, despite their poverty, she had created a magic world for him from bits of painted carboard, a candle under a tablecloth, a banquet of homemade sweets and cakes; she told him anything was possible in life as long as he desired it. But as he grew older César realized 'nothing was possible; his mother had lied' (180). She was no fairy godmother. He resented his reality, the family's poverty and, above all, his mother's passive resignation to subjection. Modelling himself on his father, he treated her with derision in a dictatorial fashion throughout adolescence and distanced himself from her in adult life. The visit to the hospital, then, when he knows she has but weeks or days to live, fills him with dread; he smells her decay, he cannot abide her silent suffering, or the idea of her death. Filled with terror he mumbles he will take her away for Christmas. But at that moment his mother turns slowly towards him, looks him in the eye, takes him by the hand, and tells him to calm down, that he should not be afraid, that it was not so bad after all:

> And so, sheltered in the solid hollow of his mother's hands, while the wolf chased the three little pigs on the television and the afternoon died through the window, César felt he was passing through a door, that he was entering an inner space where, rescued across the distances, the powerful magic of his mother shone intact. And just like when he was a boy, César let himself be calmed by her wisdom and he knew he was saved from the unknown. (185)

It is with difficulty that any other women could possibly relate to César in this way. The relationship between mother and son is unique, irreplaceable. The mother, Montero seems to argue, is man's only source of female love because only a mother demands nothing and gives all. Only in this relationship can power become a non-issue; the 'inner space' afforded by his mother is César's only possible escape from the prison-house of society.

Power is played out in spaces. The settings of the novel are predominantly the office building and César's flat, underlining the transnational capitalist invasion of private and public space and the blurring of the boundaries between them. However, three of the nine chapters take place in Nacho's home, a church, and a hospital out-patient department respectively. This is familiar Montero territory, reminiscent of *Crónica* where an office building, several flats, and a doctor's surgery are also foregrounded. In *Amado amo*, the party scene at Nacho's and the scene with the doctor serve as comic relief verging on the farcical. In the latter, for example, a paranoic César is convinced his appointment has been arranged by the firm to prove he is physically unfit and that the doctor is a spy. It culminates with a half-naked César walking along a busy corridor looking for his clothes. Montero's hallmark is wit and humour and, although macabre at times, it should not be underestimated. Her light-hearted or darker ironies only underscore the seriousness of the novel's message. It is possible, for example, that César is quite right about the appointment; similarly, his suspicion that Nacho's dog was given an item of his clothing to sniff before the party so it would masturbate against his legs and no one else's, might also be well founded. Anything is possible in the devious workings of the company. Less explicable are the absurd, surrealistic episodes of the overflowing bathtub or the accidental death of an (anarchist?) worker that invite a psychological interpretation and again point to the absurd.

Animal imagery communicates effectively the nature of power games. The analogy César draws between himself and a nervous mongrel, and between Nacho and a cocky pedigree who sniffs him out, has already been mentioned. In that same chapter (Chapter 3), César describes himself as a lamb in a lion's den (46), a wounded, bleeding cock forced to fight against a younger, more ferocious opponent (66), and (later) a guinea-pig (202). The butchery referred to by Clara in her description of the Oklahoma land run is extrapolated by César to contemporary society; 'there they all were, running desperately towards nothing, shoving . . ., kicking . . ., mutilating . . ., disembowelling a colleague because he was competing for a plot' (198). This is the law of the human jungle, the surfacing of violent animal instincts, which Montero relates to masculinity – while at the same time suggesting associations between femininity and solidarity. The aggressive pursuit of power is inextricable from desire, eroticism, and sado-masochism. Morton's tyrannical exertion of power is described as seduction, 'perhaps a necessary attribute of power', and when César thinks Morton needs him, he feels like 'an adolescent in love' (142):

> Power possessed that secret energy, that amazing alchemy: the ability to conjoin love and suffering. And so, in every subaltern there seemed to exist an urge to submit to those in authority. Like the dog that licks the hand that beats it, or the Bolshevik peasant who weeps after killing his master. Beloved master. (142–3)

Loving a girl who mistreats you, or treating badly a mother who loves you, are further examples of the inextricability of desire, fear, power, aggression, and humiliation. Fear is the inhuman substance of life; the 'substance of life was a trembling' (144).

Montero explores the idea of a morass of basic human instincts, stemming from anxiety and fear, channelled into rigid social structures in her next novel, *Temblor*. In *Amado amo*, although domination and individualism are associated with masculinity and patriarchy, and collective resistance and humiliation with femininity, it is nevertheless true that César is a victim, and César's mother the one person in the novel who possesses the magical, maternal power to conquer all. In *Temblor* Montero asks what might happen if the tyrants were women and the oppressive social organization a matriarchy? She is thus suggesting that, while there may be a male disposition to violence involving the destruction of the loved one, social hierarchies and elites based on inequalities are oppressive of their own accord. Power corrupts no matter which group wields it and, similarly, power involves its own resistance.

Several further interconnections can be made between *Amado amo* and *Temblor* having to do with power and space. In *Amado amo*, space is of paramount importance and is a prime indicator of personal worth and self-esteem. Within a highly structured but variable social organization, space is power. In the company, the directors have offices and a car park reservation. A person's lack or loss of power is precisely measured and clearly visualized in the amount of space he or she is allotted and, like power, these areas are susceptible at all times to total withdrawal, reduction, or extension. Matías loses his space in the car park and is ousted from his office to share a room with three other disgraced employees. César's office is twice reduced in size by moving the false walls so that he ends up with a 'liliputian office' (93), while the recently promoted Miguel takes over César's half of the window, his cupboard, and his piece of floor; 'punishments and awards were measured in feet of window-pane and metres of fitted carpet' (83). Thus the boundaries between the spaces are in continual flux. For a person to be treated 'en masse' rather than as an individual signifies low status and low self-esteem. This accounts for the low status associated with having to work in a panoptican-like, open-plan office and being susceptible to the gaze of those in authority.[7] The bosses effect their observations not from a single, centre point but from their offices situated around the

7. Foucault, *Discipline and Punish*, 1977, pp. 195–227.

edges of the building. They too can be seen, but only from one side.

Geometrical shapes and structures in the novel point to social stratification and isolation: for example, in Nacho's party Matías stands in the centre of a square foot of loneliness' (46) and César sees himself as a cock enclosed by a circle of spectators from which he cannot break out. The vertical axis of the organization is carefully measured in the painstakingly slow and detailed account of César going up eight floors in a lift (enclosed space) with Morton his boss (71), and then crossing the horizontal axis of the open-plan office (open, observable space) (73–4) to take refuge in his albeit tiny office (enclosed, observable space) with Conchita his resentful secretary. The denial of space means the boundaries of the self are deliberately blurred; at one point César feels as if 'Golden Line was erasing [his] existence, the same way that Stalin erased Trotsky from the pages of the Russian encyclopedia' (189). To have no space means loss of privacy, loss of an individual identity.

At one point, César wakes in the night trapped 'in that nightmare reality where he couldn't recognize himself, or understand where he was, or who he was'; he is the very essence of loneliness, the 'wound of a consciousness lost in the immensity of an alien universe' (201). The whole universe, César believes, is itself hierarchically structured. He visualizes this in eschatalogical terms: angels and archangels, cherubim and seraphim, all conspiring to elbow their way up the Celestial scale, while ranks of devils, Succubus, Incubus and Leviathans, do their best to outdo Lucifer (148). There is no escape. Even the Hare Krishna rival each other over who has the roundest shaved head (168).

Yet, as we have seen, there does exist another, magical space outside the coordinates of César's immediate reality. He senses its presence through his mother, and he aspires to capture it in art. The picture he dreams of painting is an empty room in which the protagonist is the tangible, dank, almost fluid, air. In true Platonic fashion César wants to paint light, space, and shadows, and through them represent the world. He is impeded by the bright sunlight, the harsh light of appearances and rationality which dissolves the secret mysteries of being; 'he had no idea how he could capture in a painting that metaphysical air, that nothing which was so full' (166). This is the intangible, magical world of ideas, ideals, imagination, dreams, and love; it belongs to another dimension beyond the small-minded world of 'collective pillage'

(195) in which César exists and points to idealism in the face of pragmatic materialism. This moment of enlightenment, like the one he experiences with his mother, is what makes César so tragically human, so pathetically small and yet great in his aspirations and possibilities.

If power inheres in a position in space it also inheres in language. The complex, ambiguous semiotic system at play in the firm has been referred to. A gesture, a tone, or a word, becomes a signifier loaded with meaning indicating praise or disapproval, that is, recognition or negation of personhood. In this game, those implicated must respond appropriately or lose. But a correct response depends on an accurate interpretation. This accounts for César's agonizing over the import of Morton's words in the lift: what did the largely phatic 'Hello, César. How are things?' (77–8) really mean? Taking into consideration these particular five words, the tone of voice, the corresponding gestures, the time of day, and the location where the remark was made, César concludes the question was innocuous. His fascination with language leads him to look up the verb 'to dominate' in the dictionary where he finds fifty-one synonyms listed by Montero in alphabetical order. As he reads, César feels as though he is reading a 'page of his own intimate diary' (147); he has experienced all these nuances of subjection and submission. In Foucauldian fashion, power is manifested at all levels, in all situations, in all kinds of interpersonal relationships. In the final instance, it is words and their interpretation which lead to Paula's downfall. She insists on the correct interpretation of the company's rules set down in a text César gives to her, and César is forced to put his signature to a document, drawn up by the company, indicting Paula's (mis)conduct. The company puts words into César's mouth, which will be used against Paula. The misuse of words suggests not only the lack but also the deliberate perversion of information and truth. Throughout the novel, César is only able to communicate effectively, with his mother or with himself, outside the confines of discourse. In speech, he can only communicate with himself. Increasingly, he talks to himself, but he is convinced most people do: 'it was one of those secret vices that everyone practised, like masturbation' (129). Such onanistic behaviour is symptomatic of this self-obsessed social organization and self-defeating narcissism.

The novel, then, points to the need for a new language and a new – possibly magical – space outside patriarchal culture and discourse. In the introduction to her book, *Where the Meanings Are* (New York and London, 1988), Catharine Stimpson writes: 'I have found feminism a space where meanings are . . . Feminism provides a hearing room and a reading room in which to realize how energetic women's engagements with language have been' (xii). *Amado amo* is the kind of sceptical analysis of women in man-made culture Stimpson calls for. In *Temblor* Montero attempts a reconstruction of culture to include women and gender; she attempts what Stimpson calls the 're-designing and designing of cultural spaces' (xix) and engages on a quest for different social formations codes. *Amado amo* is, to date, Montero's most postmodern novel; in *Temblor* she moves from postmodernism to fantasy.

# 6

## Flights of fantasy: the Narrative of the 1990s

### Temblor (Trembling)

*emblor*, 1990, Montero's fifth novel, continues to explore preferred themes yet it is quite unlike her previous work. In fact, the critic Juan Antonio Masoliver declared it was 'an unrepeatable novel, without precedent in Spanish narrative'.[1] On one level it is an adventure tale, a romance fantasy, and a *bildungsroman*. On another, it is an example of feminist specular fiction offering a dystopic vision of a future woman's world. Montero herself refers to the novel as an allegory, an 'emblematic fable' (Glenn, 1990, 282). *Temblor* is set in a post-holocaust age, although the reader does not know this until the final pages of the novel. The setting is strangely familar: an almost medieval landscape, populated with small villages and governed from one central, sacred institution (the Talapot tower) in the capital city, Magenta. Comparisons with ancient city cultures centering on the pyramid or temple, the scene of Aztec-like religious rituals including human sacrifice and execution, are suggested. Montero mentions her admiration of the author Ursula Le Guin, and certainly *The Left Hand of Darkness* and similar science fiction fantasies come to mind.[2] So, too, do the disturbingly futuristic worlds of Huxley, Orwell, and Montero's own *La función Delta*. The world of *Temblor*, the Empire, is a self-contained, 'other' world that does not impinge on 'reality' (the reader's here and now) in

---

1. Juan Antonio Masoliver Ródenas, '*Temblor* de Rosa Montero', *Insula*, 525, September 1990, pp. 19–20. He compares it to Alvaro Custodio's *Mil y ochenta y seis demonios*, and to Cristoph Ransmayr's *El último mundo*.
2. In a conversation with the author. Kathleen Glenn also notices similarities with Ursula Le Guin and picks out the motif of the circular journey and the idea of the end as a new beginning in her review of *Temblor*, in *ALEC*, 16, 1991, p. 401.

any way. In Rosemary Jackson's terminology, it maps a 'duplicated cosmos' (43). The novel is not so much a work of fantasy, therefore, (suggesting a distortion or inversion of reality as we know it) but a magical or marvellous romance. Only through an allegorical interpretation of the novel can the values of the 'real' world be questioned. The narrative voice is impersonal, the events distanced in time and space, the emotional involvement minimal, and reader participation negligible – as is to be expected in this genre. Like Le Guin, Montero builds up 'another universe out of elements of this one, according to dystopian fear and utopian desires' (43). Like Le Guin, too, redemption is an important theme.

The Empire has a history, known only to the power élite, and revealed only towards the end of the novel. After a nuclear explosion survivors encircling the earth on satellites returned to set up a new, egalitarian world. They succeeded for a short while but their population increased so quickly that a pecking order was soon established. This eventually privileged women for their reproductive capabilities and set apart a female élite which became the maximum authority. The female-centred power of the Empire is symbolized, paradoxically, by the great phallic Talapot tower imposing its threatening presence throughout the novel. Thus the tower-block housing the gynaecologist in *Crónica* and the cannibalistic office-world of *Amado amo* are exaggerated to fantastic proportions. Rising three hundred feet over Magenta and divided into an intricate pattern of consecutive inner rings (like Borges's 'Library of Babylonia') the tower functions as the clearly visualized structural organization not of patriarchy, as in Montero's previous novels, but of an even more destructive matriarchy. The female élite wields power despotically in a world governed by fear, violence and aggression. The High Priestess, Ocean, inhabits the uppermost central ring of the tower. Ocean is the latest of a long line of female theocrats and hopes to pass on her power to her granddaughter, Sugar Skin. However, her domain (the Empire) is in crisis; it is gradually dissolving, whole mountains turning into wisps of cloud. No child has been born for years. The power élite seem not to realize the gravity of the situation and refuse to relinquish power. Enter the protagonist of the novel, the young girl Cold Water, who through a long succession of adventures, finally saves herself and the world.

In *Temblor*, as in her other novels, Montero explores a number of issues which are not strictly feminist but more generally existential and metaphysical.[3] She inverts the savage, male-oriented world of *Amado amo*, then takes the result to its logical conclusions. In this visionary world, knowledge is still very much the 'key to power' (241) but reality itself is now no more than 'the representation of our dreams' (244). In other words, the social and political structures of the world of *Temblor* do not emerge from an objective reality but are literally the ideological constructions of a particular dominant sect. This was the case in *Amado amo* where male élites, with which men colluded, created oppressive, capitalist modes of living for themselves and for women by refusing to think differently. The reality in which the characters of *Temblor* live is similarly of their own making; it is the result of a collective delusion or, more precisely, of the delusion of a small sect which is enforced and commonly accepted. If the élite and the people would choose to think and believe differently their reality would change. As Ocean tells Cold Water towards the end of the novel, 'reality, though rebellious, ends up like our dreams' (240). This is a familiar postmodern theme, with metaphysical rather than psychological implications, and rarely articulated from a feminist perspective. Montero dispels any pretensions to a woman-centred utopia in which power relations are structured on a hierarchical, sexually defined basis. To replace patriarchy by matriarchy, to simply reverse the dominant situation, is no solution. Thus the novel constitutes a strong indictment of identity politics and Spanish difference feminism. A revolutionary feminist strategy must experiment with different options which are humanist and aim for a politics of equality. To bring about a new and better society, Montero suggests, women and men must collaborate.

Although the plot of the novel is straightforward, consisting of a sequence or series of events leading to a denouement, the cosmology of its universe is complex and semiotically rich. The novel is circular in structure; scenes are ordered chronologically, and there are few flashbacks. It is divided into four parts; the first three subdivided into numerous short sections (between fifteen and twenty), while Part IV, divided into three sections, functions as an explanatory epilogue. Part I deals with Cold Water's novitiate in Talapot until she escapes; Part II her journey to the

---

3. In the Glenn interview (*ALEC*, 1990) Montero says the novel is 'an adventure novel but metaphysical', p. 283.

North to find Oxygen, the Great Sister; Part III her time with the Uma people; and Part IV her return to Talapot, to destroy the matriarchs five years after her escape. A ten-year period is covered, from when the heroine is twelve until she is twenty-two years old. The language of the narrative is also straightforward and fairly monochord. There is much reported action but little dialogue; the characters have no psychological depth. It will be obvious from this description that *Temblor* marks a turning-point in Montero's work. Gone is the experimentation with narration and discourse, the wit and humour, the caustic repartee. *Temblor* is more solid, but less entertaining. This is a far more serious Montero, a Montero with 'gravitas', looking disenchantedly at a possible future world and offering what some feminists would consider a profoundly conservative vision. Nevertheless, in taking the leap from the familiar, contemporary world of the home and workplace, and from the realist convention, Montero shows great boldness and decision. By using a fantastic framework she can explore more incisively and imaginatively certain ideas glimpsed in her earlier novels, ideas mainly to do with the institution-alization of ideology and structures of power, and the nature of reality. *Temblor* is, therefore, conceptually richer than previous novels, but less fun.

Out of power comes resistance; out of a despotic matriarchy comes the female protagonist, Cold Water – resistance personified. The reader may well ask, to what extent is *Temblor* a feminist novel? On the one hand, it is a woman who saves the world, which is no mean feat. Cold Water receives help from men and women alike but ultimately her objective is achieved single-handedly. She is spurred on by love for her mother and anger at her mother's unnecessary death; the mother-daughter bond is as important in this novel as was the mother-son relationship in *Crónica* and *Amado amo*. All the women in the novel are intelligent and astute, and most are brave and physically strong. The history of women is important too, as is the oral transmission of a rebellious female tradition. The leaders of the clandestine rebel organization who work to overthrow the matriarchy are also women and members of the High Priestess's family: Oxygen, her sister, and Lightning, her daughter. Women, then, embody resistance and struggle against power structures. The novel is also a *bildungsroman* tracing the formation of an adolescent girl from when she starts to menstruate until she conceives a child. In this sense, as Kathleen

Glenn (1991, 401) points out, it follows Joseph Campbells's description of mythological initiation and quest motifs. Unlike Glenn, who believes Cold Water 'does not return with . . . answers to the question of how to save the world from destruction' (401), in my reading of the novel Cold Water is a girl who uses her skills and knowledge acquired in the dominant system to overthrow that same system. At the same time she grows up into a wiser, more self-aware person.

However, women also represent the established, oppressive order. Ocean, Sugar Skin, and the long dynasty of female rulers before them, are as deceitful, ruthless, cruel, and selfish as the men of any patriarchy hitherto known. And while maternal bonding may well be important to Cold Water, Ocean puts her own daughter, Lightning, to death for heading the conspiracy, while Ocean's granddaughter gives the final order in, presumably, her own mother's execution. It could be argued that these women are in every way perverse, but the novel does seem to put forward a totally anti-essentialist, feminist argument. Women do not have specific biologically defined natures or attributes which distinguish them from men: they are no less unjust, violent, and egoistic when placed in positions of power. Basic human characteristics, virtues, and vices are shared by all human beings no matter what their sex. Not surprisingly, the novel places much emphasis on the cultural construction of gender roles. Patriarchal gender roles are reversed in the world of *Temblor*. Here women are perceived as the natural rulers, as more intelligent than men and, furthemore, they possess reproductive potential. Women are believed to be naturally disposed towards the finer mental skills such as hypnosis, telepathy, and telekinesis; men, perceived as inferior, brutish beings, are prohibited from acquiring such skills. The male priests, who do wield a certain amount of authority as teachers in Talapot, cross-dress and wear long gowns like the women. What amounts to anti-sexist sexism is invalidated during the course of the novel, as is the whole concept of female supremacy. Cold Water receives crucial help from several hetero men who either die or suffer for her world-saving cause. Above all, without the uncouth Zao, Cold Water could not have become pregnant and hence restored fertility to a barren land.

A clear example of the invalidation of mere role reversal is Cold Water's relationship with her lifelong companion, Pedernal [Flint]. Both adolescents have been taken into Talapot as novices for future generations of priests and priestesses, but only Cold Water can aspire to the higher ranks and only she is taught hypnosis, because she is a woman. In the 'dialectical dialogue' (Masoliver, 19) which typifies the novel, Pedernal engages with Cold Water in a feminist-like debate on sexual discrimination; only now the usual roles are reversed:

> It's not fair, you can go into the Inner Circle because you're a woman, and I can't, just because I'm a man.
> Cold Water laughed . . .
> It's always been that way, that's the norm . . .
> Rubbish. What have you got that I haven't, how are you better than me?
> Cold Water smiled quietly in the darkness; she could think of lots of examples but she didn't want to offend her companion.
> What do you want me to say, Pedernal? . . . Of course we're different, that's clear.
> Is it? Our bodies are different. That's all . . .
> Don't be stupid, Pedernal. It's quite obvious that you have certain limitations . . . We are mothers, we are the makers of life, answered the girl with a pedantic, haughty smile.
> But we too play our part in all that, don't we?
> But there is no possible comparison. . . . It's our blood, our body, the children are ours . . . (53–4)

Cold Water goes on to explain that men are only a small ingredient in the process of human reproduction; it wouldn't matter if there was only one man as long as there were plenty of fertile women. Men are more violent, simple, and emotional and become dangerous in positions of authority, 'Because you get drunk on power; you have no sense of control or spirituality, you are biologically incapable of learning the occult powers' (55).

The point is, Cold Water does teach Pedernal hypnosis and he shows he is as capable of learning as any woman. Moreover, thanks to him she escapes from Talapot and he is tortured on her behalf. But the fact that Pedernal can practice hypnosis does not mean the power élite change their view of men. They simply allow him to become a priestess; they consider him a woman. Contemporary analogies are clear.

Echoing post-Soviet re-thinking, *Temblor* indicates two directions for the attainment of a new and better world order. First, men and women should return to basic humanist values (such as love and compassion, individual initiative and productive activity), and avoid great ideological schemes. Second, hope, vision, and an awareness of change and flux, should never be lost. Utopian ideals fossilized into the laws and dogma of oppressive ideologies thwart human desire, reason, and imagination: 'Never again the tyranny of the Law, never again brutalizing dogma: to be free, humanity needed to aspire to the omniscience of the gods. Willpower and reason created worlds', thinks Cold Water in the spirit of Nietzsche. Civilizations come and go: 'it is not the repetitive spinning of the Eternal Wheel . . . but a concatenation of different universes. Everything changed, throbbed, flowed' (250). Earlier in the novel Oxygen, the Great Sister, explains to Cold Water that there is no ultimate Order, the universe is governed by contingency, and existence is irrational. But, she adds,

> our weakness is our strength. . . . From the beginning of time human-
> ity has striven to create a destiny for itself. We are only a speck of
> cosmic dust . . . and yet we have pitched our willpower into deadly
> combat with chance. Our pride and our innocence are incalculable.

She goes further:

> That is where out greatness lies: even knowing our insignificance, we
> aspire to the highest. What makes us humans, what differentiates us
> from animals, is precisely that hardfaced ambition to be happy. To
> control our lives and to become our own gods. Like Prometheus, like
> Ulysses . . . at times we manage to influence the course of the universe.
> That is our greatest deed: to set limits to confusion. (171)

Marxist humanism is of significance in this passage and suggests a possible reading of the novel. The critique of a future society in which the masses are exploited by a minority ensconced in an imposing political institution suggests an analogy with the Communist (Soviet) state organization of the late 1980s. Arguably, this developed out of class struggle and was meant to liberate the very masses it finally oppressed. In *Temblor*, the classes or castes are sexually defined. The minority of ruling women not only controls the means of production but also the means of repro-duction. Yet they are no more liberating for all that. In fact, they make the world sterile. Thus Montero offers a further indictment of feminist essentialist positions which argue for women's control of reproduction as the key to a better future for humanity. In *Temblor* this is manifestly not the case.

The issue is explored further. Ocean suggests to the inquisitive Cold Water three reasons why the egalitarian social organization which existed prior to the matriarchy also collapsed. Despite the fact that this brave, new, democratic world lasted centuries without hierarchies of any kind, it was very boring. Then it became overpopulated. Most importantly, certain collective beliefs adhered to over the centuries and created to justify privilege began to shape the way people conceived of reality (241). In the world of *Temblor* this has to do with the 'preservative gaze', a technique originally developed for retaining an image in the mind but which became a means of keeping the (chosen) dead alive and, finally, reality real. Without the 'preservative gaze', it was thought, the world would disappear. Locke's distinction between nominal and real essence would seem to be appropriate here. The world does, indeed, start to disappear during the novel: people lose their faith in the corrupt system and their world disintegrates. Their minds are 'numbed by dogma' (170). Cold Water's task is to show for once and for all that the so-called 'truth' or Law of the Empire and its symbols – the Crystals and the Eternal Wheel – is a complete fabrication; but she must also find an alternative world-view to replace it. The analogy with Soviet state organization is suggestive. A fossilized belief-system, call it religion or ideology, leads to false consciousness and to an inability to effect change. In order to change, a different way of seeing or believing the world is necessary. The High Priestess, Ocean, suggests to Cold Water that the presence of another people on earth, another 'exotic' culture, might indicate the existence of another dream and, therefore, another reality. If that were the case, the world could be saved. This is exactly what Oxygen, the rebel leader, had advised too. Cold Water finds that 'other', but it hardly responds to a feminist utopia.

The people to whom Cold Water turns for new ideas and a different life style are the primitive cavemen, the Uma, residing in the 'Empire's' equivalent to the Third World. They live in the far North, on the margins of the Empire, and know nothing of the Law or the Crystals. Their language is simple and descriptive with few abstract concepts; they have no writing. Their society is patriarchal and led by an old chief; women – considered inferior – give birth and look after the home. Unlike the people of the Empire, the Uma are very fertile. They all die permanently and have no knowledge of the 'preservative gaze', and yet despite or because of this their world remains solid. Their dead are not hurriedly disposed of as in the Empire, rather they are buried in magnificent chambers which rival the Talapot tower in grandeur. The reader is suddenly on familiar ground, but not Cold Water whose woman-centred world is turned upside-down. She is appalled by the fact she has to obey men. In a bout of anger she hypnotises the whole tribe and from then on is treated with caution. Again, there is a certain amount of role reversal. Among the Uma Cold Water should not be allowed to indulge in masculine practices, for example, to kill animals. Of course, she was also forbidden to kill under the matriarchy for different reasons: it was considered inferior for women. But Cold Water has learned humility, self-control, and self-sufficiency, so although her new husband beats her senseless on their wedding night – as is expected of him – she stays with the Uma 'to learn the secret of your strength and perhaps that way to save my people' (180).

The secret is revealed to her when the wife of the chief's son gives birth. The scene, which takes place at night by the camp fire, with the women of the tribe chanting and singing, is witnessed by an astounded Cold Water who suddenly realizes the secret of life:

> That was it . . . that was what terrified the Uma men, what made them subject women to the most abject dependency: the power of women's bodies, the creative gift of their entrails. The strength of life. Humanity gestated in the warm insides of women, in a turbulence of grease and blood . . . .. The Uma females, even as primitive as they were, possessed the essential mystery of existence. (185–6)

What the text seems to indicate at this juncture is that, although gender roles are culturally constructed and arbitrary, and men and women are as human as each other, there is – obviously – a biological difference. Anatomy in no way shapes intelligence, personality, or ability, but women do have the power to create life. Women have the key to the survival of the human race, and the possession of this ultimate power makes all forms of subjection to men trivial in comparison. Although this may seem a concession to essentialism, men are nonetheless deemed to be a necessary part of reproduction – as Pedernal originally pointed out to Cold Water. Cold Water needs Zao to get pregnant and to save her life. What Cold Water learned from her quest was that men also play a key role in humanity's struggle for survival and that any form of hierarchical relationship in which a balance is not maintained between the sexes is ultimately destructive. As Ocean intimates, decadence sets in when the balance of life is broken, when 'the rules of the game are broken' (239). In the end, the world of *Temblor* is saved, but this new epoch in the spiral of human history does not bode well. The leader is now a man, 'El Negro' (The Black Man), one of the rebels. He is virile and ruthless. Cold Water takes herself off to be alone, out of social interaction: 'in some corner of the wide world there had to be a place for herself and her child' (249). Only the mother-child bond is of value in this desolate scenario.

The emphasis *Temblor* gives to epiphany, associated with the overwhelming power of love, and the construction of self-hood, associated with naming, links it to *Amado amo* and *El nido de los sueños*. Reference was made earlier to the scene in *Amado amo* when César realizes in a moment of magic the wonderful power of his mother's love. It lifts him to another dimension, out of the turmoil of the coordinates of time and space in which he was trapped. In *Temblor*, there is a similar scene. It is recounted to Cold Water by her Anterior (her tutor) before she enters Talapot and concerns both revelation and naming. The task of the Anteriors is to pass on to their wards the memory of one special experience. This way part of the Anterior's life survives after his or her death in the ward's memory. The child is given a second name by the Anterior based on that memory. Children, then, have two names; the one they were born with which is replaced by the one received at the age of ten from the Anterior. The bestowing of the second name represents for the child a moment of personal development and functions as a rite of passage to adulthood. The name itself, denoting another's memory, and the ritualistic recounting of that experience, means the child has assimilated another person's key experience. This can mean that men, such as Mo, possess the memories of women (a reversal of the usual situation in which women possess the memories, traditions, and histories of men). The child Talika, then, must separate from mother and home to become Cold Water.

What that name entails is explained to Cold Water by her dying Anterior: the Anterior is lying on her bed next to her husband one spring afternoon after having made love. The sun shines through the window and she perceives, in a brief moment of revelation, the very throb of life: the perfect geometry of the sun's rays on the wall, and the room and all its objects extraordinarily defined. She sees life's very substance. For a moment time stands still. She is overwhelmed with happiness and plenitude. She drinks a glass of iced water to cool herself down, 'And I thought: every time I drink iced water I will remember there was an afternoon when I was able to hold time still' (13). The experience is momentous, hence the memory and Cold Water's name. Language produces (rather than reflects) concepts of reality and the power to name shapes those conceptualizations. Cold Water's view of the world is transformed by the incorporation of her Anterior's experience and knowledge. For her, naming – the assumption of matrilineal identity – involves notions of transcendence. The potential of human love to reach plenitude of another dimension is, as it were, planted as a seed in her mind. Her task is to make it grow.

Cold Water experiences a similar revelation when she is the arms of a man (Mo), and the sense of wonder she feels encourages her to go on with her struggle. She watches a tiny caterpillar make its way up a tree trunk, 'advancing with difficulty, almost imperceptibly'. 'It moved with so much determination, so much infinite certainty', and that caterpillar, she muses,

> was a daughter, a granddaughter and a great granddaughter caterpillar; mother, grandmother and great grandmother of creatures like herself. All with the same genetic pattern, the identical segments . . . Cold Water closed her eyes, dizzy with the implacable order of the world . . . No, the world could not end, said Cold Water to herself, amazed by so much harmony. (128)

It is this microcosmic life-force, female and reproduced through matrilineality, which invokes universal harmony.

The novel, then, posits the substitution of the symbolical name-of-the-father, and all it subsumes, for the name-of-the-mother, matronyms, matriarchal law, matrilineal identity and language (naming) as entrance into matriarchy. Yet the formulation of the female life-force into rationalized power structures is destructive. The problem is how to channel those forces into ordered chaos or, in Oxygen's words, how to 'set limits to confusion' (171). There is no obvious solution. The novel presents a bleak picture of future social organization; Cold Water rejects society altogether when she takes herself off to some remote corner. Only one source of hope is suggested, and that is motherhood and the mother-child bond. Again, Montero seems to be clearing a space between essentialist and non-essentialist positions. This space is fantastic, and as fantasy it is 'disenchanted'; it 'betrays a dissatisfaction with what "is", but its frustrated attempts to realize an ideal make it a negative version of religious myth'.[4] It is hardly surprising that the text asks many questions but suggests few solutions. Ritualistic naming, double names, and double identities (important in *Crónica* and *Te trataré* as we have seen) link *Temblor* to Montero's subsequent novel for children, *El nido de los sueños*. Here the young protagonist also has two names: the one she is known by in the real world, Gabriela, and the one she calls herself in her world of fantasy, Balbalú. Again, in *El nido* the girl must undergo a journey of initiation, a rite of passage, in order to outgrow her name and the self it denotes. It is this rift between signifier and signified, name and meaning, which Montero's fantastic literature of the 1990s explores from a woman-centred perspective.

## *El nido de los sueños* (*The Nest of Dreams*)

Montero published this short novel for children, *The Nest of Dreams*, in 1991. Beautifully illustrated, it came out in Siruela's collection the 'Third Age'. The riddle of the Sphinx provides the epigraph for the novel; the Third Age referring to the mature adult. Similarly, the wording on the book jacket stresses this is Montero's first book 'for readers of all ages'. The book, then, like *Alice in Wonderland*, can be read at several levels: from an adventure story for children, to a tale of fantasy with surrealistic, psychological and ontological implications. In *El nido* Montero continues to explore several issues she engaged with in *Temblor*. The heroine is a young girl who embarks on a circular journey of initiation and shows her mettle by saving a situation despite a series of obstacles. The girl has two names, as did Cold Water; one, Gabriela, belongs to the real world, and the other, Balbalú, to Gabriela's fantasy world. Again, questions relating to the nature of reality are raised; in this story reality is perceived as the creation of human desire and imagination. Language is crucial in this process: to name is to create; language is the means of producing meaning. And, again, the construction of feminine identity through an adolescent rite of passage is a prime concern. However, there is one main

4. Rosemary Jackson, *Fantasy. The Literature of Subversion*, London and New York, 1981, p. 18.

difference between these two works of fantasy. Unlike *Temblor*, a narrative of the magical and marvellous, *El nido* has to do with the uncanny and the objectification of unconscious anxieties. *El nido* is concerned with the dreams and delusions of the psyche of one individual and her subjective reality, while *Temblor* explores the trickier concept of collective delusion or ideology.

The world of *El nido* falls within what Todorov termed the fantastic/uncanny (Jackson, 32); that is, it recounts strange events which have a subjective origin. The narrative unfolds on two planes indicated by the incongruous chapter numbering. The story begins and ends in a contemporary, real world (Chapters I, II and III), while the fantastic adventures take place in the world of dreams, or rather, nightmares (Chapters 1–8, followed by another Chapter 1) in a section located between Chapters II and III. The resulting structure is a circle within a circle. The text explores in greater detail a comment made by Ocean in *Temblor*: 'reality ends up adapting itself to our dreams, and sometimes to our nightmares' (241). Certainly, the heroine's wishes come true. However, her dream-world turns out to be a dystopic and horrific, psychic reality. A literal rendition of this oneiric world produces a didactic dream narrative in which a girl does not step through a threshold as such but becomes trapped in a dangerous game of her own making. She cannot escape her own mental schemes, the labyrinth of her mind. Gabriela learns a lesson: not to envy others but to be confident and happy with what she has and with who she is. To be able to do this, though, she first has to gain a sense of self. Thus the story can be read as one of female psychological development. The protagonist brings together the various con-flicting images of her self, still separated at the outset of the adventure. Her self-image is twofold: the intrepid Balbalú (of the unconscious or imaginary) and the faceless Gabriela (of the conscious or real). Her conscious image of herself, an unattractive, boring girl with her feet in the clouds, responds to the image she perceives reflected by the gaze of others. The story recounts the maturation of a subject with low self-esteem who gains a sense of self and psychological vitality. Having learned the grass is not greener on the other side, Gabriela is able to grow up.

As is usual in this genre the story is told in the third person by a distanced narrator in the realist convention. Fairy-tale motifs centre on the wood or magical forest. The story begins with Gabriela, the sixth of eleven children, being abandoned by her family in a dark, cold forest like a lost babe. It is all a mistake; the family had merely not missed her and had started for home. They return and all is well. While she is alone in the wood, however, Gabi becomes acutely aware of how lonely she is; she receives little attention from her busy mother, is the odd one out among her siblings because she is the middle child, and has few friends at school. She dislikes herself and her humdrum home in a fifth floor flat. She is particularly jealous of a classmate, a girl called Reyes, who is an only child, lives in a detached house on an up-market estate, has a room of her own, and is clever and pretty.

Gabi rejects her banal reality for a world of fantasy where she is someone else, Balbalú. The more introverted Gabi becomes, such as after being left in the woods, the more she invents. Her imaginary world has its basis in reality as we know it and in the language used to describe that reality. However, like the Anteriors of *Temblor*, Gabriela assumes the power of naming. She renames the familiar buildings and streets of the area where she lives to create a female-defined, imaginary landscape which is the inverse of her everyday world. For example, the motorway is renamed Orgen in the fantasy world and becomes a black river ('orgen' is 'negro' [black] back to front). The world of Balbalú, rather than being the mirror-image of the one Gabi inhabits, is the reverse side of the mirror. The dark and nasty river of oil, Orgen, is still strangely reminiscent of a motorway, and the witch, Mencar, is very like Carmen the school janitor's wife. The naming of each portion of the imaginary world involves a ritual whereby Gabi writes out the new name on a piece of paper. Once labelled, the place (a building, a road, a gully) becomes part of her psychic landscape, 'once a place was named that place lasted for ever' in the 'geography she had invented' (25); 'to name a place' was 'to create it' (26). As in *Temblor*, language (the unconscious) creates reality; the distinction between nominal and real or ontological essence is maintained. But as the gap between name and meaning widens, so reality slips into nightmare.

Gabi's nightmare starts when she names the block of flats where she lives 'Zascatún', the city of ruins. Her motivation is revenge on her family for leaving her in the woods. This deep desire and the ritualized naming process result in the imaginary dominating the symbolic. What she imagines comes 'true', and home becomes a wasteland. The destruction of the family, society and the logic of conventional reality allows Gabi to enter the uncanny – the space of repressed anxieties and fears – as Balbalú. Like Dorothy in the film and book *The Wizard of Oz*, Gabriela is accompanied by strange creatures, a dog and an old chair, who have voices and personalities. Boundaries between the human, animal, and inanimate are thus broken down, differences collapse in a threatening, grotesque world. Balbalú's psycho-mythical journey of self-discovery takes her from the ruins of her former home to her dream's desire, 'The nest of dreams', which is the house where Reyes lives in the middle of a wooded estate guarded by keepers. A series of obstacles must be overcome in a world where the familiar has been transformed into the unfamiliar, and yet remains intact as if in an inverted allegory. First, Balbalú must cross the evil Orgen river (motorway) which threatens to engulf her. Then, mad, flying creatures (tennis balls) attack her on the flat, red desert (tennis court). With the help of Mencar, the witch, Balbalú escapes into the wood surrounding the 'nest'. She meets the ferocious dragons (the keepers) of the estate. A knight in shining armour (her school friend Carlos) helps her. Finally, she sees the house in the centre of the wood and, like Hansel and Gretel, approaches it unsuspectingly. By then she has learnt that 'the landscapes she had invented turned out to be, seen from inside, frankly sinister' (73), and that there exists only one means of escape from her nightmare. This involves destroying the pieces of paper on which the invented names are written. Once the sign, the written word, is destroyed, so too is the imagined reality.

The protagonist's most revealing experiences, inscribed in spectral imagery, involve her own self-image. While crossing the Orgen, Balbalú sees her reflection in the dark liquid; the reflection mocks her and tries to pull her into the murky depths. Narcissism, cast as evil, threatens to destroy the developing self. On another occasion, in Mencar's cave, the witch holds up a magnifying glass to Balbalú and tells her she can see two girls in it, one with no face and one with her feet in the clouds: 'they are just the same as you, they are half made or half unmade, and they look very sad' (76). Double identity and the 'divided self' are thus foregrounded once more and, as Rosemary Jackson writes, 'it is precisely this subversion of unities of "self" which constitutes the most radical transgressive function of the fantastic' (83). However, when she finally reaches her dream's desire, the house in the wood, Balbalú sees her reflection in water. This time it is not grotesque or fractured, but upside-down, suggesting a coherent self-image but skewed. These scenes all point to the unconscious projections of hidden anxieties and distorted representations of one's own image. Mencar also reminds Balbalú she has a past history; the secret is to know her origins, then she will know her destination (77). This was something Bella had to come to terms with in *Te trataré* when she attempted to remember the house she grew up in. It brings into question the girl's relationship with the family and her mother in particular.

At the crisis-point of the dream narrative Balbalú is propelled inside the head of Reyes, an only child with an over-protective mother. Balbalú finds she can hear Reyes thinking and – much to her surprise – she realizes Reyes is as unhappy as she is. Reyes envies Gabriela because Gabi is free, independent, and has numerous siblings. Reyes is so unhappy she paints a picture of a train with a rock on the line so the train will crash. Balbalú escapes from Reyes's head and finds herself on that very train travelling on the railway of her own invention. The train passes what was Gabriela's house and she sees herself looking out of her bedroom window in the 'real' world. This time her image of herself is whole and undistorted. Escaping imminent destruction on the train, Balbalú is plunged into a strange cloud. She has lost her bearings completely (in *Temblor* Cold Water suffers a similar experience when she loses all sense of time and space in the cloud of nothingness). She looks down at herself once more: she cannot see her own face, of course, but she can see her feet in the clouds. This final image of herself joins her previous self-image with the image the gaze of others reflect back. She has constructed an identity by resolving her multiple selves into one unified subject.

Only after throwing three sixes is Balbalú able to leave the world of contingency and land back at the beginning of the frightening game of her own invention. Her adventures are over, but as the Goose reminds her, hers is not the only game. Other (existential) games involve death. But, 'if you want something strongly enough you'll achieve it' (131), says the Goose. Gabi wants to go home and she manages to do so by re-creating the 'real' world through language. She sticks a label 'Gabriela' on the door of her block of flats and, as this is the first time she has ever written out her name in full, the implication is she accepts her newly constructed identity. She returns to the family, to her mother, a wiser and grown-up girl. She feels 'sure and satisfied' (146). Next time, she thinks, she will invent an ocean. Montero reads the story thus:

through her imagination the girl discovers things about herself. In this sense there is an initiation process. *The girl dreams herself as she is* [sic] and she learns that desire is something which is always outside of ourselves, that it is an unreachable fantasy . . . She intends to go on inventing and thanks to invention and the wisdom of fantasy she grows up, becomes more mature, and is happier in the end (my italics).[5]

A feminist reading of another kind might be more ambiguous. First, the family unit of patriarchal society is reaffirmed; its destruction does not bode well for the adolescent girl. Many feminists would consider the site of the girl's femininity ('the girl . . . as she is') to be outside symbolic, patriarchal social relations and the language that empowers them. But this world is depicted as horrific and life-threatening. Second, the skewed images of the girl's reflected self in the dream narrative suggest representations which falls outside those of masculine-defined rationality (indeed, suggest the negative of such representations) and yet they too are horrific. Arguably, it is precisely to the chaotic, fluid, and variable world of the unconscious and the feminine libidinal economy that the girl should look to undermine phallocentric constraints. On the other hand, it could be argued that the protagonist has no other option than to do what she does during her developmental journey, that is, to encounter the dark desires and fears of the unconscious and resolve them by renewing her place in the signifying chain of language. Only within signification, only in a world which makes sense, can she avoid psychosis and death and live constructively. Gabriela compromises, then, and returns to the world as we know it. But the fact that she is now aware she can 'escape' through her imagination to another infinite plane of reality suggests that her journey has not been in vain.

### Bella y oscura (Beautiful and Dark)

The above two works of fantasy, one metaphysical the other psychological, explore reconstructions of femininity and inversions of patriarchal relations in the unreal worlds of the marvellous and uncanny. Both are subversive to a degree, but neither offers a workable, feminist alternative for the society we

5. Catherine Davies, 'Entrevista a Rosa Montero (Madrid, 22 de enero de 1993)', *JHR*, 1, 1992–3, pp. 383–8.

live in. Montero's most recent novel, *Bella y oscura* (*Beautiful and Dark*), 1993, eschews the epic landcapes and metaphysical flights of *Temblor* as well as the psychoanalytical focus of *El nido* but is equally open-ended and enigmatic, purportedly combining the urban realism of *Te trataré* with the fantasy of *Temblor* (book jacket and interview with Montero, *JHR*, 1993).

In what is predominantly a realist novel, an adult, female narrator recounts in the first person a singular episode of her childhood, her first learning step in the process of growing up. Baba, after having spent some years in an orphanage, is taken to live with her grandmother, aunt, uncle and cousin, to await the return of her father. Several months later, towards the end of the novel, the father finally meets his daughter with unexpected results. Meanwhile, Baba has experienced, on the one hand, the harsh reality of the urban underworld and, on the other, the marvellous magic of the strange Lilliputian figure, Airelai. It is through Airelai (a character reminiscent of Torbellino in *Temblor*) that magic is introduced into an otherwise contemporary world. The book jacket, displaying the lurid exaggerations of a painting ('The Street') by George Grosz, reaffirms connections with 'magical realism' in as much as the German expressionists first coined the term. However, Montero denies her novel has anything to do with the magical realism of Latin American authors Gabriel García Márquez or Isabel Allende (*JHR* interview) and, indeed, the magic of *Bella y oscura* is shown to be no more than fake illusion.

The story is set in a Barrio (district) on the margins of a large city, next to the rubbish tips, the shanty towns, and the airport. It is focalized through the innocent Baba who gradually discovers (along with the reader) first, her family's dark, criminal past and, second, the web of deceit spun by the dwarf, Airelai. The imposing grandmother, Doña Bárbara, the cruel uncle, Segundo, his meek wife, Amanda, and astute child, Chico, are virtually confined to the Barrio and are constantly threatened by gangs and thugs from the surrounding violent world, as were the women in *Te trataré*. They live in a boarding house, bought on arrival in the Barrio, and Segundo and Airelai, magicians by profession, make a living by staging a nightly performance in a club owned also by the family. Time passes and they all wait patiently for Máximo, Doña Bárbara's eldest son and Baba's father, to escape from jail and meet them. The wait is interminable and dangerous: Segundo disappears and returns with his cheek deeply scarred; Airelai turns to prostitution so the family can survive in his absence; the house where they are staying burns down in a fire probably started by Segundo; Doña Bárbara dies soon after having lost all her belongings; Chico – petrified of his father – runs away; and Baba is accosted by 'El Portugués' who wants her to find out where Segundo is hiding a large sum of money. Knowledge of the money gradually comes to light. By accident, Baba discovers Segundo's hiding place and confides in Airelai. At last, Máximo escapes from jail and returns, not so much to see his daughter (who he speaks to only briefly), but to recover the money and make off with his lover, Airelai. In a final showdown, Airelai shoots Segundo and she and Máximo escape with the money on a plane bound for Canada while the unsuspecting Baba still waits patiently for her father in the village square. But Segundo had planted a bomb in the case full of money and the plane explodes over the Barrio. Baba, who sees the explosion in the night sky, believes it is her lucky Star (Estrella) come at last. On this note of calm and tragic irony the novel ends.

Although three-quarters of the novel's thirty-two short sections are told by Baba, two sections are narrated by Chico (recounting his escape from the Barrio and describing the murder of Segundo) and six sections by the inimitable Airelai. It is Airelai's presence and voice which counter the drab and sordid world of dirty dealings and crime. The exotic tales, ancient myths and legends she recounts intersect the here and now of the realist narrative with flashes of timeless wonder; her words create a world of beauty and transcendence in the midst of horror. She tells Baba of her life in the exotic East, tales of children who speak in the womb, of magic charms, prodigies, and prelapsarian bliss. Above all, she confesses her passion for the man she is waiting for. As Baba grows up, she acquires through Airelai a feminist consciousness of her own worth, innate power, and potential. But what Baba perceives as magic and fantasy is, for the reader, no more than fallacy and deception. Through sleight of words Airelai constructs her own illusory identity through discourse; as she says herself, people can 'narrate themselves', they 'invent their own existence' (22), 'often the story of an event is more real than reality' (81). The magic show with Segundo is an obvious example of illusion, but as deceptive are the so-called charms cast on 'El Portugués' and Segundo, and the dwarf's apparent faith in the lucky Star. If, from the point of view of the naive narrator, Airelai is the personification of perfection, she can also be read as a not so wonderful manipulator with a gift for spinning tales. However, a one-sided reading would defeat the objective of the novel. Airelai represents ambivalence; she is a goddess and a devil (83) claiming 'we humans all have within us the potential for being divine and diabolical' (82–3), she is a mundane prostitute and a fabulous sorcerer, she embodies life itself, she is 'a miniature of life' (52), beautiful and dark. Thus notions of absolute truth, and polarities of goodness and evil are destabilized. In a Nietzschean sense, moral values are seen to depend on who is speaking and where. The four adult characters who propel the action forward (Doña Bárbara, Airelai, Segundo, and Máximo) are both good and bad (only the children are innocent) and their pursuit of knowledge (the whereabouts of the money), power, and immortality leads to murder and malice. At the same time, however, as in *Temblor, Amado amo* and *La función Delta*, the women glimpse brief moments of sublime beauty and love. As Montero says, 'what I wanted to capture . . . was the fascination and the splendour [of life] and, at the same time, the horror that hides beneath' (*JHR* interview). The unfixing of essential truths and the affirmation of ambivalence is continued throughout the novel in the recurrent contrasts of dark and light. The Barrio, the club, the red-light district, and the house are all ordinary, banal places in the light of day but at night they are both magical and dangerous, mysterious and sordid. Darkness can connote the revelation of beauty, as the house in the moonlight (48), and light indicate the masking of ugliness, as in Violet Street where women make money from 'dirty things' (171) under gaudy, fluorescent lights. A single image of light and dark recurs in several contexts signifying unreachable desire and perfection: sunlight sparkling on the surface of dark water (a lake, pond, fountain). But beauty is no absolute state, it depends on the viewer's perception. Doña Bárbara, for example, sees in the dirty water of a fountain 'the liquid reflection of the sun, that sparkle of gold . . . on the slimy, dusty, black surface of the stagnant water' (132). In other words, as Airelai says, 'hell is not a place but a state. A poison we carry within us' (120). In the Barrio 'everything is relative' (66). Nevertheless, the grandmother and the dwarf do experience moments of sublimity and thus dare to defy their 'inevitable' (148), 'unavoidable' (149) biological destiny. Airelai, furthermore, has the gift to recreate beauty with words. In a world where language is detached from representation, where moral values are slippery, and reality no more than shifting surface images of light and dark, women survive and are transfigured through the power of words and the power of love.

Given these philosophical premises, can *Bella y oscura* be considered a feminist novel? First, three of the four adults living in the house are women. At one point, when Segundo disappears, with the exception of the boy Chico, they form an all-female community. The grandmother and Airelai are strong, positive role models for both Baba and Chico. Even Chico wants to grow up like Doña Bárbara (137) who confronts two cut-throats with a gun, the same gun Airelai uses to kill Segundo. Together, the women brave the threats from outside the home, not by attacking, but by resisting. They put on a 'demonstration of strength' by carrying on with their lives as if everything were normal (89). In addition, they have hidden individual strengths. The tall and manly grandmother, who throughout the novel is associated, like a witch, with cats and graveyards, draws her vigour from memory. After the tangible signs of those memories (photographs, letters, clothes) are burned in the fire, she slowly dies. One memory in particular enables her to rise above mortal decay and imperfection, the memory of love. 'I was always bad, less so with him. I was always too big and clumsy, less so with him. I was always selfish, less so with him', she muses, 'Unfortunate are those who have never known love' (75). Love is beauty, and Doña Bárbara resists death by absorbing the beauty of nature, by watching the play of sparkling light on the surface of water. More important in this respect is Airelai. Like the grandmother she is valiant and intelligent, but she is also beautiful, ageless, and fantastic. Her power stems also from the memory of love. She remembers watching her lover (presumably Máximo) asleep:

> And in those moments the world acquired a perfect geometry, a visible order which I felt I could understand. I was in my place, in the exact place which corresponded to me in the universe, in the same way as all the other creatures of the planet were in their precise place . . . I could see and understand everything in that moment of equilibrium . . . I was always weak, less so with him. I was always a dwarf, less so for him. (149)

Airelai has two further sources of strength: awareness and

language. She knows she is small, unlike the majority of people; 'that is my power, consciousness' (53). Her greatest gift, however, is 'the magic power' (80) of language. Because she spoke in the womb, she claims, she was chosen to be a goddess as a child. What all gods have in common is 'the word', 'with words they created worlds' (80). This way Airelai creates herself as well as visions of wonder and hope for Baba. Generally speaking, then, women are associated with strength, beauty, care, and intrigue; men with violence, cruelty, ugliness and lust. Sisterhood is important; together the women of the family resist male violence, unlike the wife of El Portugués who is forced to bury her child alive. Motherhood and mothering is less important. Doña Bárbara is a bad mother to Segundo, Baba's dead mother is mentioned only briefly, and Airelai cannot conceive. Only the close relationship between Amanda and her son Chico points to a better future; indeed, apart from Baba, they are the sole characters to survive.

Nothing, not even love, is without its dark side in this novel. Baba has to learn that lesson, too. Doña Bárbara speaks of love but she is cruel to her son. Airelai is beautiful but treacherous. Love may well lead the dwarf to clairvoyance, but it also leads to ruthlessness. As she says, and demonstrates, 'I would be capable of anything: of murder and treachery' for love (149). Passion is an illness of the soul, 'a bright evil which deceives you with its sparks of colour while it devours you' (146). Sexual pleasure is related to pain and death (149). Language, the very substance of illusion, constantly deceives. Airelai's maestro was trapped and killed by his own words (22). 'The word made us accursed and human' (181), declares Airelai in her version of the fall of Man. According to this legend, Paradise was inhabited by giants living in perfect symbiosis with dwarves who they carried on their backs. The understanding between each couple was such that there was no need for language. The creatures were immortal, without gender; 'they lacked sex, I mean gender did not exist' (179). But one dwarf loved its corresponding giant so much that it wanted to remember their moments of pleasure and to do so drew a scene on the bark of a tree. Thus was constituted a sign, a memory, time, and the past, and from this, desire and anguish hitherto unknown. Desire lay in the dwarf's mouth and became language, the dwarf's first words to the giant being 'I want you to tell me you love me'. At that point Paradise was lost. After the advent of words, memory, and time, human beings were incomplete parts always desiring the whole. Language, then, 'is evidence of our humanity' (181) and our limitations. Like love, it is a double-edged weapon. Baba experiences the deception of language and love when finally, after months of waiting, she meets Máximo. Before moving on, the father speaks one word to her, Baba, a word which brings her memories of pre-oedipal bliss and the pain of its loss. The word 'Baba' is itself deceptive. Baba had thought it her secret name for herself, but on the photograph her father gives her of her grandmother as a child she reads 'To Daddy, from Baba'. Baba was Doña Bárbara's name. Baba's final act of defiance is to destroy the image and the words by dropping the photograph in the fountain, thus making way for her own identity. Ultimately, she draws her strength not from her father – who has betrayed her – or her grandmother, but from her faith in the Lucky star, the product of Airelai's words. The appearance of the star, in fact the exploding plane, enables Baba to believe 'life is sweet and that our desires are always fulfilled'. Faith may be deceit, but illusion and reality are commensurate.

If, from a feminist point of view, language, love, and illusion are slippery concepts, less so is the female body. Airelai refers to women's innate potency as 'the power of the transition to life and to death, blood, and what has no words' (125) and compares it to men's power which is 'of rust and iron, causality and territory' (126). She uses the natural force of menstrual blood in certain potions, and – as a prostitute – she uses her sexuality to charm men. Similarly, women's strength lies in hidden rather than revealed knowledge. To survive, they must keep secrets 'because our outer appearance responds to what others know of us, but really we are what others don't know we are . . . I am above all, what you don't know about me' (96). Baba's almost esoteric knowledge, learned from Airelai, is quite different from her cousin Chico's. The astute and street-wise Chico, who cannot understand Airelai, accuses Baba of not knowing anything because 'you're a girl' (32), by which he means the unwritten laws of the Barrio, his territory, the here and the now of the real world. But even in these cases affirmations of feminism are dubious. As already mentioned, Airelai's charms do not work – menstrual blood notwithstanding, her Lucky star is a disaster, she deludes Baba. Chico entertains no such delusions regarding his father, mother or Airelai. He is the only one to escape from the Barrio, by using his wits; he is the one who brings his family's welfare to the notice of the proper authorities; he is the only witness of the final showdown to survive and to tell Baba the 'truth' of her father's and Airelai's betrayal. Perhaps the novel's message is as inconclusive as Airelai's: 'Men are an enigma for women and women for men. Males and females are separate, secret planets turning slowly in the blackness of the universe; and when their orbits cross, sparks fly' (176).

# Conclusion

I n her book *Mujer y poder político* (*Woman and Political Power*), 1992, leading Spanish feminist Lidia Falcón attributes the demise of the Feminist Movement of the 1970s and 1980s in Spain (and elsewhere) primarily to internal dissension (See introduction). She indicates three main points of conflict: Marxist versus difference feminists; hetero versus lesbian feminists; double militancy feminists versus independents. In her account, difference (lesbian, independent) feminism is rendered completely apolitical, whereas political feminism implies heterosexuality, and left-wing party membership (534). Social feminists of 'double militancy' persuasion, she writes, 'became the worst enemies of feminism' (520).

Falcón is well known for her outspoken, often extreme views and most women writers distance themselves from her ideas (Nichols, 156–7). Nevertheless, it is interesting to note how Montserrat Roig and Rosa Montero took on board these very same issues and focused on the relationship between socialism, feminism, and political and domestic organization, particularly in their early work. These writers voiced a strong inside critique not only of the sexist practices of left-wing political parties but of other, more obvious Spanish patriarchal institutions (from the family and the Church, to the nightclub and the workplace). They thus questioned and subverted traditional male-centred relations, values and myths. Roig's political sortie was more sustained, perhaps, because she was five years older than Montero and had already published two works of fiction before Franco's death in 1975. She experienced censorship directly and had participated more fully in the political turmoil of the 'transition' period. By the early 1980s, however, the topic of double militancy and the politicization of private lives is a less urgent topic in the work of both writers. Higher on their agenda were issues relating to the construction of gender roles, male and female desire and sexuality,

Conclusion

female subjectivity, power, and the possibilities of different, woman-centred forms of social organization. Towards the end of the decade, both Roig and Montero gradually distanced themselves from their early realist, semi-confessional narrative and began to experiment more boldly with pastiche, allegory and fantasy. This tendency bears out indications of a similar more general movement from realism to fantasy, horror, the gothic and the bizarre in the European female-authored novel of the 1980s.[1] It is useful at this point to refer to Rosa Montero's lucid account of the development of female-authored fiction in the West ('Escribiendo en la luna' ['Writing on the Moon']) in which she pinpoints four stages in the 'conquest of the literary voice' (8): first, the pre-twentieth-century 'dark-ages', when women writers were obliged to imitate men to achieve success; second, the more recent 'search for one's own space' represented by Virginia Woolf; third, the post-1950s (post-1960s in Spain) period when, for the first time and thanks to women's social advancement, women writers were no longer perceived as the exception to the rule; and fourth, the most recent stage, 'the conquest of creative freedom' (11). In the 1960s, 'testimonial' or semi-autobiographical, confessional literature predominated. 'It was as if we needed to talk of our reality; of those murmurs which had never been considered voices previously. I am thinking of one novel which is emblematic in this sense: Doris Lessing's *The Golden Notebook*' (9). Such novels, Montero writes, were characterized by their realism, pessimism, and rejection of romantic love; the women were inevitably lonely and the men harmful. She includes her first two novels in this category and clearly we could include Roig's trilogy too. Montero continues: 'this confessional literature restricted me. I needed more space, more imagination' (10). Like the other women writers of her generation, she began to experiment. 'We women novelists, in Spain and elsewhere, are starting to write all kinds of works in all kinds of genres; historical, suspense, erotic, westerns, fantastic, allegorical, satirical or realist . . . The world is ours' (11). Although this is certainly the case, arguably the early work of both writers – the hybridization of Roig's narrative collage and the chaotic breathlessness of Montero's chronicle – was more formally

1. See C. Davies, 'Foreword', in *The Language of a Thousand Tongues. Contemporary European Fiction by Women*, special issue of *Forum for Modern Language Studies*, 28, 4, 1992, pp. 301–3.

Conclusion

transgressive than the later fiction. Certainly the later works were more readily accepted into the literary canon.

Roig's *oeuvre* is firmly positioned within the Catalan literary tradition and veers back, again and again, to questions involving the representations of history and national identity from a woman-centred perspective. Montero is more concerned with postmodern systems of thought, with moral and existential choices in a hostile and alienating contemporary world. As indicated in the Introduction, to explain the present Roig looks too the past, Montero to the future. Interestingly, despite obvious differences, the figure of the mother is important in the work of both authors. Lidia Falcón, on the other hand, theorizes women's seeming incapacity for solidarity in terms of political and symbolical matricide. The 'mother-figure' has been killed off throughout history and in everday life, she claims; accordingly, women do not share a group identity or a class consciousness. They embrace 'the ideology of genocide . . . which they are led to . . . by the patriarch' (435). But, as we have seen, the mother is clearly reinscribed and reclaimed in the fiction of Montserrat Roig and Rosa Montero. Roig deconstructs the traditional bourgeois Catalan family in order to free the voices of its women (mothers, daughters, sisters) silenced for generations. The relationships between all members of the fictional families – especially between mothers and daughters – are fraught with repressed antagonism; family unity is exposed as a myth sustained by the compliance of women who hide their inner worlds from public view. Roig's long-term project was outlined in the moving epilogue to the early work ¿*Tiempo de mujer?*, entitled 'Daughter and Granddaughter of Silence'.

> Daughter and granddaughter of silence, little by little my clamour turns to words. A sorceress cradled in what she knows, I search for the precise word, the precise voice to give shape to what was never before expressed.
>
> Daughter and granddaughter of silence, my words only gather what has impregnated the innerweavings of walls, words banished from yellowing sheets and from bedcovers that smell of thyme and lavender, deathly sobs that returned skywards in the smoke of all the kitchens of the world, the words that come to me across the centuries and from bedrooms of fearful silence, through the net curtains that droop with boredom.
>
> I only transmit messages, the messages of sorceresses who died sighing for a diabolical love, the messenger of so many words which

faded before they were born, that hung in the air, words that waited for the breath of art. I am yours, quiet words, daughters and granddaughters of silence, I return to you without vanity or pretence. If you like, I will be small, they would say ephemeral. But you and I know that perhaps the moment has arrived to recover the instant when the earth was licked by water. I know in my house, in my little room, you have kept the secret safe, a secret they would say is childish. But you and I know the secret has not died of starvation nor has it been destroyed by the hunter's fire. And that is why the mother will not disappear, nor the grandmother, nor the great grandmother. Thanks to you I am no longer Ariadna, I have become Teseo, but a Teseo who will be free and will remember that Araidna existed; he will not renounce her.

Thanks to you, words that were never expressed through art, today I dare to go alone into the labyrinth. You guide my silences and the clamour that at last sounds. Now I know the labyrinth is not the prison they said was my destiny, but that the labyrinth marks the existence of us all. Now, at last, I do not fear the labyrinth. (299–300)

Roig opens the doors of the Eixample houses and gives public expression to the words of the female occupants, for too long ignored or disdained. She considers new ways in which women can relate to each other outside the 'bars'['rejas'] of imposed social and familial paradigms ['patronos'] (*Dime que me quieres*, 41). Moreover, the Eixample house not only represents female oppression; it stands for class inequality because it is a microcosm of hierarchical social division (*Dime*, 51). And by challenging the Catalan bourgeois family Roig undermines the very foundations of Catalan nationalism. Señor Malagelada, the most traditional of Catalanists, is also the most outrageous transgressor of 'civilizing' family values. Zeus-like, he creates his own offspring and perpetuates his own values through incest with his daughter. Finally, he must accept the 'idea that an ideal Catalunya does not exist' (*Dime*, 168). In her last three works of fiction in particular Roig questions the basic tenets of a middle-class, Catalan nationalist exclusivism. Catalan women such as Mar ('Mar') and Virginia (*La voz melodiosa*) search for an alternative order – without success. In this sense, although Roig's work forms part of the Catalan literary canon it is also highly critical of the nationalist programme and consequently multiply subversive. Women's voices are certainly heard and heeded but not all Catalan critics like what women say. Women's discourse endangers the cohesion of the collectivity. From a radical feminist perspective, Roig tentatively considers lesbian alternatives. She writes, in *Dime que me quieres*: 'today we women have discovered female friendship, female complicity, and shared secrets at last . . . and we have confused friendship with love. Love is too cruel to possess the tenderness of friendship . . . I love women, some women, too much to fall in love' (*Dime*, 13–14). In her fiction, the female characters (often the narrators and the implied author) find it difficult to abandon equality politics altogether and suffer from a social conscience. Radical feminism is important but identity politics alone is not the answer.

Montero's fiction is more varied, moving from social realism to parody, fantasy and magical realism. Her narrative style, though, remains predominintly realist. Her fiction is less self-conscious than Roig's, but – like Roig – she raises a range of important feminist issues for public debate; women's control of reproduction, male violence, sexual harassment, matriarchal power, and female sexuality and desire. Her first novel exposed the subjection of women in post-Franco Spain. She, too, presents an inside critique of double militancy and suggests the possibility of 'another way of relating to others . . . other ways of living' (*La función Delta*) although homosexuality is kept very much in the margins, represented by secondary characters such as Cecilio and Tadeo, or Paulo Pumilio. Several recurring features distinguish Montero's work as a postmodern reworking of feminism. It inscribes diversity, engages in a critique of a patriarchal systems of thought and de-legitimizes master-narratives and cultural myths. The characters consistently reconstruct their shifting identities by the frequent name-changing and theatrical performance. But the feminist perspective is not lost. Women are shown to be consistently oppressed by insidious social structures and ideologies. Montero offers two apparently contradictory solutions: one is transcendence (thus reinstating the Enlightenment modern project) and the other is motherhood without matriarchy (thus reinstating difference without essentialism). The interrelated discourses of metaphysics and biology thus make for another feminist alternative.

In Montero's novels the hard-pressed characters experience an almost mystical, transcendental moment of revelation when they glimpse eternity. Lucía sees eternity, César has a vision of plenitude which he wants to capture in his painting, and Corcho

Conclusion

Quemado [Burnt Cork, the tutor] witnesses a moment of perfection in *Temblor*, 'I tried to remember that there was a moment one afternoon when I was able to stop time' (13). These passages inscribe what one critic calls 'a vision of "moreness"' (Gunew, 344). There *is* a truth, a perfection, another order to which humanity (men and women) can aspire, manifested through epiphany. It is neither socialist nor matriarchal, it defeats categories, but it does have something to do with the overwhelming power of love, mother-love, and the mother-child bond. Cold Water's glimpse of eternity is directly associated with matrilineality when she sees the caterpillar advancing (128). The despairing César holds his mother's hand and is transported to another dimension. Bella, Lucía, and Gabriela all take strength from their mothers and their childhood home. Empowerment of the mother, however, does not legitimize essentialism; the dystopic vision in *Temblor* is a vigorous indictment of matriarchy, feminist elitism, and essentialism. It puts paid to the idea of a mere inversion of patriarchal relations.[2] In fact, by the time *Bella y oscura* is published, even motherhood is no longer of significance in Montero's work. Montero does not envisage strategies for women to counter hegemonic power games or existential angst. The transcendent mother-figure is certainly reinscribed in feminist discourse but as a mystical enigma. As in Roig's work, a feminist politics is deferred.

Celia Amorós (Professor of Philosophy in the Complutense University, Madrid) believes that feminism is an ethics and should take into account 'all the other forms of alienation and exploitation'.[3] The writings of Montserrat Roig and Rosa Montero ratify this view. Radical feminism, as understood by Anglophone feminists, is apparently incommensurate to Spain; identity politics must be inflected by equality politics to be taken seriously as we have seen. This bears out Gisela Kaplan's view (*Contemporary Western European Feminism*, 1992) that difference feminism's celebration of innate gender-specific 'special qualities' verges on fascist attitudes to women, and therefore 'seems to surface only in countries which have not experienced fascism first hand' (30).

2. Gabriela in *El nido de los sueños* takes a psychological trip outside the symbolic into the (female) imaginary. But this other world, though fluid and chaotic, is horrific and life-threatening. Gabriela, like the narrator of 'Mar', must renew her place in signification.
3. C. Amorós, *Hacia una crítica de la razón patriarcal* (*Towards a Critique of Patriarchal Reason*), Barcelona, 1985 and 1991, p. 328.

Conclusion

In those that have, difference feminism is considered revisionist and right-wing.[4] The historical reasons for the absence of a strong, independently organized Spanish feminist movement have been mentioned already. Women-only groups were associated with Catholic, right-wing organizations which also stressed innate female attributes and mothering. Women's liberation was identified with social-democratic reform, in the 1930s and 1980s, and with clandestine, left-wing parties, trade unions and civil rights in the intervening period.[5] Spain's second-wave feminists were jailed and exiled and, in this respect, were unique in Europe (Kaplan, 209, mentions the Greeks too). What has been described as a system of 'strong honour shame sanctions' and 'rigid sex-stereotyping' (Kaplan, 209) meant that Spanish feminists were also attempting to abolish an entire 'macho' moral code. Politics, the science of government, is important in the Hispanic world and, as Lynn Segal points out, 'no clear political strategies follow from our either embracing or rejecting gendered identity as such' (Segal, 85). The fiction of Roig and Montero textualizes this tricky process of sexual politics in a Spanish context.

Western feminism in general is at an impasse and the fiction studied here reflects this. Caught between subjectivity and social responsibility, the individual and the collectivity, feminisms are in search of new formulations and writing practices. This impasse has much to do with Western feminism's uneasy relationship with postmodernism. Like radical feminism, postmodernism rejects Enlightenment thought and universality. Instead it posits diversity, difference, play. From the perspective of form, Rosa Montero's work is exemplary in this sense. Postmodernism and radical feminism share an interest in representation, in the deconstruction of the individual bourgeois subject, and in women's desire. But postmodernism also rejects the unitary subject *tout court*, truth, and essentialism. It is precisely a notion of absolute transcendence and of individual agency that Rosa Montero attempts to recuperate in her fiction. As Sabina Lovibond argues (*NLR*, 1989)

4. Consideration must also be given to the problematic cultural transposition of the sex/gender system and of the essentialist /constructionist distinction in Spain. Romance languages do not have a term which corresponds to the English word 'gender'. In Spain therefore, gender is not immediately perceived as constructed but as natural. There is a cultural resistance to constructionism as the word 'sexo' conflates gender and sex and essentializes both.

5. See M.A. Durán, *Mujer y sociedad en España (1700–1975)*, p. 396–7.

feminism may well critique Western philosophy and masculinity as transcendence, but can it afford to dispense with the Enlightenment altogether? Ultimately, feminism is a modern project. This is self-evident after reading, for example, Maria Aurèlia Capmany's *El feminismo ibérico* (*Iberian Feminism*), 1970, or Anabel González's *Los orígenes del feminismo en España* (*The Origins of Feminism in Spain*), 1980. Feminism needs the free circulation of ideas, educated and informed women, a cultural critique of traditional role models, and control of one's life and body. What hope did feminism have in a Spain which was rural, Catholic, and underdeveloped? What hope does it have when, in 1987, 50 per cent of young women between the ages of fifteen and twenty-four are unemployed (*Women in the European Community*, 108)? Emancipatory narratives, therefore, are important in Spain – especially if, in the case of Montero, the female protagonist is young. Moreover, as Linda Hutcheon argues (*The Politics of Postmodernism*), feminism wants to go further than simply de-legitimize and de-naturalize; it wants change. Feminism 'goes beyond making ideology explicit and deconstructing it'; it argues 'a need to change that ideology, to effect a real transformation', and 'that can only come with a transformation of patriarchal and social practices' (168). Rosa Montero takes this on board fully in *Temblor*. The problem with postmodernism is that it has not theorized agency; 'it has no strategies of resistance that could correspond to the feminist ones'. It is political but ambivalent, it can be perceived both as 'complicity or critique' and recuperated by Right and Left. The analogies with radical feminism are clear. Social identities are not necessarily political identities. Social identities do not 'spring from' gender, class, race, but from 'a sense of belonging to specific social and historical milieux' writes Lynn Segal (*NLR*, 1991, 86). This becomes clear from a reading of Montserrat Roig's work. Social movements '(particularly as conceived by the theorists of difference) can offer little more than the enjoyment of an endless game of self-exploration played out on the great board of Identity' (91). Hence Gabriela's desire to get back to reality, away from the illusive 'nest of dreams'. The utopian counter-argument is acknowledged by Kaplan. She concedes that 'if we were to discuss issues of a new *identity*, then all these perspectives take on a different meaning. In *that* context even the 'special value perspective . . . will have a place' (31). As we have seen, Montserrat Roig and Rosa Montero continually grapple with these difficult issues of feminine identity, agency, and power in their fiction.

In Spain, then, the impressive achievements of socialism and feminism, of a politics of equality, have not been sufficient to radically displace phallocentricity or to enable the materializtion of a new order, what Campioni and Grosz refer to as 'a completely different perspective on problems of truth, reason, reality, and knowledge' (Gunew, 392). In this sense Spain is no different from any other country. Literature, for its part, is neither political theory nor social science. For that reason it can negotiate the conflicts and ambiguities of both. Here I have studied the work of two Spanish women writers, openly sympathetic to socialism and the women's movement, to trace in their fiction the textualization of feminine identity and the subversion of the socialist feminist discourse they publicly espoused. Creative practice unties paradoxes and defies polarities; it simultaneously reflects on the past and imagines the future. It breaks down verbal and conceptual barriers and shifts the site of difference. Hence the importance of the work of Montserrat Roig and Rosa Montero for feminist discourse and theory, in Spain and elsewhere. As Roig wrote:

> If we didn't contemplate life as a representation we couldn't bear it. We need a few lies to imagine we're pursuing a few truths . . . Writing is a pleasure, a privilege. And, if you like, revenge. Or a miracle . . . because there will always be another person, cut off and perplexed, who will read us and, while reading, that person will create a different, better, almost perfect work of literature. That's when the reader's pleasure starts and our work ends. (*Dime*, 12, 59)

# *Bibliography*

*A Montserrat Roig en homenatge/Homage to Montserrat Roig,* Generalitat de Catalunya, Departament de Cultura, Barcelona, 1992

Abad, Mercedes, et al, 'Conversando con Mercedes Abad, Cristina Fernández Cubas y Soledad Púertolas: "Feminismo y literatura no tienen nada que ver"', *Mester,* XX, 2, 1991, pp. 157–65

Acín, R., *Narrativa o consumo literario (1975–1987),* Zaragoza, 1990

Alba, N., 'Entrevista con Rosa Montero', *Ventanal: Revista de Creación y Crítica,* 14, 1988, pp. 81–100

Alborg, C., 'Metaficción y feminismo en Rosa Montero', *Revista de Estudios Hispánicos,* 22, 1, 1988, pp. 67–76

——, 'Cuatro narradoras de la transición', *Nuevos y novísimos. Algunas perspectivas críticas sobre la narrativa española desde la década de los 60,* (eds) Ricardo Landeira, Luis T. González del Valle, Boulder, Colorado, 1988, pp. 11–27

Alcobendas Tirado, María Pilar, *Commission of the European Communities: The Employment of Women in Spain,* Luxembourg, 1984

Alonso, Santos, *La novela en la transición,* Madrid, 1983

Alvarado Florián, Victor, 'A propósito de "Before the Civil War" de Montserrat Roig', *Ventanal: Revista de Creación y Crítica,* 14, 1988, pp. 159–69

Amell, Samuel and García Castañeda S., *La cultura española en el posfranquismo,* Madrid, 1988

——, 'El motivo del viaje en tres novelas del posfranquismo', in *Estudios en homenaje a Enrique Ruiz-Fornells,* Eerie, 1990, pp. 12–17

Amorós, Celia, *Hacia una crítica de la razón patriarcal,* Barcelona, 1985

Bayón, Miguel, 'Mujeres escritoras: la mirada que va desde el rincón', *Cambio 16,* 24 November 1986, pp. 149–52

Bellver, C., 'Montserrat Roig and the Penelope Syndrome', in M.

Servodidio (ed.), *Reading for Difference*, 1987, pp. 111–22
——, 'Montserrat Roig: A Feminine Perspective and a Journalistic Slant', in R.C. Manteiga (ed.), *Feminine Concerns in Contemporary Fiction by Women*, Potomac, 1988, pp. 152–68
Bou, Enric, 'Montserrat Roig *L'hora violeta*', *Serra d'or*, March 1981, p. 166
——, 'La literatura actual', *Història de la literatura catalana*, vol. 2, (eds) Martí de Riquer, Antoni Comas, Joaquim Molas, Barcelona, 1988, pp. 355–420
——, 'Magia y lección', *El País*, 12 November 1991, p. 41
Broch, Alex, *Literatura catalana dels anys setanta*, Barcelona, 1980
——, 'La búsqueda interrumpida', *La Vanguardia*, 10 November 1991, p. 33
Brown, Joan L., 'Rosa Montero: from Journalist to Novelist', in Joan L. Brown (ed.), *Women Writers of Contemporary Spain. Exiles in the Homeland*, London and Toronto, 1991, pp. 240–57
Cadenas, C. B., 'Historia de tres mujeres', *Nueva Estafeta*, May 1980, pp. 76–7
Capmany, M. A., *El feminismo ibérico*, Barcelona, 1970
Carandell, Josep Maria, 'Para siempre joven', *El País*, 12 November 1991, p. 41
Castellanos, Jordi, 'Montserrat Roig. El temps de les cireres, *Serra d'or*, June 1977, pp. 397–9
Castells, F., 'Montserrat Roig: Escriptora Compromesa', *Serra d'or*, February 1977, p. 26
Ciplijauskaité, Biruté, *La novela femenina contemporánea (1970–1985)*, Barcelona, 1988
Corbalán, P., 'Una mirada crepuscular', *El Sol*, 7, X, 1990
Davies, C., 'Interview with Rosa Montero', *Journal of Hispanic Research*, 2, Spring 1993, pp. 383–8
——, 'The sexual representation of politics in Hispanic feminist narrative', in *Feminist Readings on Spanish and Latin American Literature*, L. Condé and S. M. Hart (eds), Lewiston, 1991, pp. 107–19
——, 'Foreword', *The Language of a Thousand Tongues: Contemporary European Fiction by Women*, special issue of *Forum for Modern Language Studies*, 28, 4, 1992, pp. 301–3
de Miguel Martínez, Emilio, *La primera narrativa de Rosa Montero*, Salamanca, 1983
de Riquer, M., Comas, A., Molas, J., *Història de la literatura catalana*, II, Barcelona, 1988

Bibliography

Díaz-Pérez, Janet, 'L'hora violeta', *World Literature Today*, 55, 1981, p. 659

Dominguéz, M., 'Bolero. Golpe bajo el corazón', *Cambio 16*, 19 April 1993, p. 59

Durán, M. A., et al, *Mujer y sociedad en España (1700–1975)*, Madrid, 1982

Durán, M. A., and Gallego, M. T., 'The women's movement in Spain and the new Spanish democracy', *The New Women's Movement. Feminism and Political Power in Europe and the USA*, (ed.) D. Dahlerup, London, 1986

Encinar, Angeles, 'Escritoras españolas actuales: una perspectiva a través del cuento', *Hispanic Journal*, 13, 1992, pp. 181–92

Evora, Tony, 'Boleros con sabor', *Cambio 16*, 28 June 1993, i–iv

Falcón, Lidia, *Mujer y poder político*, Madrid, 1992

Fernández Santos, Angel, 'Rosa Montero: Narrar es una inutilidad necesaria', *El País*, 21 November 1983

Ferreras, J. I., *La novela en el siglo XX (desde 1939)*, Madrid, 1988

Foucault, M., *Discipline and Punish*, London, 1977

Galerstein, C. L. (ed.), *Women Writers of Spain. An Annotated Bio-Bibliographical Guide*, New York, 1986

Gascón Vera. E., 'Rosa Montero ante la escritura femenina', in M. Servodidio (ed.), *Reading for Difference: Feminist Perspectives on Women Novelists of Contemporary Spain*, special issue of *Anales de la Literatura Española Contemporánea*, 12, 1987, pp. 59–77

Gerling, David Ross, 'Review of *La hora violeta*, 1980', *Anales de la Literatura Española Contemporánea*, 8, 1983, pp. 243–5

Gil Casado, P., *La novela deshumanizada española (1958–1988)*, Barcelona, 1990

Glenn, K.M., 'Victimized by Misreading: Rosa Montero's *Te trataré como a una reina*', in M. Servodidio (ed.), *Reading for Difference: Feminist Perspectives on Women Novelists of Contemporary Spain*, special issue of *Anales de la Literatura Española Contemporánea*, 12, 1987, pp. 191–201

——, 'Reader expectations and Rosa Montero's *La función Delta*', *Letras Peninsulares*, 1, 1988, pp. 87–96

——, 'Authority and Marginality in Three Contemporary Spanish Narratives', *Romance Languages Annual*, 1990, 2, pp. 426–30

——, 'Conversación con Rosa Montero', *Anales de la Literatura Española Contemporánea*, 15, 1990, pp. 275–83

——, 'Review of *Temblor*', *Anales de la Literatura Española Contemporánea*, 16, 1991, p. 401

{ 185 }

González, A., *Los orígenes del feminismo en España*, Madrid, 1980

Gould Levine, L., 'The Censored Sex. Woman as Author and Character in Franco's Spain', in *Women in Hispanic Literature. Icons and Fallen Idols*, (ed.) Beth Miller, Berkeley, 1983, pp. 289–315

Gunew, Sneja (ed.), *A Reader in Feminist Knowledge*, London and New York, 1991

Humm, M., *Border Traffic. Strategies of Contemporary Women Writers*, Manchester, 1992

Jackson, Rosemary, *Fantasy. The Literature of Subversion*, London and New York, 1981

Kaplan, G., *Contemporary Western European Feminism*, New York and London, 1992

Lovibond, Sabina, 'Feminism and Postmodernism', *New Left Review*, 178, 1989, pp. 5–28.

Manteiga, Roberto C., 'The Dilemma of the Modern Woman: A Study of the Female Characters in Rosa Montero's Novels', in R.C. Manteiga et al (eds), *Feminine Concerns in Contemporary Spanish Fiction by Women*, Potomac, 1988

Martínez Cachero, J. M., *La novela española entre 1936 y 1980*, Madrid, 1985

Masoliver Ródenas, Juan Antonio, '*Temblor* de Rosa Montero', *Insula*, 525, September 1990, pp. 19–20

Mayoral, Marina (ed.), *El oficio de narrar*, Madrid, 1990

Molas, Joaquim, 'Montserrat Roig. *El temps de les cireres*', *Els Marges*, 11 September 1977, pp. 123–5

——, 'Vida y literatura: un mismo designio de amor y libertad', *La Vanguardia*, 10 November 1991, p. 31

Monegal, A., 'Entrevista con Rosa Montero', *Plaza: Revista de Literatura*, 11, 1986, pp. 5–12

Montero, Rosa, *España para tí para siempre*, Madrid, 1976

——, *Crónica del desamor*, Madrid, 1979; *Absent Love. A Chronicle*, trans. Cristina de la Torre and Diana Glad, Nebraska U.P. , 1991

——, *La función Delta*, Madrid, 1981. *The Delta Function*, trans. Kari Easton and Y. Molina Gavilán, Nebraska U.P. , 1991

——, *Cinco años de país*, Madrid, 1982

——, 'Paulo Pumilio', in *Doce relatos de mujeres*, (ed.) Ymelda Navajo, Madrid, 1982, pp. 69–73

——, *Te trataré como a una reina*, Barcelona, 1983

——, 'Nunca pensé casarme', *La mujer feminista*, 21, November–December 1985, pp. 7–10

——, *Amado amo*, Madrid, 1988
——, *Temblor*, Madrid, 1990
——, *El nido de los sueños*, Madrid, 1991
——, *Bella y oscura*, Barcelona, 1993
——,'Escribiendo en la luna', unpublished paper
Moreno, Sebastián, 'Entrevista. Rosa Montero', *Tribuna*, 25 July 1988
Moxon-Browne, Edward, *Political Change in Spain*, London and New York, 1989
Myers, Eunice D., 'The Feminist Message: Propaganda and/or Art? A Study of Two Novels by Rosa Montero', in Roberto C. Manteiga et al (eds), *Feminine Concerns in Contemporary Spanish Fiction by Women*, Potomac, 1988, pp. 99–133
Navajo, Ymelda (ed.), *Doce relatos de mujeres*, Madrid, 1982
Navarro, J. M., 'El lenguaje coloquial en *Te trataré como a una reina*', in Joppich, K. H., Hillen, W. (eds), *Lengua, literatura, civilización en la clase de español*, Bonn, 1986, pp. 13–24
Nichols, Geraldine C., *Escribir, espacio propio: Laforet, Matute, Moix, Tusquets, Riera y Roig por sí mismas*, Minneapolis, Minnesota, 1989
——, *Des/cifrar la diferencia. Narrative femenina de la España contemporánea*, Madrid, 1992
Obiol, María J., 'De puño femenino', *El País*, 5 August 1985, p. v
Oller, Dolors, 'Signos perdurables', *El País*, 12 November 1991, p. 41
Ordóñez, Elizabeth J., 'Reading Contemporary Spanish Narrative by Women', in *Anales de la Literatura Española Contemporánea*, 7, 1982, pp. 237–51
——,'Inscribing difference: "L'écriture féminine" and New Narrative by Women', in M. Servodidio (ed.), *Reading for Difference*, 1987, pp. 45–58
——, *Voices of Their Own. Contemporary Spanish Narrative by Women*, London and Toronto, 1991
Oropesa, S., 'El encuentro con la otredad: "Estampas bostonianas" de Rosa Montero', in Fernández Jiménez, J., Labrador Herraiz, J. J., Valdivieso, T. L. (eds), *Estudios en homenaje a Enrique Ruiz-Fornells*, Eerie, 1990, pp. 472–8
Oyarzun, L.A., 'Eroticism and Feminism in Spanish Literature after Franco: *Los amores diurnos* de Francisco Umbral and *Crónica del desamor* de Rosa Montero', *Mid-Hudson Language Studies*, 4, 1981, pp. 135–44
Palmer, Paulina, *Contemporary Women's Fiction: Narrative Practice*

*and Feminist Theory*, New York and London, 1989

Perez, J., 'Review: Montserrat Roig *L'hora violeta*', *World Literature Today*, 55, 1981, p. 659

Piñol, R. M., 'Entrevista con Montserrat Roig: La etapa de *L'hora violeta* ya queda para mi muy lejana', *La Vanguardia*, 7, X, 1989

Riera, Carme, 'Literatura femenina.¿Un lenguaje prestado?', *Quimera*, 18, 1982, pp. 9–12

Rogers, Elizabeth S., 'Montserrat Roig's *Ramona, adiós*: A Novel of Suppression and Disclosure', *Revista de Estudios Hispánicos*, 20, 1986, pp. 103–21

Roig, Montserrat, *Molta roba i poc sabó ... i tan neta que la volen*, Barcelona, 1971 [*Aprendizaje sentimental*, trans. Mercedes Nogués, Barcelona, 1981]

——, *Ramona, adéu*, Barcelona, 1972 [*Ramona, adiós*, trans. Joaquim Sempere, Barcelona, 1980]

——, *Retrats paral.lels I*, Barcelona, 1975, *II*, 1976, *III*, 1978

——, *Los hechiceros de la palabra*, Barcelona, 1975

——, *Rafael Vidiella, l'aventura de la Revolució*, Barcelona, 1976

——, *El temps de les cireres*, Barcelona, 1977 [*Tiempo de cerezas*, trans. Enrique Sordo, Barcelona, 1978]

——, *Els catalans als camps nazis*, Barcelona, 1977 [*Noche y niebla. Los catalanes en los campos nazis*, trans. C. Vilaginés, Madrid, 1978]

——, *Personatges I, II*, Barcelona, 1978, 1979

——, *L'hora violeta*, Barcelona, 1980 [*La hora violeta* trans. Enrique Sordo, Barcelona, 1980]

——, *¿Tiempo de Mujer?*, Barcelona, 1980

——, *Carnes de mujer*, Barcelona, 1981

——, *Mujeres en busca de un nuevo humanismo*, Madrid, 1981 [*El feminismo*, Barcelona, 1984]

——, *Mi viaje al bloqueo. 900 días de la lucha heroica de Leningrado*, Moscow, 1982

——, *L'òpera quotidiana*, Barcelona, 1982 [*La ópera cotidiana*, trans. Enrique Sordo, Barcelona, 1983] ('The Everyday Opera. Selections', trans. J. M. Sobrer, in *On Our Own Behalf. Women's Tales from Catalonia*, ed. Kathleen McNerny, Nebraska U.P. , Lincoln, 1988)

——, *L'agulla daurada*, Barcelona, 1985 [*La aguja dorada*, Barcelona, 1985]

——, *Barcelona a vol d'ocell*, Barcelona, 1987

——, *La veu melodiosa*, Barcelona, 1987 [*La voz melodiosa*, trans. José

Agustín Goytisolo, Barcelona, 1987]

——, *El cant de la joventut*, Barcelona, 1990 [*El canto de la juventud*, trans. Joaquim Sempere, Barcelona, 1990]

——, *Digues que m'estimes encara que sigui mentida*, Barcelona, 1991 [*Dime que me quieres aunque sea mentira*, trans. Antonia Picazo, Barcelona, 1992]

——, *Reivindicació de la senyora Clito Mestres. Seguit de El Mateix Paisatge*, Barcelona, 1992

——, *Un pensament de sal, un pessic de pebre: dietari obert 1990–1991*, Barcelona, 1992

——, *L'art de la memòria*, Olot, 1992

'Rosa entre espinas. En su tercera novela, Rosa Montero aborda un mundo ajeno', *Cambio 16*, 19 December 1983, p. 167

Sánchez Arnosi, Milagros, *'La hora violeta'*, *Insula*, 36, April 1981, p. 8.

Sarrias, C., 'La juventud en la literatura castellana actual', *Razón y Fe*, July–August 1984, pp. 25–31

Segal, Lynn, 'Whose Left? Socialism and Feminism in the Future', *New Left Review*, 185, 1991, pp. 81–91.

Servodidio, M. (ed.), *Reading for Difference: Feminist Perspectives on Women Novelists of Contemporary Spain*, special issue of *Anales de la Literatura Española Contemporánea*, 12, 1987

Sobejano, Gonzalo, 'La novela poemática y sus alrededores', *Insula*, 464–5, 1985, p. 1, p. 26

Sosnowski, Saul, 'Manuel Puig. Entrevista', *Hispamérica*, 1 May 1993

Stimpson, Catharine, *Where the Meanings Are*, New York and London, 1988

Sullà, Enric, 'Sobre *Ramona, adéu*. Fuga en gris', *Serra d'or*, July 1973, pp. 467–8

Suñén, Luis, 'La realidad y sus sombras: Rosa Montero y Cristina Fernández Cubas', *Insula*, 446, 1984, p. 5

Talbot, Lynne K., 'Entrevista con Rosa Montero', *Letras Femeninas*, 14, 1988, pp. 90–6

Threlfall, M., 'The Women's Movement in Spain', *New Left Review*, 151, May–June 1985, pp. 44–73

Torres, Maruja, 'Una luchadora', *El País*, 11 November 1991, p. 29

Torres, S. E. and S. Carl King (eds), *Selected Proceedings of the Thirty-Ninth Annual Mountain Interstate Foreign Language Conference*, Clemson, South Carolina, 1991

Tsuchiya, Akiko, 'Montserrat Roig's *La ópera cotidiana* as Histiographic Metafiction', *Anales de la Literatura Contemporánea*, 15, 1990, pp. 145–59

Valls, Fernando, 'Sobre *El canto de la juventud* de Montserrat Roig', *Insula*, 531, March 1991, p. 25

Vázquez Montalbán, Manuel, *Barcelonas*, London, 1992

*Women in the European Community*, Luxembourg, 1992

Zatlin, Phyllis, 'Review of *Crónica del desamor* and *La función Delta*', *Hispanófila*, 84, May 1985, pp. 121–3

——, 'Women Novelists in Democratic Spain: Freedom to Express the Female Perspective', in M. Servodidio (ed.), *Reading for Difference*, 1987, pp. 29–43

——, 'Passivity and Immobility: Patterns of Inner Exile in Postwar Spanish Novels Written by Women', *Letras Femeninas*, 14, 1988, pp. 3–9

# Index